From Participants in the

TEXT READING PROGRAM

If it were not for these enlightening Text commentaries, we would still be floundering in an intellectual soup. The soup was mighty tasty, but was difficult to get our teeth into without these brilliant observations, comparisons, and analogies. We know this is a vast body of work that has been given us and we are grateful from the bottom of our hearts.
—SYLVIA AND CAP LYONS

A very powerful tool to keep me on track, reading and absorbing just a few pages each day. This process has been an invaluable source of inner peace during this past year.
—CONNIE PORTER

Robert Perry and Greg Mackie are experts at making the sometimes challenging Text not just understandable, but rich with meaning and poignancy. This is a priceless gift to anyone who wants to fully understand the awesome teachings of *A Course in Miracles*. I can think of no better form of support than this!
—JULIA SIMPSON

The Text commentaries offer insights I could not have had alone, because of the deep understanding Robert and Greg have.
—DIETRUN BUCHMAN

An amazing journey into the genius and magnitude of this material. Don't miss this opportunity.
—SHARON EDWARDS

Robert and Greg's insights illuminate Text principles like never before.
—LORETTA M. SIANI, PH.D

I have studied the Text and read it through at least once a year for the last 19 years. I thought I knew it pretty well. However this year has been a real eye-opener. Many of those little question marks I made in the margins have been erased. I shall be forever grateful for this year of Text study.
—WENDY FINNERTY

After 20 years with the Course, I now understand it on a much different level.
—ULLA WALLIN

Robert and Greg's intelligence, insight, and wit, create a fun climate of spiritual scholarship that helps make the Text more intelligible and alive. They're extraordinarily gifted.
—AMY ELLISON

The clear and down-to-earth commentary has helped me connect with the Text as never before.
—NANCY NEVITT

Robert and Greg have a tremendous comprehension of the Course and provide down-to-earth explanations. I know of no better way to learn the message of the Text than this program.
—JAN WORLEY

Translates the beautiful poetry of the Course's Text into everyday common language, making the valuable meaning of each sentence easily understood.
—KATHERINE LATORRACA

Previously, I had never succeeded in completely reading the Text. Participating was the best thing that I did for myself this year.
—DAVID COLWELL

There is nothing else in my years of studying the Course that has helped me so much!
—GEORGE PORTER

I can honestly say I'll finally complete the reading of the entire Text—and I've been at this for 20 years!
—BARBARA OLSON

Robert and Greg's insights helped me understand and assimilate the Course's otherwise complex and difficult passages. I will do this again next year, and the next, and the next. This program is amazing.
—JO CHANDLER

Your program has been a revelation.
—DON DE LENE

I would like to say that this year has been too amazing to actually put into words.
—KATHY CHOMITZ

Having studied the Course faithfully for 28 years, I never imagined the insights and miracles I would receive from these commentaries on the Text!
—MIRKALICE GORE

I can truly say that this program has made an incredible difference to my life. I wholeheartedly recommend it.
—DAVID FLEMING

Nothing less than totally inspiring.
—REV. JERRY CUSIMANO

THE ILLUMINATED TEXT

Commentaries for Deepening Your Connection with
A Course in Miracles

Robert Perry & Greg Mackie

VOLUME 5

 CIRCLE PUBLISHING

Published by Circle Publishing
A division of the Circle of Atonement
P.O. Box 4238 * West Sedona, AZ 86340
(928) 282-0790 * www.circleofa.org
circleoffice@circleofa.org

Cover design by Thunder Mountain Design and Communications
Design & layout by Phillips Associates UK Ltd
Printed in the USA

ISBN 978-1-886602-36-6

Library of Congress Cataloging-in-Publication Data

Perry, Robert, 1960-
 The illuminated text : commentaries for deepening your connection with A course in
miracles / Robert Perry & Greg Mackie.
     p. cm.
 Includes bibliographical references.
 Summary: "Provides in-depth analysis of the Text of A Course in Miracles"--
Provided by publisher.
 ISBN 978-1-886602-36-6
1. Course in Miracles. 2. Spiritual life. I. Mackie, Greg, 1963- II. Title.
 BP605.C68P455 2010
 299'.93--dc22

                                    2009039354

CONTENTS

Commentaries on Chapter 20: THE VISION OF HOLINESS

Commentaries on Chapter 21: REASON AND PERCEPTION

FOREWORD

The Text is the foundation of *A Course in Miracles*. Doing the Course is simply a process of learning and internalizing its thought system, and the Text is where that thought system is laid out. It is an unparalleled spiritual tour de force. Careful study of it will change your outlook in ways that perhaps nothing else can.

Many students, however, find the Text to be very hard going. Many do not finish it, and even those who make it through, perhaps repeatedly, wish they had a deeper grasp of what they were reading.

For this reason, in 2006, the Circle of Atonement offered the Text Reading Program. This was a year-long tour through the Text of *A Course in Miracles* with commentary on each paragraph, written by myself and Greg Mackie, both teachers for the Circle. Before each weekday, we would send out to all the participants via e-mail the reading for that day. This would usually consist of a single section from the Text, accompanied by our commentary as well as practical exercises.

We often supplemented these sections with material from the Urtext, the original typescript of the Course. Our experience was that, especially in the early chapters of the Text, material from the Urtext that was eventually edited out was very helpful and clarifying. So when we felt it was useful, we included this Urtext material in brackets, and let it inform our commentary. We also indicated where a word had been emphasized in the Urtext, as this too often added clarity.

Note: In this volume, words that were originally emphasized in the Urtext are <u>underlined</u>. So when you see an underlined word here, know that that word was emphasized in the Urtext, but that emphasis was not included in the eventual published Course, which included fewer emphasized words. Again, we did this because quite often that emphasis from the Urtext would add clarity.

The reason we developed this program has a bit of history to it. In 2000, we offered a local program in Sedona that included a daily Text class, using a schedule that took us through the entire Text in a year of weekday readings. (On the sixth and seventh days, we rested!) Our friend, student, and colleague John Perry attended that program. When it ended, he began guiding people through the Text using the same schedule, only doing so online. He sent out the Text material for a given day and interspersed it with his own clarifying comments. In fall 2005 he felt guided to suggest we do something similar. Our guidance told us to go ahead, and so that's what we did. Without John's suggestion, however, it is safe to say we never would have done this.

2006, the year of the program, was an intense one. I would write commentaries for three weeks. Then I got a breather for a week while Greg wrote the commentaries. And then the schedule started over. Each day we wrote the commentary that needed to go out the next day. In addition, we led a weekly phone class for participants, in which we summarized the previous week's sections. (The recordings are still available to students who sign up for the online version of the Text Reading Program.)

The response to our program far exceeded our expectations. We have included a few edited comments at the front of the book, but if you want to read the unadulterated student reactions, straight from the various horses' mouths, then go to www.circlepublishing.org and click on the link for the Text Reading Program. During the year of the program, and actually ever since, we have had consistent requests that we put this material into published form.

So here it is, presented in book form as a multi-volume set. We hope you find these commentaries illuminating, and that they do indeed deepen your understanding of the spiritual masterpiece, *A Course in Miracles*.

Robert Perry
September 2009
Sedona, Arizona

Commentaries on Chapter 18

THE PASSING
OF THE DREAM

I. The Substitute Reality
Commentary by Greg Mackie

1. To substitute is to <u>accept instead</u>. If you would but consider exactly what this entails, you would perceive at once how much at variance this is with the goal the Holy Spirit has given you, and would accomplish <u>for</u> you. To substitute is to <u>choose between,</u> renouncing one aspect of the Sonship ["aspect of the Sonship" was apparently added by the editors] <u>in favor</u> of the other. For this <u>special</u> purpose, one is judged more valuable and the other is <u>replaced</u> by him. The relationship in which the substitution occurred is thus fragmented, and <u>its purpose split</u> accordingly. To fragment <u>is to exclude,</u> and substitution is the strongest defense the ego has for separation.

This section is all about substitution, and it begins with a succinct definition: "To substitute is to accept instead." Here, the specific substitution is judging one aspect of the Sonship more valuable than another and using him to replace the other. In the special relationship, we substitute one special person for the entire Sonship, "forsaking all others" as the traditional wedding vows say. In T-17.V, we saw a form of substitution that tempts those in the rough early stages of a holy relationship: dumping the partner and substituting another special relationship, or at least taking some of our problems to another substitute relationship to be "solved" there.

All this substitution is completely at odds with the goal of truth at the center of the holy relationship. Inherent in the goal of truth is the acceptance of everyone, but when we substitute our purpose is split: we accept some and reject others. A relationship dedicated to wholeness is now fragmented as substitution introduces exclusion into it. Substitution is a powerful separation device—in fact, it is "the strongest defense the ego has for separation."

2. The Holy Spirit never uses substitutes [Ur: The Holy Spirit *never* substitutes]. Where the ego perceives one person as a <u>replacement for</u> another, the Holy Spirit sees them joined and indivisible. He does not judge <u>between</u> them, <u>knowing</u> they are one. Being united, they

3

are one <u>because they are the same</u>. Substitution is clearly a process in which they are <u>perceived as different</u>. One would <u>unite;</u> the other <u>separate</u>. <u>Nothing</u> can come <u>between</u> what God has joined and what the Holy Spirit sees as one. But everything *seems* to come between the fragmented relationships the ego sponsors to destroy.

The Holy Spirit accepts no substitutes. Instead of seeing people as truly different and picking and choosing between them, He sees them as the same: one, united, indivisible. We still have specific relationships with particular people, of course, but relationships the Holy Spirit has joined work together in harmony: "All relationships are seen as total commitments, yet they do not conflict with one another in any way" (T-15. VI.1:3). Nothing can come between us in the Holy Spirit's relationships, but as we all know, *everything* seems to come between us in the ego's relationships.

> 3. The one emotion in which substitution is impossible is love. [Ur: But] Fear involves substitution by definition, for it is love's <u>replacement</u>. Fear is both a fragmented <u>and fragmenting</u> emotion. It <u>seems</u> to take many forms, and each one seems to require a <u>different</u> form of acting out for satisfaction. While this appears to introduce quite variable <u>behavior,</u> a far more serious effect lies in the fragmented <u>perception</u> from which the behavior stems. <u>No one is seen complete</u>. The body is emphasized, with special emphasis on certain parts, and <u>used as the standard for comparison</u> of acceptance or rejection [Ur: for either acceptance or rejection of suitability] for acting out a special <u>form</u> of fear.

The Holy Spirit's "accept no substitutes" stance is the way of love. But fear, the only alternative to love in the Course's view, is itself a substitute: our substitute for love. It fragments because it is rooted in differences. It takes many different forms, requires many different behaviors to act out and, most importantly, is rooted in the perception of differences.

The substitution process is like the Energizer bunny: It keeps going and going and going. I mentioned earlier that in the special relationship, we substitute one person for the entire Sonship. Well, it just keeps getting worse. We continue to substitute, first substituting that person's body for the whole person, and then even substituting certain preferred body parts for her whole body. This then becomes the standard by which we choose one person over the other. Our selection process is something akin to the

Miss America swimsuit competition. The lucky winner gets to have a special relationship with us, a relationship which, being the antithesis of love, is nothing more than fear in love's clothing.

One more comment: We may object to this material about emphasizing body parts on the grounds that we *are* attracted to people's inner qualities, not just sexy legs and washboard abs. That's true, but even people's inner qualities are associated with and expressed by certain body parts. If you love someone for his intelligence and way with words, then to a large extent he is a brain and a mouth to you.

> 4. You who believe that God is fear made but <u>one</u> substitution. It has taken many forms, because it was the substitution of illusion for truth ["of illusion for truth" was apparently added by the editors]; of fragmentation for wholeness. It has become so splintered and subdivided and divided again, over and over, that it is now almost impossible to perceive it once was one, and still <u>is</u> what it was. That <u>one</u> error, which brought truth to illusion, infinity to time, and life to death, was all you ever made. Your whole world rests upon it. Everything you see reflects it, and every special relationship that you have ever made is <u>part</u> of it.

All of our substitutions are just different forms of the primordial substitution that started it all: the substitution of fragmentation for wholeness that happened when we chose "the tiny, mad desire to be separate, different and special" (T-25.I.5:5) over the oneness of Heaven. This brought with it all the reversals that make up our world: illusions replaced truth, time replaced infinity, death replaced life. And since this error was the replacement of wholeness with fragmentation, it never stopped fragmenting, producing all the different forms of substitution we've been talking about and many more. Precisely because this one error has taken so many different forms, we no longer see that all those substitutions that define our relationships and make up our world are simply manifestations of a single unfortunate mistake.

> 5. You may be surprised to hear [Ur: You have expressed surprise at hearing] how <u>very</u> different is reality from what <u>you</u> see. You do not realize the magnitude of that <u>one</u> error. It was so vast and so <u>completely</u> incredible that from it a world of total unreality *had* to emerge. What else <u>could</u> come of it? Its fragmented <u>aspects</u> are fearful enough, as you begin to <u>look</u> at them. But nothing you have seen <u>begins</u> to show

you the enormity of the <u>original</u> error, which seemed to cast you out of Heaven, to shatter knowledge into meaningless bits of disunited perceptions, and <u>to force you to make further substitutions</u>.

I'm sure I speak for many when I say that even after years of studying the Course, I'm still amazed by how big a gap there is between what seems real to me and the reality the Course describes. The more traditional depiction of Heaven in Christianity, with its angels and pearly gates and streets of gold, is nothing more than an elevated version of things I'm already familiar with. The Course's Heaven, in contrast, is utterly, staggeringly different. The reason for this huge gap, we are told here, is that we simply don't have a clue how big that original error really was. It appeared to cast us out of Heaven like Lucifer and shatter the seamless oneness of Heaven into billions of tiny, separate pieces. The reversal was so profound that a completely upside-down world simply *had* to emerge from it. Once substitution got started, it was the proverbial snowball rolling down the hill, gaining momentum until we ended up with an entire substitute reality.

> 6. That was the first projection of error outward. The world arose to hide it, and became the screen on which it was projected and drawn between you and the truth. For truth extends <u>inward,</u> where the idea of loss is meaningless and only <u>increase</u> is conceivable. Do you <u>really</u> think it strange that a world in which <u>everything</u> is backwards and upside down arose from this projection of error ["projection of error" was apparently added by the editors]? <u>It was inevitable.</u> For truth brought to <u>this</u> could only remain within in quiet, and take no part in all the mad projection by which this world was made. Call it not sin but madness, for such it was and so it still remains. Invest it not with guilt, for guilt implies it was accomplished <u>in reality</u>. And above all, *be not afraid of it.*

The "first projection of error outward" was the original error described above: the first substitution, the substitution of fragmentation for the wholeness of Heaven, which appeared to shatter Heaven. Then, we made the world to hide the error, which I think means to hide the *source* of the error: our own minds. Projecting the error onto an external world makes the error seem to be an external reality independent of our minds, which (seemingly) renders us powerless to do anything about it. Not only does the world hide the error in this way, but it also hides the *truth* by (apparently) standing between us and the truth. It is no surprise, then, that this world is the exact opposite of truth. Truth has nothing to do with all this crazy projection.

Does this sound scary to you? It sure does to me. The Course calls the instant in which all this seemed to happen "the time of terror" (T-26.V.13:1), and says that deep down we feel unimaginable guilt for the "crime" of shattering Heaven. But Jesus implores us here to "*be not afraid of it.*" It was not a real crime against Heaven but only a crazy dream, and therefore not a cause for guilt. Thank God!

> 7. When you seem to see some twisted form of the original error rising [Ur: rise] to frighten you, say only, "God is <u>not</u> fear, but Love," and it will disappear. <u>The truth will save you</u>. It has <u>not</u> left you, to go out into the mad world and so <u>depart from you</u>. Inward is sanity; <u>insanity</u> is <u>outside</u> you. You but <u>believe</u> it is the other way; that truth is <u>outside</u>, and error and guilt within. Your little, senseless substitutions, touched with insanity and swirling lightly off on a mad course like feathers dancing insanely in the wind, <u>have</u> no substance. They fuse and merge and separate, in shifting and totally meaningless patterns that need not be judged at all. To judge them <u>individually</u> is pointless. Their tiny differences in form are no <u>real</u> differences at all. <u>None of them matters</u>. *That* they have in common and nothing else. Yet what else is <u>necessary</u> to make them all the same?

Because we think we really shattered Heaven, deep down we believe that the pristine truth of Heaven has left us for good and within us is nothing but a corrupt, sinful nature. Yet it is really the other way around: The truth of Heaven remains within us and it is insanity that is foreign to our true nature, and thus outside it. All our crazy substitutions are merely meaningless nightmares with no substance at all. Truth will save us from all of them, if we will simply look within and find it.

Application: Think of something that frightens you. Whatever it is, it is but a "twisted form of the original error" that substituted fear for love. Now, reverse that error by saying, with as much conviction as you can, "*God is **not** fear but Love*," and watch that error disappear.

> 8. Let them all go, dancing in the wind, dipping and turning till they

disappear from sight, far, far <u>outside</u> of you. And turn you to the stately calm within, where in holy stillness dwells the living God you never left, and Who never left you. The Holy Spirit takes you gently by the hand, and retraces <u>with</u> you your mad journey <u>outside</u> yourself, leading you gently back to the truth and safety within. He brings all your insane projections and the [Ur: your] wild substitutions that <u>you</u> have placed <u>outside</u> you to the truth. Thus He <u>reverses</u> the course of insanity and restores you to reason.

Application: Bring to mind more of your fears, "your little, senseless substitutions," and do the following visualization.

First, imagine that all these fears are tiny feathers, light and insubstantial.
You have them all in your hands as you stand outdoors on a windy day.
Now, let them all go.
Watch them dance in the wind, dipping and turning until they disappear from sight.

Now, turn to the stately calm within,
the quiet center, the inner altar, where God dwells in holy stillness.
Let the Holy Spirit take you by the hand
and retrace your mad journey outside yourself,
leading you gently back to the truth and safety within.
There, you see that He has brought all those feathers you released
and placed them upon the altar to truth.
Watch them now disappear for good in the light of truth.

9. In your relationship with your brother, where He has taken charge of everything at your request, He has set the course inward to the truth you <u>share</u>. In the mad world <u>outside</u> you nothing <u>can</u> be shared but only <u>substituted</u>, and sharing and substituting have <u>nothing</u> in common in reality. Within yourself you love your brother [Ur: Within yourselves, you love each other] with a perfect love. Here is holy ground, in which no substitution [Ur: substitutes] can enter, and where only the <u>truth</u> in your brother [Ur: about each other] can abide. Here you are joined in

God, as much together as you are with Him. The original error has not entered here, nor ever will. Here is the radiant truth, to which the Holy Spirit has committed [Ur: to which the Holy Spirit submitted] your relationship. Let Him bring it here, where *you* would have it be. Give Him but a little faith in your brother [Ur: each other], to help Him show you that no substitute you made for Heaven can keep you from it.

Now we return to the central focus of all these sections: the holy relationship. It is through the holy relationship, in which two people have joined together in the goal of truth, that all of our insane substitutes for truth are undone. In the holy relationship, the Holy Spirit is guiding us inward to the truth we share. The world outside is only a mad world of substitution, but deep within the two of us is holy ground. Here we already love each other with a perfect love. Here no substitution has ever entered. Here we are already perfectly joined with God and with each other. Here is only the radiant truth that is the Holy Spirit's goal for our relationship. All we have to do to let Him bring our relationship here is have a little faith in each other. Is that too much to ask for a reward so great?

10. In you there is no separation, and no substitute can keep you from your brother [Ur: each other]. Your reality was <u>God's</u> creation, and <u>has</u> no substitute. You are so firmly joined in truth that only God is there. And He would <u>never</u> accept something else <u>instead</u> of you. He loves you both, equally and as one. And as He loves you, so you <u>are</u>. You are <u>not</u> joined together in [Ur: by] illusions, but in the Thought so holy and so perfect that illusions cannot remain to darken the holy place in which you stand together. God is with you, my brother [Ur: brothers]. Let us join in Him in peace and gratitude, and accept His gift as our most holy and perfect reality, which we share in Him.

Beneath all the madness generated by the original error, our reality remains as it always was. There is no separation and no substitution, nor are there any illusions. We are still God's creations, firmly joined with each other and with Him, loved by Him equally and as one, forever abiding on holy ground. Jesus wants so dearly for us to realize that God is with us!

Application: This is a great paragraph to read as a personal message to you. I recommend doing that right now, inserting your name at various appropriate points.

> 11. Heaven is restored to all the Sonship through your relationship, for in it lies the Sonship, whole and beautiful, safe in your love. Heaven has entered quietly, for all illusions have been gently brought unto the truth in you, and love has shined upon you, blessing your relationship with truth. God and His whole creation have entered it together. How lovely and how holy is your relationship, with the truth shining upon it! Heaven beholds it, and rejoices that you have let it come to you. And God Himself is glad that your relationship is as it was created. The universe within you stands with you, together with your brother. And Heaven looks with love on what is joined in it, along with its Creator.

In the midst of all this beautiful poetry, I want to step back and remember what a seemingly ordinary event is at the heart of this: two people joining in a common goal. Helen and Bill's joining didn't look spectacular on the surface. It was just two people who were fed up with petty arguments and office politics, two people who were asking that question made famous by Rodney King: "Can we all get along?" A worthy goal, but nothing out of the ordinary.

Or so it seemed, for this was *no* ordinary event. It sparked a holy relationship, a joining so great in its power that "Heaven is restored to all the Sonship through your relationship." When they joined, literally everyone joined with them: God, Heaven, and all of God's creation. The entire universe rejoiced at the loveliness and holiness of two people joining together in the shining light of truth. Of course, all this happens when *any* two people join in a truly common goal, one that transcends our usual self-interest. Have you done this with someone in your life? If so, remember that however ordinary that joining may look to you, it has a far greater impact on all of creation than you could ever realize.

> 12. Whom God has called should hear no substitutes. Their call is but an echo of the original error that shattered Heaven. And [Ur: For] what became of peace in those who heard? Return with me to Heaven, walking together with your brother out of this world and through another, to the loveliness and joy the other holds within it. Would you still further weaken and break apart what is already broken and

hopeless? Is it <u>here</u> that you would look for happiness? Or would you not prefer to <u>heal</u> what has been broken, and join in making whole what has been ravaged by separation and disease?

Long ago, we made the original substitution of fragmentation for wholeness that seemingly shattered Heaven. Do we want to keep swinging the hammer and break the shards of Heaven into even smaller pieces, or do we want to put them back together again? If the latter, we need to stop engaging in substitution *now*. After all, our current substitutions are nothing more than different forms of that original error. So, we need to stop substituting one special person for the entire Sonship. We need to set aside that Miss America swimsuit competition through which we substitute one person for another by judging who has the best body parts. We need to resist the temptation to dump our holy relationship partner and substitute another relationship in which our ego's goals can be met.

Jesus calls us to the alternative: Walk together with him and with our holy relationship partner through the real world and back to Heaven. Through this journey, we "heal what has been broken, and join in making whole what has been ravaged by separation and disease." Isn't this more likely to bring us peace and happiness than all of our crazy substitutions?

> 13. You have been called, together with your brother, to the most holy function this world contains. It is the <u>only</u> one that has no limits, and reaches out to every broken fragment of the Sonship with healing and uniting comfort. This is offered <u>you</u>, in your holy relationship. Accept it <u>here</u>, and you <u>will</u> give as you have accepted [Ur: and received]. The peace of God is given you with the glowing purpose in which you join with your brother. The holy light that brought you and him together <u>must</u> extend, as <u>you</u> accepted it.

"The most holy function this world contains" is the healing of the entire Sonship, putting the fragments of Heaven back together again (in awareness, of course—Heaven was never actually shattered). Each holy relationship is given this function. Joining in the goal of truth brought the peace of God to our relationship. We accepted it; now our function is to give it, for it is part of the very nature of the light we received to extend to others. We are not meant to be only a light to each other. Our holy relationship is meant to be a light to the world.

II. The Basis of the Dream
Commentary by Robert Perry

1. Does not a world that seems quite real arise in dreams? Yet think what this world is. It is clearly <u>not</u> the world you saw <u>before</u> you slept. Rather it is a <u>distortion</u> of the world, planned solely around what you would have <u>preferred</u>. Here, you are "free" to make over whatever <u>seemed</u> to attack you, and <u>change</u> it into a <u>tribute</u> to your ego, which was outraged by the "attack." This would not be <u>your</u> wish unless you saw yourself <u>as one</u> with the ego, which <u>always</u> looks upon itself, and therefore on you, as <u>under</u> attack and highly <u>vulnerable</u> to it.

This paragraph begins a discussion that, as you can see, is about ordinary nighttime dreams. It is primarily about wish-fulfillment dreams, those dreams that gave the word "dream" its other meaning of "something wished for."

I just had one of these sorts of dreams a few hours ago. I recently read a book by a bestselling author whose work affected me deeply. I found his website and wrote him a message of thanks, to which he responded with a brief, polite reply. I was surprised even at that, given how besieged he is with both praise and attack. And that was that.

In the dream I had, however, things turned out very differently. He had been wrongly jailed and escaped, and I became almost his primary support in his desperate attempt to avoid the law. At the end of the dream, in a room with him and a few close supporters, I was giving a discourse on a topic which, though I didn't mention it, I felt could have been dealt with better in his book.

What really produced this dream? Jesus says that my ego was outraged by not being able to have more contact with this author, so in my sleep I changed everything around, remaking the situation into a tribute to my ego.

2. Dreams are chaotic <u>because</u> they are governed by your conflicting wishes, and therefore they have <u>no</u> concern with what is true. They are the best example you could have of how perception can be utilized

to substitute illusions for truth. You do not take them seriously on awaking because the fact that reality is so <u>outrageously</u> violated in them becomes apparent. Yet they <u>are</u> a way of <u>looking</u> at the world, and <u>changing</u> it <u>to suit the ego better</u>. They provide <u>striking</u> examples, both of the ego's <u>inability</u> to tolerate reality, and of your willingness to <u>change</u> reality on its behalf.

When we waken from a dream, we don't take it seriously because we can see how chaotic and crazy it was, how outrageously it violated our waking reality. Yet doesn't that say something about the place in us that dreams come from? This place must be chaotic, filled with conflicting wishes. And it must have no concern for reality; only for what it wants. If reality doesn't suit this childish place in us, then we set about making a fantasy reality that does.

3. You do not find the differences between what you see in sleep and on awaking disturbing. You recognize that what you see on waking is blotted out in dreams. Yet on awakening, you do <u>not</u> expect it to be gone. In dreams *you* arrange everything. People <u>become</u> what you would have them be, and what they do <u>you</u> order. No limits on substitution are laid upon you. For a time it seems as if the world were <u>given</u> you, to make it what you wish. You do <u>not</u> realize <u>you</u> are <u>attacking</u> it, trying to triumph over it and <u>make</u> it serve you.

We assume that dreams are this bubble of unreality; kind of like Las Vegas—what happens there, stays there. Inside this bubble, for a time, the world is ours to control with impunity. Everyone in the dream is a puppet on our string. Of course, in the dream, we don't realize this. For instance, I wasn't conscious in my dream that I was making it all happen. Yet who else could it have been? Even further from my mind was the fact that I was taking the daytime reality, the one that did not fully honor my ego, wrestling it to the ground, and putting it under my boot. Now *I* was on top.

4. Dreams are perceptual temper tantrums, in which you literally scream, "<u>I want it thus!</u>" And thus it seems to be. And yet the dream can<u>not</u> escape its origin. Anger and fear pervade it, and in an instant the illusion of satisfaction is invaded by the illusion of terror. For the dream of your ability to <u>control</u> reality by substituting a world that <u>you</u>

> prefer *is* terrifying. Your attempts to <u>blot out</u> reality are <u>very</u> fearful, but <u>this</u> you are <u>not</u> willing to accept. And so you <u>substitute</u> the fantasy that <u>reality</u> is fearful, <u>not</u> what you would <u>do</u> to it. And thus is guilt <u>made real</u>.

I love that first line! It says that dreams come from the screaming two-year-old within. This enraged toddler was not treated in a sufficiently kingly manner before, and so now he is going to climb the throne and issue some decrees: "I want it *thus!*"

Yet how, in this wish-fulfillment approach to dreams, can you explain nightmares? Jesus' explanation is actually very similar to what parenting experts say about the need for authority and boundaries in a child's life. They say that the child who rules the household is terrified by his own power run amok, and this makes him ultimately quite afraid and insecure. This fear, Jesus says, is what invades our dreams. Now we see ourselves surrounded by a fearful dream world, yet this is only our own fantasy of being punished for our "sin" of trying to control the universe. Thinking this dream is real, we become unconsciously convinced that we really did sin.

> 5. Dreams show you that you <u>have</u> the power to make a world as you would have it be, and that <u>because</u> you want it you <u>see</u> it. And <u>while</u> you see it you do <u>not</u> doubt that it is real. Yet here is a world, clearly <u>within</u> your mind, that <u>seems</u> to be outside. You do <u>not</u> respond to it as though you made it, nor do you realize that the emotions the dream produces <u>must</u> come from you. It is the <u>figures</u> in the dream and what <u>they</u> do that seem to <u>make the dream</u>. You do not realize that you are making them act out <u>for</u> you, for if you did the guilt would not be theirs, and the illusion of satisfaction would be gone.

Over and over the Course has told us that we make the world we see. It even tells us that, in a very literal sense, we made the physical universe. Yet, we ask, how can this really be true? Jesus' answer is simple: Look at your dreams. They show that you have the power to make a world as you would have it be. True, you don't seem to be the one making it. The dream seems to happen to you. The figures (people) in the dream do things to you and thereby cause emotions in you. But face it: you're the one doing it all. It's your dream. You're pulling the strings on those dream figures, making them do things that you want done, making them cause emotions that you want to experience. If you yourself did those things and chose those emotions, you would feel guilty. So you have them do it all for you.

> In dreams these features are not obscure. You seem to waken, and the dream is gone. Yet what you fail to recognize is that what <u>caused</u> the dream has <u>not</u> gone with it. Your <u>wish</u> to make another world that is <u>not</u> real <u>remains</u> with you. And what you seem to <u>waken</u> to is but another <u>form</u> of this same world you see in dreams. All your time is spent in dreaming. Your sleeping and your waking dreams have different forms, and that is all. <u>Their content is the same</u>. They are your protest <u>against</u> reality, and your fixed and insane idea that you can <u>change</u> it. In your <u>waking</u> dreams, the special relationship has a special place. It is the means by which you try to make your <u>sleeping</u> dreams <u>come true</u>. From this, you do <u>not</u> waken. The special relationship is your <u>determination</u> to keep your hold on unreality, and to <u>prevent</u> yourself from waking. And while you see more <u>value</u> in sleeping than in waking, you will <u>not</u> let go of it.

Here is the chilling part: When we waken, even though the dream is gone, whatever crazy thing in us produced that weird dream is *still there*. Whatever produced my dream of being an intimate confidant and helper of a famous author is still in me. That the dream has ended means nothing, for its cause remains.

Why, then, do I assume that this thing in me is turned off once I'm awake? How do I know it isn't operating right this second? How do I know it isn't dreaming the world I see around me right now? According to Jesus, that is exactly what is happening. My nighttime dreams are my fantasy protest against the daytime dream, and the daytime dream is my fantasy protest against true reality. All my time is spent in dreaming.

One more point: In my daytime dream, the special relationship is my attempt to make my (nighttime) dreams come true. In other words, special relationships, like nighttime dreams, are wish-fulfillment episodes in which I try to triumph over my humiliating daytime life. Many pages of commentary could be written on this one remarkable insight. All I want to draw out here is Jesus' main point: If special relationships are an attempt to make sleeping dreams into our reality, they must also be an attempt to make *sleep* into our reality. They are our attempt to never wake up.

Application: Think of a special relationship in your life, one you are heavily invested in. First ask yourself how this relationship is your attempt to triumph over other situations in your life that didn't treat you right. Then picture, at the heart of the relationship, you as a child having a tantrum and screaming:

> *I want it my way!*
> *I want my sleeping dreams to come true.*
> *I want to never wake up.*

6. The Holy Spirit, ever practical in His wisdom, <u>accepts</u> your dreams and uses them as means for <u>waking</u>. <u>You</u> would have used them to remain <u>asleep</u>. I said before [Ur: We once said] that the first change, before dreams disappear, is that your dreams of fear are changed to <u>happy</u> dreams. That is what the Holy Spirit does in the special relationship. He does <u>not</u> destroy it, nor snatch it away from you. But He <u>does</u> use it differently, as a help to make <u>His</u> purpose <u>real</u> to you. The special relationship will remain, <u>not</u> as a source of pain and guilt, but as a source of joy and freedom. It will <u>not</u> be for you alone, for therein lay its misery. As its <u>un</u>holiness kept it a thing apart, its <u>holiness</u> will become an offering to everyone.

The Holy Spirit doesn't say, "Get rid of those dreams!" That would be His temper tantrum in response to ours. Instead, He accepts that we are dreaming and says, "While you dream, can we perhaps change the purpose? Can we use your dreams as means for wakening?" He does this by preserving our special relationships but changing their purpose. They thus remain special in form, but they acquire increasing holiness in content. Rather than an exclusive club with the threatening title "We'll Show Them," they become lovely little charities called "We'll Serve Them."

Application: Think about a special relationship in your life and ask yourself which slogan fits it better—"We'll Show Them" or "We'll Serve Them."

7. Your special relationship will be a means for <u>undoing</u> guilt in

16

everyone blessed through your holy relationship. It will be a happy dream, and one which you will <u>share</u> with all who come within your sight. Through it, the blessing the Holy Spirit has laid upon it will be <u>extended</u>. Think not that He has forgotten anyone in the purpose He has given you. And think not that He has forgotten <u>you</u> to whom He <u>gave</u> the gift. He uses everyone who calls on Him as means for the salvation of everyone. And He will waken everyone through you who offered your relationship to Him. If you but recognized His gratitude! Or mine through His! For we are joined as in one [Ur: as one in] purpose, being of one mind with Him.

Here is what makes the holy relationship so different from the special relationship. The special relationship is our vengeance on a world that didn't bow down before the sacredness of our ego. It is our way of saying, "Look, you *&%$#. In spite of all you did, I got the love I wanted. Me and my love have something so special that you couldn't even understand it, and you certainly can't share in it."

The holy relationship makes the opposite statement: "The Holy Spirit has laid a gift in this relationship, a gift so holy that it could only be for everyone. The two of us are its trustees, and we hope you will allow us the privilege of offering it to you, for that is why it was given us." When two people actually accept this purpose, however imperfectly, they gain the eternal gratitude of Jesus and the Holy Spirit.

8. Let not the dream take hold to close your eyes. It is not strange that dreams can make a world that is unreal. It is the *wish* to make it that is incredible [Ur: The *wish* to make it *is* incredible]. Your relationship with your brother has now [Ur: Your relationship has] become one in which the wish has been <u>removed,</u> because its purpose has been changed from one of dreams to one of truth. You are not sure of this because you think it may be <u>this</u> that is the dream. You are so used to choosing among dreams you do not see that you have made, at last, the choice between the truth and *all* illusions.

What is unbelievable is not that we can make an entire unreal world. Rather, what is unbelievable is the *wish* to do so. This twisted wish to bend reality to our ego's whim lies at the heart of the special relationship. Yet in the holy relationship, that wish to control reality has been replaced by the wish to wake up to reality as it is. If you have had a relationship in which this has happened, you probably know that it is extremely tempting to think that this new journey, this joint quest to wake up, is the pie-in-the-sky fantasy. You may not realize that, instead, you have at last made the choice to leave all fantasies behind.

> 9. Yet Heaven is sure. This is no dream. Its coming means that you have chosen truth, and it has come because you have been willing to let your special relationship meet its conditions. In your relationship the Holy Spirit has gently laid the real world; the world of happy dreams, from which awaking is so easy and so natural. For as your sleeping and your waking dreams represent the same wishes in your mind, so do the real world and the truth of Heaven join in the Will of God. The dream of waking is easily transferred to its reality. For this dream reflects your will joined with the Will of God. And what this Will would have accomplished has never *not* been done.

When truth finally shows up, after all our asking, we have this odd way of being too busy to answer the door, or too annoyed at this "intrusion" to let our guest in. That is what happens when a holy relationship is formed. We don't realize that this is truth showing up at our door, ready to take us on a journey to Heaven. We don't realize that here, laid in the heart of this relationship, is the real world, held out to us. All we need do is take hold of this gift, and Heaven will be ours. For just as our sleeping and waking dreams stem from the same wish in our mind, so the real world and Heaven stem from the same Will in God's Mind. When we claim one, we gain the other, and discover that it has always been ours.

III. Light in the Dream
Commentary by Robert Perry

1. You who have spent your life [Ur: lives] in bringing truth to illusion, reality to fantasy, have walked the way of dreams. For you have gone from waking to sleeping, and on and on to a yet deeper sleep. Each dream has led to other dreams, and every fantasy that seemed to bring a light into the darkness but made the darkness deeper. Your goal was darkness, in which no ray of light could enter. And you sought a blackness so complete that you could hide from truth forever, in complete insanity. What you forgot was simply that God cannot destroy Himself. The light is *in* you. Darkness can cover it, but cannot put it out.

What a sad picture. This, too often, is the sobering reality behind our "every day, in every way, I'm getting better and better." We see certain people go through the kind of process Jesus sketches above, but they are symbols for all of us. Think of the addicted gambler, who starts out with his life together, but then gets bitten by the bug. He begins chasing fantasies of the big win. He tells himself that, despite his losses, he knows exactly what he's doing. He has epiphanies in which how to win is revealed to him with perfect clarity, yet these only lead to more loss. His life unravels more and more, even though he doesn't see it. He has no idea that he is actually being driven not by the will to win, but by some hidden self-destruct mechanism.

This gambler's story is our story. We started out in truth, with God, and somewhere we veered off into dreams and fantasies. We told ourselves that we'd make it all work, that we'd make our dreams come true. But we were really motivated by a deep self-destruct mechanism inside. Yet we forgot that no part of God can destroy itself. We *cannot* find total darkness because light is the fabric of our being.

2. As the light comes nearer you will rush to darkness, shrinking from the truth, sometimes retreating to the lesser forms of fear, and sometimes to stark terror. But you will advance, because your goal is the advance from fear to truth. [Ur: *You know this.*] The goal you accepted is the goal

19

of knowledge, for which you signified your willingness. Fear seems to live in darkness, and when you are afraid <u>you have stepped back</u> [away from light, into darkness]. Let us then join quickly in an instant of light, and it will be enough to remind you that your goal <u>is</u> light.

Now, on our long, slow spiral into darkness, a light has turned on. Perhaps that light is the Course coming into our life, or perhaps we had an otherworldly experience. In the context of this section, the light is our joining with another person in a holy relationship. Whatever the form, that light represents our setting the goal of getting out of the dark.

Now if your whole goal has been complete darkness, and you then set the goal of light, you are going to be in a profoundly divided state. The closer you get to the light, the more your old goal of darkness will pull at you, causing you to recoil. How do you know when you are recoiling? When you are afraid. When you feel that fear, join with Jesus in an instant of light, a holy instant, to get you back in touch with your real goal.

> 3. Truth has rushed to meet you since <u>you</u> called upon it. If you knew Who [based on the context, I would say this is Jesus] walks beside you on the way that <u>you</u> have chosen [Ur: on *this* way], fear would be impossible. You do <u>not</u> know because the journey into darkness has been long and cruel, and you have gone deep into it. A little flicker of your eyelids, closed so long, has not yet been sufficient to give you confidence in yourself, so long despised. You go <u>toward</u> love still hating it, and <u>terribly</u> afraid of its judgment upon you. And you do <u>not</u> realize that you are <u>not</u> afraid of love, but only <u>of what you have made of it</u>. You are advancing to love's <u>meaning</u>, and away from <u>all</u> illusions in which you have surrounded it. When you retreat to the illusion <u>your fear increases</u>, for there is little doubt that what <u>you</u> think it means *is* fearful. Yet what is that to us who travel surely and very swiftly <u>away</u> from fear?

The darkness into which we have retreated is, in part, made of our illusions of what love is. Through the lens of these illusions, we see God, standing there at the end of the journey, as a typical special relationship partner. As we go toward Him, stumbling, faltering, seesawing back and forth, we envision Him tapping His foot in impatience, judging the hell out of us, searching His memory to see if there was ever a more hopeless spiritual seeker than us. We ourselves carry this same cruel perception of us, for after all, this perception exists only in our own mind. In fact, the whole journey is one of realizing that we fear love only because of what we've projected onto it, not because of what it really is. When we recoil from the light, we are retreating back into our frightening illusions of what love means. When we advance, we are shedding those illusions.

Our saving grace is that we are not walking toward the light alone. An embodiment of the light is walking beside us. This seems to be Jesus (though the "Who walks beside you" is not entirely clear). To appreciate the significance of this, imagine yourself on a long journey by foot to a distant and unfamiliar kingdom. Now imagine the same journey, but your traveling companion is the king of that kingdom. Which journey will you feel more secure on?

> 4. You who hold your brother's [Ur: each other's] hand also hold mine, for when you joined each other you were <u>not</u> alone. Do you believe that I would <u>leave</u> you in the darkness that you agreed to leave <u>with</u> me? In your relationship is this world's light. And fear <u>must</u> disappear before you now. Be tempted not to snatch away the gift of faith you offered to your brother. You will succeed only in frightening yourself [Ur: yourselves]. The gift is given forever, for God Himself received it. You <u>cannot</u> take it back. <u>You have accepted God.</u> The holiness of your relationship is established in Heaven. You do not understand <u>what</u> you accepted, but remember that your understanding is <u>not</u> necessary. All that <u>was</u> necessary was merely the *wish* to understand. That wish was the <u>desire to be holy</u>. The Will of God <u>is</u> granted you. For you desire the only thing you ever had, or ever were.

When Helen and Bill took each other's hand, they were simultaneously taking the hand of Jesus and agreeing to leave the darkness with him. We can readily imagine someone making a pact with the devil without realizing she was doing so. Helen and Bill's situation is the reverse of that; this is two people making a pact with *Jesus* without knowing it. Once made, Jesus will honor this pact forever, even if the two people are constantly looking for ways out.

That is what is happening here. Helen and Bill, by joining in a common goal, have given each other the faith that they can reach that goal. But now they are wishing they could take that gift back. Jesus, however, standing behind the counter, informs them that this gift is nonreturnable, for God Himself received it.

The fact is that they have no idea what they accepted in that holy instant, but that's all right. They don't need to understand. In accepting the goal of holiness, they embraced the *wish* to understand, the *goal* of understanding. In return, all of the knowledge and Will of God was placed in their relationship, a priceless gift waiting to be unwrapped by them.

> 5. Each instant that we spend together will teach you that this goal is possible, and will strengthen your <u>desire</u> to reach it. And in your desire lies its accomplishment. <u>Your</u> desire is now in <u>complete</u> accord with all the power of the Holy Spirit's Will. No little, faltering footsteps that you may take can separate your desire from His Will and from His <u>strength</u>. I hold your hand as surely as you agreed to take your brother's [Ur: each other's]. <u>You will not separate</u>, for I stand with you and walk with you in your advance to truth. And where we go we carry God with us.

Imagine again that you're on that journey to that remote kingdom with its king. The kingdom is a true Shangri-La and its king is the epitome of everything it stands for. However, you are journeying largely with your eyes closed, and so most of the time you are not aware that he walks with you. At the opening of the journey, you experienced a brief flicker of your eyelids, and thus caught sight of him next to you. Yet now that you are well into the journey, your footsteps are faltering. How can you strengthen your footsteps? By having more flickers of your eyelids, in which you briefly glimpse the presence of that wondrous king with you.

Application: Think of whatever lack of hope you feel on your journey. Think of how far away the goal of God seems. Then realize that if you could only open your eyes—your real eyes—you would see Jesus right there beside you. Say to him,

> *Jesus, I acknowledge your presence.*
> *You are here with me now.*
> *Let us join quickly in an instant of light.*
> *This will remind me that my goal is light*
> *and that my guide is sure.*
> *I **will** get there.*

6. In your relationship you have joined with me in bringing Heaven to the Son of God, who hid in darkness. You have been willing to bring the darkness to light, and this willingness has given strength to everyone who would <u>remain</u> in darkness. Those who would see *will* see. And they will join with me in carrying <u>their</u> light into the darkness, when the darkness in them is <u>offered</u> to the light, and is removed forever. My need for you, joined <u>with</u> me in the holy light of your relationship, is <u>your</u> need for salvation. Would I not give you what you gave to me? For when you joined your brother [Ur: each other], you answered <u>me</u>.

You are actually traveling with another darkness dweller like yourself, as well as with the king. On this journey, there is much more going on than you may realize. Your progress has given all those people back in the land of darkness the hope that they can make it, and therefore given them willingness to set out on the journey themselves. And that is the king's ultimate agenda, to get all of them out of darkness and into the kingdom of light, where they can see. He knows that the more light you find, the more you will bring this light back into the darkness, to illumine all those who are still stuck there like you used to be. And so the king is deeply grateful for the journey you have set out on. He looks at the two of you and sees, not two people saved, but *everyone* saved.

7. You who are now the bringer [Ur: bringers] of salvation have the function of bringing light to darkness. The darkness in you <u>has</u> been brought to light. Carry it back <u>to</u> darkness, from the holy instant to which you <u>brought</u> it. We are made whole in our desire to make whole. Let not time worry you, for all the fear that you and your brother experience is really past. Time has been readjusted to help us do, together, what your separate pasts would hinder. You have gone <u>past</u> fear, for no two minds can <u>join</u> in the desire for love without love's joining <u>them</u>.

It is not enough to bring our darkness to the light, to be dispelled. That is just the beginning. We are not whole until we carry the light back into the darkness, where our brothers are still chained. This is the function given every holy relationship.

As they faced this task, no doubt Helen and Bill thought, "How can we help them? We are still stuck in our own stuff. All those ego patterns from the past are still gripping us, making us afraid, keeping us apart." Jesus responds, "Don't worry. I have adjusted time. That future in which the two of you have gone past all your ego patterns is here now. It is an actual presence shining at the heart of your relationship. And you can draw on it now to help the people I send you."

> 8. Not one light in Heaven but goes with you. Not one Ray that shines forever in the Mind of God but shines on you. Heaven is joined with you in your advance to Heaven. When such great lights have joined with you to give the little spark of your desire the power of God Himself, can you remain in darkness? You and your brother are coming home together, after a long and meaningless journey that you undertook apart, and that led nowhere. You have found your brother [Ur: each other], and you will light each other's way. And from this light will the Great Rays extend back into darkness and forward unto God, to shine away the past and so make room for His eternal Presence, in which everything is radiant in the light.

Now we can see the full picture. There are two people who both took that long, slow spiral into darkness that we saw in the first paragraph. They both meandered into ever deeper darkness, increasingly alone in their own private hell. But now they have found each other, and together they are slowly, haltingly making their way out of the darkness.

To them, however, this just seems like one more version of the hopelessness that has characterized everything. For even though this is the journey to light, they seem hopeless at it. The spark of their desire is too faint amid the stifling gloom. They believe they are going in circles.

What they don't realize is that Jesus holds their hands and walks with them. And all the lights of Heaven go with them and shine on them. With these great lights joining them, the spark of their desire becomes immeasurably strengthened. It blazes forth like a beacon, lighting the way in front of them. Its Rays then extend back into darkness, lighting the way for all those left behind. Those same Rays also extend forward, shining away the past that would clog the road in front of them, and thus making "room for [God's] eternal Presence, in which everything is radiant in the light." Can they really fail?

IV. The Little Willingness
Commentary by Robert Perry

1. The holy instant is the <u>result</u> of your determination to be holy. It is the *answer*. The desire and the willingness to let it come <u>precede</u> its coming. <u>You</u> prepare your mind for it <u>only</u> to the extent of <u>recognizing</u> that you want it above all else. It is not necessary that you do more; indeed, it is necessary that you realize that you can<u>not</u> do more. Do not attempt to give the Holy Spirit what He does <u>not</u> ask, or you will add the ego to Him and <u>confuse the two</u>. He asks but little. It is <u>He</u> Who adds the greatness and the might. He <u>joins</u> with you to make the holy instant far greater than you can understand. It is your realization that you <u>need</u> do so little that enables <u>Him</u> to give so much.

This section is about how to invite the holy instant, and how not to. Here in the first paragraph, Jesus explains that to have a holy instant, you have to desire it above all else, you have to be willing to have it come, and you have to be determined to have the fruit of it: holiness. You prepare for it, in other words, by putting your mind into a state of pure asking for it. This is the little that you give to the process. The Holy Spirit gives the rest.

It is essential, Jesus says here, that you give only your little part, that you don't attempt to give more. Anything more that you try to give actually takes away from your invitation. This naturally raises the question: What is the more that we try to give?

2. Trust not your good intentions. They are not enough. But trust <u>implicitly</u> your willingness, whatever else may enter. Concentrate only on this, and be <u>not</u> disturbed that shadows surround it. <u>That is why you came</u>. If you could come <u>without</u> them you would not <u>need</u> the holy instant. Come to it not in arrogance, assuming that <u>you</u> must achieve the state its coming brings with it. The miracle of the holy instant lies in your willingness to let <u>it</u> be what it is. And in your willingness for <u>this</u> lies also your acceptance of yourself as <u>you</u> were meant to be.

I believe that this paragraph, which has been a favorite of many Course students, is easily misunderstood. Here is what I think it really means:

Do not rely on your good intentions to make you holy and therefore worthy of the holy instant. Your "good" intentions are simply not good enough. They are tainted with ego. What will bring the holy instant instead is your willingness to let it come. Rely on this willingness, and do not be disturbed that it is surrounded by shadowy intentions, by unholy intentions. That is why you are coming to the holy instant—to have those healed. If you didn't have those dark intentions, you wouldn't need the holy instant. It is arrogance to think that in order to have the holy instant, you must give yourself the holiness that only it can give you. Just be willing to let it be what it is, and in doing so you will also accept yourself as you were meant to be.

> 3. Humility will <u>never</u> ask that you remain content with littleness. But it <u>does</u> require that you be <u>not</u> content with less than greatness that comes <u>not</u> of you. Your difficulty with the holy instant arises from your fixed conviction that you are not <u>worthy</u> of it. And what is this but the determination to <u>be</u> as you would <u>make yourself</u>? God did not create His dwelling place unworthy of Him. And if you believe He cannot enter where He wills to be, you <u>must</u> be <u>interfering</u> with His Will. You do not need the strength of willingness to come from you, but only from <u>His</u> Will.

Now the "more" that we try to add to gain the holy instant is clear: We try to make ourselves worthy of it. We assume that we are not worthy of it, and that, consequently, God is withholding it from us. Let's be honest: Isn't that assumption somewhere in our mind? If only we were holier, we think, we would have holy instants all the time. Why else isn't God giving us the juice?

This paragraph makes clear that this sense of unworthiness is a false humility. Real humility does not acknowledge unworthiness. Rather, it refuses to be content with anything less than the greatness God gave us. Our sense of unworthiness, rather than humility, is actually our determination to be the sinner we made ourselves, in rejection of the holiness that God created in us. Our "humility" is the defiance of Lucifer, not the meekness of Mary.

> 4. The holy instant does <u>not</u> come from your little willingness alone. It is <u>always</u> the result of your <u>small</u> willingness <u>combined</u> with the unlimited power of God's Will. You have been wrong in thinking

that it is needful to prepare yourself for Him. It is impossible to make arrogant preparations for holiness, and not believe that it is up to you to establish the conditions for peace. God has established them. They do not wait upon your willingness for what they are. Your willingness is needed only to make it possible to teach you what they are. If you maintain you are unworthy of learning this, you are interfering with the lesson by believing that you must make the learner different. You did not make the learner, nor can you make him different. Would you first make a miracle yourself, and then expect one to be made *for* you?

It's almost as if Jesus is inside our mind, as he dissects our attitudes around the holy instant. Here is what we are thinking: "I decide what it takes to have a holy instant, and what it takes is making myself holy. It is the holy who are granted holy instants. Therefore, I must make myself into a different person. I must transform my unworthiness into worthiness. This is how I need to prepare myself for the holy instant. I must make a miracle for myself and turn myself into a holy and deserving person. Then God will make a miracle for me; then He'll give me the holy instant."

Please read that statement again and try to see yourself in it, even if it does not represent your conscious thoughts. Can you see it in your attitudes? Realize that whatever you see of it in you is just the tip of the iceberg. Whether you can see it or not, this statement dominates your attitudes.

Now notice that every single sentence in this statement is soaked with arrogance, the arrogance of thinking we decide how high the bar is set, the arrogance of thinking we have to remake the self that God created, the arrogance of trying to do God's job for Him.

5. You merely ask the question. The answer is given. Seek not to answer, but merely to receive the answer as it is given. In preparing for the holy instant, do not attempt to make yourself holy to be ready to receive it. That is but to confuse your role with God's. Atonement cannot come to those who think that they must first atone, but only to those who offer it nothing more than simple willingness to make way for it. Purification is of God alone, and therefore for you.

Notice all the ways in which Jesus points out the circularity of our attempts to earn our way into holy instants. We are trying to answer our own question. We are trying to make ourselves holy in order to be given holiness. We are trying to make a miracle for ourselves, so that one can then be given us. We are trying to atone first, so that Atonement can come to us. We are trying to purify ourselves, so that God can purify us.

This is ridiculous. It's as if we are cleaning the house before the cleaning lady arrives, worried that unless the house is already clean, we won't be worthy of her. This is crazy. Why can't we just relax and let God give to us?

> Rather than seek to prepare <u>yourself</u> for Him, try to think thus:
>
> *I who am host to God <u>am</u> worthy of Him.*
> *He Who <u>established</u> His dwelling place in me created it as He would*
>   *have it be.*
> *It is <u>not</u> needful that I make it ready for Him, but only that <u>I do not</u>*
>   *<u>interfere</u> with His plan to <u>restore</u> to me my own <u>awareness</u> of my*
>   *readiness, which is eternal.*
> *I need <u>add</u> nothing to His plan.*
> *But to <u>receive</u> it, I <u>must</u> be willing <u>not</u> to substitute my own <u>in place</u> of*
>   *it.*

This is a powerful practice for inviting the holy instant. We'll practice it at the end, but for now I just want to explain its meaning.

What I am is host to God; therefore, I must be worthy of Him being my Guest.

He Who established His guest room in me created it as He would have it be. It is His space and it is holy. I have no say in it.

I don't have to make this space in me ready for Him. In this place, I am eternally ready. I just need to not interfere with His plan to bring this eternal fact to my awareness.

I don't need to add anything to His plan.

But to receive it, I must not replace it with my plan, which is to give ***myself*** *the readiness that He has already created in me.*

> 6. And that is all. Add <u>more</u>, and you will merely <u>take away</u> the little that is asked. Remember <u>you made guilt</u>, and that your plan for the <u>escape</u> from guilt has been to bring Atonement <u>to</u> it, and <u>make salvation fearful</u>. And it is <u>only</u> fear that you will add, if you prepare <u>yourself</u> for

love. The preparation for the holy instant belongs to Him Who gives it. <u>Release</u> yourself to Him Whose function <u>is</u> release. Do <u>not</u> assume His function <u>for</u> Him. Give Him but what He asks, that you may learn how <u>little</u> is your part, and how great <u>is His</u>.

The practice that Jesus has given us is carefully designed to help us give our willingness to receiving the holy instant and *give nothing else*. We tend to want to give our willingness *plus* our attempts to make ourselves worthy. This practice takes a razor and cuts off that excess. The problem with the excess is that it reflects *our* plan for escaping guilt, which is to atone for it through sacrifices designed to establish our goodness. This is a fearful system. Do we really want to inject fear into our search for the pure love of the holy instant?

> 7. It is this that makes the holy instant so easy and so natural. <u>You</u> make it difficult, because you insist there <u>must</u> be more that you need do. You find it difficult to <u>accept</u> the idea that you need give so <u>little</u>, to receive so much. And it is very hard for you to realize it is <u>not</u> personally insulting that <u>your</u> contribution and the Holy Spirit's are so <u>extremely</u> disproportionate. You are still convinced that your <u>understanding</u> is a powerful contribution <u>to</u> the truth, and <u>makes it what it is</u>. Yet we have emphasized that <u>you</u> need understand nothing. Salvation is easy <u>just</u> *because* it asks nothing you cannot give <u>right now</u>.

Here we can see the arrogance in our "humility." We want to contribute more to the holy instant than the Holy Spirit asks. We don't want our part in it to be so much smaller than the Holy Spirit's. We want our deep understanding to make the holy instant what it is. The fact that our part is so small we find personally insulting. Here, then, is the real issue behind our "humble" desire to clean ourselves up for God. Our supposed humility is really just old-fashioned pride.

Jesus used the phrase "personally insulting" no less than three times, and always around this same basic issue. In the Urtext, he said that the real means for perfect comfort is already provided and does not involve any effort at all on our part. Then he said, "[Your] egocentricity usually misperceives this as personally insulting." In the Manual, he speaks of giving up our own judgment as the prerequisite for receiving the Holy Spirit's judgment. He then says that this giving up "is usually a fairly slow process not because it is difficult, but because it is apt to be perceived as personally insulting" (M-9.2:4).

> 8. Forget not that it has been your decision to make everything that is natural and easy for you impossible. [Ur: What you believe to be impossible *will be*, if God so wills it, but *you* will remain quite *unaware* of it.] If you believe the holy instant is difficult for you, it is because you have become the arbiter of what is possible, and remain unwilling to give place to One Who knows. The whole belief in orders of difficulty in miracles is centered on this. Everything God wills is not only possible, but has already happened. And that is why the past has gone. It never happened in reality. Only in your mind, which thought it did, is its undoing needful.

Here at the end of the section, we can fully appreciate the real reason behind our desire to make ourselves worthy of the holy instant. We are trying to play God. God says, "I will that you have the holy instant. Therefore, it must be natural and easy, and in fact it must already *be*." We respond, "No, sorry, I am the arbiter of what is possible, and I say that it is difficult, for it means reconfiguring my whole nature."

This is the real story here. We want to be in charge. We want to know better than God. We want to be in control of what we are. And we want to decide what is easy and what is hard. Are we willing to give all this up, to stop playing God? Are we willing to let God be God?

Application: I strongly recommend taking some time with the holy instant practice Jesus gives us in this section. Take fifteen or even thirty minutes if you can. Have this page in front of you. Read a line from the practice, fix it in your mind, and then close your eyes and say it to yourself, slowly and meaningfully. Then open your eyes and fix the next line in your mind, and close your eyes and say it to yourself. I have included my explanations of each line, just for clarity's sake. I'm not suggesting you repeat these to yourself, but you can if you like.

You will be strongly tempted, after you go through this once or twice, to just close your eyes and relax. I strongly encourage you to not do that. You'll only be depriving yourself. Instead, keep going through the practice. My experience is that it slowly gains in power with each new pass through.

IV. The Little Willingness

I who am host to God am worthy of Him.

(What I am is host to God; therefore, I must be worthy of Him being my Guest.)

He Who established His dwelling place in me created it as He would have it be.

(He Who established His guest room in me created it as He would have it be. It is His space and it is holy. I have no say in it.)

It is not needful that I make it ready for Him, but only that I do not interfere with His plan to restore to me my own awareness of my readiness, which is eternal.

(I don't have to make this space in me ready for Him. In this place, I am eternally ready. I just need to not interfere with His plan to bring this eternal fact to my awareness.)

I need add nothing to His plan.
But to receive it, I must be willing not to substitute my own in place of it.

(But to receive it, I must not replace it with my plan, which is to give myself the readiness that He has already created in me.)

V. The Happy Dream
Commentary by Robert Perry

1. Prepare you *now* for the undoing of what never was. If you already <u>understood</u> the difference between truth and illusion, the Atonement would <u>have</u> no meaning. The holy instant, the [Ur: your] holy relationship, the Holy Spirit's teaching, and all the means by which salvation is accomplished, would have no purpose. For they are all but <u>aspects</u> of the plan to change your dreams of fear to happy dreams, from which you waken easily to knowledge. Put yourself <u>not</u> in charge of this, for you can<u>not</u> distinguish between advance and retreat. Some of your greatest advances <u>you</u> have judged as failures, and some of your deepest retreats <u>you</u> have evaluated as success.

We need to see this first paragraph as the continuation of the final paragraph of the last section. In that context, the first sentence means this: The holy instant will undo the past, which never existed in the first place. Don't prepare for a holy instant in the future by trying to make yourself worthy of it. Prepare for it now by merely desiring it and being willing for it to come to you.

This undoing of your illusions must be done for you, simply because you don't know the difference between truth and illusion. If you did, you wouldn't need the holy instant, the holy relationship, or the Holy Spirit's teaching. Their whole purpose is to exchange your illusions for the truth. Given that you can't distinguish truth from illusion, you also can't distinguish advance from retreat.

Application: Think of one of your failures, at least a failure in your eyes. Then consider that it might have been one of your greatest successes. Then think of one of your successes in life, as you have viewed success. Then consider that it might have been one of your deepest retreats. Now ask yourself, "Do I really want to put myself in charge of telling illusions from truth?"

2. Never approach the holy instant <u>after</u> you have tried to remove all

32

fear and hatred from your mind. That is *its* function. Never attempt to <u>overlook</u> your guilt <u>before</u> you ask the Holy Spirit's help. That is *His* function. Your part is only to offer Him a <u>little</u> willingness to <u>let</u> Him remove all fear and hatred, and to <u>be</u> forgiven.

These sentences repeat the theme of the last section: Don't try to clean yourself up for the holy instant. That is *its* job. Just offer your willingness to receive a gift you could never give yourself.

On your little faith, joined with <u>His</u> understanding, <u>He</u> will build your part in the Atonement and <u>make sure</u> that you fulfill it easily. And <u>with</u> Him, <u>you</u> will build a ladder planted in the solid rock of faith, and rising even to Heaven. Nor will you use it to ascend to Heaven alone. 3. Through your holy relationship, reborn and blessed in every holy instant you do <u>not</u> arrange, thousands will rise to Heaven <u>with</u> you. Can <u>you</u> plan for <u>this</u>? Or could you <u>prepare</u> yourself [Ur: *yourselves*] for such a function? Yet it <u>is</u> possible, because God wills it. Nor will He change His Mind about it. The means and purpose <u>both</u> belong to Him. You have accepted one; the other will be provided. A purpose such as this, <u>without</u> the means, <u>is</u> inconceivable. <u>He</u> will provide the means to <u>anyone</u> who <u>shares</u> His purpose.

The Course says over and over again that when two come together in a holy relationship, they will be given a joint special function, a place in the larger plan that they fulfill together. With the Holy Spirit's help, they will build a ladder to Heaven, and then ascend this ladder, with thousands of others climbing up behind them. If this sounds like flowery hyperbole, remember that Jesus was speaking directly to Helen and Bill, and that this very moment, as you read the Course, you are climbing the ladder they built.

This naturally makes one wonder: What will be my ladder, whom will I build it with, and who will climb it once we've built it?

The main theme here is that we are not in charge of this function. How could we ourselves possibly plan to bring thousands up the ladder with us? As the first paragraph said, we just don't have the requisite understanding. The Holy Spirit, therefore, contributes the understanding. We contribute our *faith*, our trust in Him and in our brother. That faith is the foundation. It is the solid rock in which our ladder is planted .

Such a function may seem impossible, "Yet it is possible, because God wills it." If we will only accept the goal, God will provide the means. We merely receive the means; we don't have to invent them.

> 4. <u>Happy dreams come true,</u> <u>not</u> because they are dreams, but only because they are <u>happy</u>. And so they <u>must</u> be loving. Their message is, "Thy Will be done," and <u>not,</u> "I want it otherwise." The alignment of means and purpose is an undertaking <u>impossible</u> for you to understand. You do not even realize you <u>have</u> accepted the Holy Spirit's purpose as your own, and you would merely bring unholy means to its accomplishment. The little faith it needed to change the purpose is all that is required to <u>receive</u> the means and <u>use</u> them.

I love that first line. It means, "Happy dreams awaken us to the truth beyond the dream, not because they are dreams, but because their happiness comes from acceptance of the truth." The usual notion of "dreams coming true" implies that we have successfully forced our wishes onto reality; we have successfully screamed "I want it thus!" (II.4:1). Yet this is not what makes happy dreams happy. Indeed, what the Course means by "the happy dream" is *not* a set of "happy" circumstances in the dream. Rather, it is a state of mind in the dream in which we accept reality *beyond* the dream. The happiness comes from accepting reality as God created it, not as we would bend it. At the core of the happy dream, then, is the acknowledgment, "Thy Will be done." That is why happy dreams awaken us to reality.

The alignment of means and purpose is a major theme in the holy relationship discussions. We have this holy goal (the purpose), but how do we actually get there (the means)? We don't really understand the goal and don't even truly realize we have accepted it. How, therefore, can we be expected to devise the means that fit it? Any means we came up with would only express our unholy mindset. Rather, we need to *receive* the means, just as we received the goal.

> 5. It is no dream to love your brother as yourself. Nor is your holy relationship a dream. All that remains of dreams within it is that it is still a <u>special</u> relationship. Yet it is <u>very</u> useful to the Holy Spirit, Who *has* a special <u>function</u> here. It will become the <u>happy</u> dream through which He can spread joy to thousands on thousands who believe that love is fear, <u>not</u> happiness. Let Him fulfill the function that He <u>gave</u> to your relationship by <u>accepting</u> it [the function] <u>for</u> you, and <u>nothing</u> will be wanting that would make of it what He would have it be.

34

Don't think that your holy relationship is just some pie-in-the-sky dream. Don't think that coming to love your brother as yourself is just some idealistic fantasy. You can get there. You *will* get there. Just let the Holy Spirit be in charge. If you do, He will turn it into a happy dream—a dream with happy content, a special relationship with holy content. And then He will use it to spread happiness to thousands and thousands of your brothers who are afraid of the love that would make them happy. In the happy love between the two of you, they will see the happiness they have denied themselves.

> 6. When you feel the holiness of your relationship is threatened by anything, stop instantly and offer the Holy Spirit your willingness, in spite of fear, to let Him exchange this instant for the holy one that you would rather have. He will never fail in this. But forget not that your relationship is one, and so it must be that whatever threatens the peace of one is an equal threat to the other. The power of joining [Ur: and] its blessing lies [Ur: lie] in the fact that it is now impossible for you or your brother [Ur: for either of you] to experience fear alone, or to attempt to deal with it alone. Never believe that this is necessary, or even possible. Yet just as this is impossible, so is it equally impossible that the holy instant come to either of you without the other. And it will come to both at the request of either.

Jesus has spoken of the relationship being "reborn and blessed in every holy instant you do not arrange." Here is how some of those holy instants may come about. First, you feel the holiness of your relationship threatened—conflict comes into the relationship. We will always at first try to solve this conflict in our way, either through more primitive strategies, such as blaming, manipulating, or placating, or through "enlightened" strategies, such as active listening, skillful compromise, or setting boundaries. Instead, Jesus says, "stop instantly." Stop trying to solve it your way and ask for a holy instant. This is one of the hardest things to do in a conflict—to stop trying to solve it our way.

We ask for this holy instant not just for the sake of ourselves, but for the sake of both. For now that we have joined in a holy relationship, our underlying oneness becomes manifest on the surface. In a holy relationship, we share the same state of mind, more so than in a special relationship. Thus, fear in one will quickly become fear in both, and a holy instant in one will be experienced by both.

7. Whoever is saner at the time the threat is perceived should remember how deep is his indebtedness to the other and how much gratitude is due him, <u>and be glad</u> that he can pay his debt by bringing happiness to both. Let him remember this, and say:

I desire this holy instant for myself, that I may <u>share</u> it with my brother, whom I love.
It is not possible that I can have it <u>without</u> him, or he without me.
Yet it is <u>wholly</u> possible for us to <u>share</u> it <u>now</u>.
And so I choose <u>this</u> instant as the one to offer to the Holy Spirit, that His blessing may descend on us, and keep us <u>both</u> in peace.

I cannot overstate the importance of this practice. We did an entire weekend workshop on it in 2002. It is not only a holy instant practice, but also a conflict-resolution practice. It doesn't look like one, because it is done *internally* by *one* person. That doesn't fit our idea of what will resolve conflict. The point is that this practice embodies an entirely different approach to conflict resolution. I have tried to capture that approach, in contrast to the usual approach, in the following table.

THE PRACTICE	ACIM APPROACH	EGO'S APPROACH
I desire this holy instant for myself,	I heal the conflict by momentarily *forgetting* the specific issue and experiencing a holy instant. I rise above the battleground.	I try to solve the conflict on its level, by fixing the outer issue. I stay on the battleground.
that I may share it with my brother,	I heal my experience of the conflict as a gift to both of us, out of love for my brother.	I change your mind so that *your* change can alleviate the conflict between us.
whom I love.	I remember that my love for you is more important than this issue, and that this love has the power to heal this issue.	This current issue becomes, for the time being, more important than the love between us.

THE PRACTICE	ACIM APPROACH	EGO'S APPROACH
It is not possible that I can have it without him, or he without me.	I remember that our interests are the same. If either of us is to experience Heaven now, we will have to go there together.	I assume that our interests are in conflict, which means that one or both of us must lose, or that we must creatively find a single form that can accommodate our essentially warring interests.
Yet it is wholly possible for us to share it now.	I remember that, even though we seem to be in hell, we truly can unite in Heaven *now*. I trust that you can do that with me.	I assume that until this outer form is fixed, we have to both stay in hell. Even if I decide to walk to Heaven, I don't trust you to go there with me.
And so I choose this instant as the one to offer to the Holy Spirit,	Remembering this, I come to a decision. I don't have to wait for outer resolution. I am not trapped by the issue's past. I can choose a holy instant *now*.	I am powerless to be at peace now. I have to wait until the outer issue is solved and the past is redressed.
that His blessing may descend on us,	Without His help we will stay stuck in the conflict. With His help, we can share a holy instant.	I can handle this. If I let the Holy Spirit in, He may get in the way of this thing being solved the way it ought to be.

THE PRACTICE	ACIM APPROACH	EGO'S APPROACH
and keep us both in peace.	The miracle restores us to a peace that is not dependent on the resolution of this issue, a peace that has an eternal basis. This peace *is* the solution, for the real problem was thinking that our peace and our unity were tied to this issue.	I would love us to both have peace, but we simply can't until you change and this conflict is resolved. Our peace and our unity are at the mercy of this specific issue.

Application: How, then, do we do this practice? Even though it is designed for use within a holy relationship, it can be used in any relationship. I suggest the following steps:

1. Write it out on a card and keep the card with you.
2. When you notice conflict in the relationship, stop trying to solve it your way.
3. Find some innocent excuse to remove yourself from the room for a few minutes.
4. Take out the card and repeat the lines in your mind over and over, slowly and sincerely, until you feel the anger and fear lift and peace come over you.
5. Return to the situation and express the content of your new perception in some form that is genuinely helpful and loving (not filled with spiritual superiority).

If you try this (and especially if it succeeds), please consider sending me the story.

VI. Beyond the Body
Commentary by Robert Perry

This is a difficult section to understand. It talks about a sick relationship with our body that few of us are in touch with. Even once you understand what it's saying, it may be hard to identify that as going on inside of you. My advice is to simply stretch in that direction. Try to understand it and try to suspend your disbelief about this going on inside of you. This section communicates essential aspects of the Course's teaching on the body.

> 1. There is nothing outside you. That is what you must ultimately learn, for it is the [Ur: for it is in that] realization that the Kingdom of Heaven is restored to you. For God created only this [the Kingdom], and He did not depart from it nor leave it separate from Himself. The Kingdom of Heaven is the dwelling place of the Son of God, who left not his Father and dwells not apart from Him. Heaven is not a place nor a condition. It is merely an awareness of perfect oneness, and the knowledge that there is nothing else; nothing outside this oneness, and nothing else within.

If we will only realize that there is nothing outside of us, we will also realize that the Kingdom of Heaven is ours—it too is within us. God created only one thing—the Kingdom—and since He created us, we then must be part of that Kingdom, and it must be inside of us. The Kingdom is our dwelling place, our true home. When we realize that we are one with it, we will also realize we are one with God. For the Kingdom itself is "merely an awareness of perfect oneness," the awareness that everything within the Kingdom is one and that there is nothing beyond this oneness.

Application. Repeat:

> *There is nothing outside me.*
> *Therefore, the Kingdom is not outside me.*
> *And there is nothing outside the Kingdom.*
> *I am one with the Kingdom and it is one with me.*
> *And there is nothing outside this oneness.*

2. What could God give but knowledge of Himself? What else is there to give? The belief that you could give and get something else, something outside yourself, has cost you the awareness of Heaven and [Ur: the loss of knowledge] of your Identity. And you have done a stranger thing than you yet realize. You have displaced your guilt to your body from your mind [Ur: *minds*]. Yet a body cannot be guilty, for it can do nothing of itself. You who think you hate your body deceive yourself. You hate your mind [Ur: *minds*], for guilt has entered into it [Ur: them], and it [Ur: they] would remain separate from your brother's, which it [Ur: they] cannot do.

The whole problem is our belief that there is something else, something outside of us, something outside the oneness of Heaven, something besides the knowledge of God. Our days are spent pursuing this something else, and this pursuit has cost us the awareness of Heaven. It has cost us everything.

We feel guilty for throwing away oneness in favor of separation. We feel guilty for being separate from our brothers. And this guilt causes us to hate our bodies. I hate to say it, but you do hate your body. Hatred of the body is an important theme in the Course and in this section. We may think we love our bodies because (perhaps) they are young and healthy and beautiful. We may think we hate our bodies because (more likely) they are unattractive and failing.

Neither of these, however, are at the deep level at which the Course is talking. At this level, *all* of us hate our bodies, without exception. At this level, we remember being a Son of God, and it feels unnatural to us to be separate from anything. We dimly sense that we chose this separation, and we hate ourselves—our mind—for doing so. We believe our mind has turned evil. Yet this belief is excruciating, so we displace our guilt (for choosing separation) onto our body. We think, "It's the fault of this barrier of flesh around me. It has made me separate. It has walled me off from my brothers. If it weren't for it, I would still be one with them." In short, we blame separation on the body.

3. Minds are joined; bodies are not. Only by assigning to the mind the properties of the body does separation seem to be possible. And it is mind that seems to be fragmented and private and alone. Its guilt, which keeps it separate, is projected to the body, which suffers and dies because it is attacked to hold the separation in the mind, and let it

40

not know its Identity [Ur: unity]. Mind cannot attack, but it can make fantasies and direct the body to act them out. Yet it is never what the body does that seems to satisfy. Unless the mind believes the body is actually acting out its fantasies, it will attack the body by increasing the projection of its guilt upon it.

This material sounds impenetrable, but it is conveying important truths. Minds, by nature, are joined with each other. Bodies, by nature, are separate from each other. So, to feel separate, we must see minds *as if* they were bodies, as if they were separate objects with space in between them. Isn't that how we functionally regard minds as we interact with the minds in other people?

Then we feel guilty for choosing separation (as we just saw), and project responsibility for this onto the body (as we just saw). It is this guilt that makes the body get sick, grow old, and die, because this guilt is a psychic attack on the body by a mind that is so powerful it *made* the body in the first place. In displacing guilt onto the body, we are really trying to displace our whole problem onto the body, so that we see the problem as being bodily, and never address the problem in the mind. This way, we will never *correct* the problem in the mind.

Just as the mind uses the body to produce the illusion of separation, so it uses the body to produce the illusion of attack. The mind cannot really attack—how can one part of a unified field attack another?—and so to give itself the illusion that it can attack, the mind directs the body to attack. It says to the body, "Go out there, Body, and raise hell and make my dreams come true." But the important thing is still the mind. The important thing is the mind's *belief* that the body is actually making its dreams come true. Unless it believes this, it will attack the body with even more guilt: "You miserable body! You were supposed to make all my fantasies into reality, but you have utterly failed me!"

4. In this, the mind is clearly delusional. It cannot attack, but it maintains it can, and uses what it does to hurt the body to prove it can. The mind cannot attack, but it can deceive itself. And this is all it does when it believes it has attacked the body. It can project its guilt, but it will not lose it through projection. And though it clearly can misperceive the function of the body, it cannot change its function from what the Holy Spirit establishes it to be. The body was not made by love. Yet love does not condemn it and can use it lovingly, respecting what the Son of God has made and using it to save him from illusions.

The mind is using the body to deceive itself, in two ways. First, by using the body to attack and then by attacking the body, the mind thinks it has proved to itself that it *can* attack. But it can't. How can a mind that is one with everything attack anything?

Second, the mind projects its guilt onto the body and thinks it has thereby gotten rid of the guilt. This projection amounts to blaming the body for two things: for making the mind separate *and* for the attacks the body carries out. In regard to the latter, we tell ourselves, "I wouldn't attack except for this animal body with its drives for aggression, sex, food, pleasure and all its insatiable needs."

If we put these two deceptions together, the mind is using the body to produce a single massive deception: "I, the mind, can attack with impunity." The nasty things my body does prove that I can attack, and the fact that my body is really to blame for those things proves that I am innocent of those attacks. We need to realize that both parts of this are a lie. I cannot attack, and I cannot feel innocent while I attempt to attack.

We also need to realize that all of this is a fundamental misperception of what the body is for. It is not for attack. It is for love. Its real function is to be used to communicate love to our brothers. If we use it for that, even though it is an illusion, it can *save* us from illusions, including the illusion of itself.

> 5. Would you not have the instruments of separation [bodies] <u>reinterpreted</u> as means for salvation, and <u>used</u> for purposes of love? Would you not welcome <u>and support</u> the shift from fantasies of vengeance to <u>release</u> from them? Your <u>perception</u> of the body can clearly be sick, but project not this upon the body. For your wish to make destructive what <u>cannot</u> destroy can have no <u>real</u> effect at all. [Ur: And] What God created is only what He would have it be, being His Will. You <u>cannot</u> make His Will destructive. You can make <u>fantasies</u> in which your will <u>conflicts</u> with His, but that is all.

While we use the body to separate and act out our fantasies of vengeance, we have merely chosen a sick perception of the body. We haven't actually accomplished what we set out to. We haven't changed our mind into something evil. We haven't made a corrupt will that clashes with God's holy Will. We haven't really accomplished anything, except to descend into madness. Why not, then, let the purpose we give our body be changed for us?

6. It is insane to use the body as the scapegoat for guilt, <u>directing</u> its attack and <u>blaming</u> it for what you wished it to do. <u>It is impossible to act out fantasies</u>. For it is still the <u>fantasies</u> you want, and they have nothing to do with what the body does. <u>It</u> does not dream of them, and they but make <u>it</u> a liability where it <u>could</u> be an asset. For fantasies have made your body your "enemy"; weak, vulnerable and treacherous, worthy of the hate that you invest in it. How has this served you? You have <u>identified</u> with this thing you hate, the instrument of vengeance and the perceived source of your guilt. <u>You</u> have done this to a thing that has no meaning, proclaiming it to be the dwelling place of God's Son, and turning it <u>against</u> him.

To make sense of this paragraph—which is an extremely difficult one—let's imagine that the body is a beloved robot that you have invented. First, you program it to attack, and once it does, you then blame it for what it did. Second, you have it act out your fantasies. It goes to a bar and picks up the greatest looking girl in the place. Has it really acted out your fantasy? For the fantasy is in your mind, while the robot is just a mindless piece of machinery. Third, let's say it gets home after a late night with this girl, and you can tell it has roughed her up (which you also programmed it to do). So in disgust you take a hammer to it and beat it up. It ends up full of dents and with one of its mechanical eyes hanging out. Now you feel bad, because you identify with this battered robot. Owning such a worthless robot makes your self-esteem go down a few notches.

Does any of this make any sense? Yet how you relate to the robot in this story is how you relate to your own body.

Application: Imagine a deep place in your mind, where you dimly remember being God's Son, an infinite being. In this place, you still carry some of the sense of grandeur of your former estate. How would you look on your body from this place? Might you not resent feeling cooped up inside this tiny, fragile, fleshy cell? Might you not feel as if you were an ocean that had been stuffed into a grain of sand? Might you not want to blame this grain of sand for your fall from your exalted estate? And might this blaming not be an attempt to displace onto it your guilt over your *own* choice to fall?

Now observe this body saying or doing something attacking. Might you not be tempted to blame the body for this attack? Might you not be inclined to think that this body has made you not yourself—made you small and petty, and filled you with alien physical urges and instincts? Wouldn't this be a convenient explanation for why you attacked? "The body made me do it!"

Finally, imagine that in this place, you truly hate the body for making you separate and turning you into an attacker. Realize that the mind that is doing the hating is the all-powerful mind of God's Son. What might the hatred of a mind that powerful do to this body? As a result of this psychic attack, see your body malfunction and break down in various ways. See it grow weak. See it shrivel up. Finally, see it die. Then realize that this is the real story behind all of your body's sickness and aging and death.

> 7. This is the host of God that *you* have made. And neither God nor His most holy Son can enter an abode that harbors hate, and where you have sown the seeds of vengeance, violence and death. This thing you made to serve your guilt stands between you and other minds. The minds *are* joined, but you do not <u>identify</u> with them. You <u>see</u> yourself locked in a separate prison, removed and unreachable, incapable of reaching out as being reached. You <u>hate</u> this prison you have made, and would destroy it. But you would <u>not</u> escape from it, leaving it unharmed, <u>without</u> your guilt upon it.

We have a choice. We can say, "I hate this body. It leaves me trapped inside this skull, lonely and isolated, unable to really reach other minds. It makes me do things I regret. It makes me a sinner, imprisoned within this wall of flesh." Or we can say, "I'm not in this body, nor have I ever been. It is to blame for nothing in my life. It is just a communication device, nothing more. And since I am outside this body, I am joined with other minds already."

> 8. Yet only thus *can* you escape. The home of vengeance is not yours; the place you set aside to house your hate is <u>not</u> a prison, but an <u>illusion of yourself</u>. The body is a limit imposed on the universal communication that is an eternal property of mind. But the communication is <u>internal</u>. Mind reaches to <u>itself</u>. It is *not* made up of different <u>parts</u>, which reach each other. It does not go <u>out</u>. Within <u>itself</u> it <u>has</u> no limits, and

there is nothing <u>outside</u> it. It encompasses <u>everything</u>. It encompasses you <u>entirely</u>; you within it and it within you. There <u>is</u> nothing else, anywhere or ever.

Remember the opening line of this section: "There is nothing outside you." If there is nothing outside you, then you are by nature in communication with everything, with all of infinity, at once. Communication, then, is internal. It is communicating with another mind that is inside the same oneness that you are.

The body is a limit on this natural state. While in the body, it appears that communication is an instance of your mind going outside itself to make contact with another mind, one that is walled off in its body just as you are walled off in yours.

> 9. The body is <u>outside</u> you, and but <u>seems</u> to surround you [it doesn't really surround you], shutting you off from others and keeping you <u>apart</u> from them, and them from you. <u>It is not there.</u> There <u>is</u> no barrier between God and His Son, nor can His Son be separated from Himself except in illusions. This is <u>not</u> his reality, though he believes it <u>is</u>. Yet this could <u>only</u> be if God were wrong. God would have had to create <u>differently</u>, and to have separated <u>Himself</u> from His Son to make this possible. He would have had to create <u>different</u> things, and to establish different <u>orders</u> of reality, only <u>some</u> of which were love. Yet love must be forever like itself, changeless forever, and forever <u>without</u> alternative. And so it is. <u>You</u> cannot put a barrier around yourself, because God placed none between <u>Himself</u> and you.

This paragraph says the same thing in different ways: There is no barrier around yourself, separating you from others and from God. Your body is not there. You may reply that that sounds inspiring, but your body obviously *is* there. You are experiencing it. And you are clearly shut up inside of it.

But do you know that all that is true? In your dreams at night you have a body, which you experience, and which shuts you off from others in your dream. But is that body really there? And does it really surround you? How do you know that your "real" body is not like your dream body? What if your "real" body isn't really there at all?

Application: Think of that earlier thought experiment, where you

45

imagined hating the body for making you a separated sinner. Now say to yourself,

> *The body is not there.*
> *There is no barrier around myself.*
> *I am free of it. Thank God I am free.*
> *I am still God's Son.*
> *I am still as God created me.*

10. You can stretch out your hand [Ur: Your hand can stretch out,] and reach to Heaven. You whose hand is joined with your brother's [Ur: You whose hands are joined] have begun to reach beyond the body, but not outside yourself [Ur: yourselves], to reach your shared Identity together. Could This [shared Identity] be outside you? Where God is not? Is *He* a body, and did He create you as He is not, and where He cannot be? You are surrounded only by Him. What limits can there be on you whom He encompasses?

How can you stretch out your hand and reach to Heaven? You can reach out and take your brother's hand. By truly joining with another, the two of you can reach within yourselves, to find your shared Identity (Christ) together. This Identity is inside of you, where God is, and where all of reality is.

You are not surrounded by the body. You are surrounded by God. If what surrounds you is tiny, which the body is, then you must be tiny. But if what surrounds you is infinite, which God is, then you must be infinite as well.

11. Everyone has experienced what he would call a sense of being transported beyond himself. This feeling of liberation far exceeds the dream of freedom sometimes hoped for in special relationships. It is a sense of actual escape from limitations. If you will consider what this "transportation" really entails, you will realize that it is a sudden unawareness of the body, and a joining of yourself and something else in which your mind enlarges to encompass it. It becomes part of you, as you unite with it. And both become whole, as neither is perceived as separate. What really happens is that you have given up the illusion of a limited awareness, and lost your fear of union. The love that instantly

replaces it <u>extends</u> to what has freed you, and <u>unites</u> with it. And while this lasts you are <u>not</u> uncertain of your Identity, and would not limit It. You have escaped from fear to peace, asking no questions of reality, but merely <u>accepting</u> it. You have accepted this <u>instead</u> of the body, and have <u>let</u> yourself be <u>one</u> with something beyond it, simply by <u>not</u> letting your mind be limited <u>by</u> it.

12. This can occur <u>regardless</u> of the physical distance that <u>seems</u> to be between you and what you join; of your respective positions in space; and of your differences in size and seeming quality. Time is not relevant; it can occur with something past, present or anticipated. The "something" can be <u>anything</u> and <u>anywhere</u>; a sound, a sight, a thought, a memory, and even a <u>general</u> idea <u>without</u> specific reference. Yet in every case, you join it without <u>reservation</u> because you love it, and would <u>be</u> with it. And so you rush to meet it, letting your limits melt away, suspending <u>all</u> the "laws" your body obeys and gently <u>setting them aside</u>.

13. There is no violence at all in this escape. The body is <u>not</u> attacked, but simply <u>properly perceived</u>. It does not limit you, merely because <u>you</u> would not have it so. You are not really "lifted out" of it; it cannot <u>contain</u> you. You go where you would be, <u>gaining</u>, <u>not</u> losing, a sense of Self [Ur: self].

What exactly is Jesus talking about here? I think he is talking about moments of losing yourself and feeling transported, as you enjoy nature, or get lost in a beautiful memory, or listen to music that you love, or even contemplate a profound idea. In each case, there is something that you love without reservation. There is no threat in it, just attraction. And so you forget about your body and even your "self," and you mentally join with this object of your love. You, in a sense, enlarge to become one with it. What you are now encompasses both you and it.

Think about your own such moments. I don't think they need to be particularly exalted or holy. I remember as a teenager, I would get home from school; the house would be empty. I would put the headphones on, crank up the volume, lay back on the couch, and listen to "Dazed and Confused" by Led Zeppelin. And I did lose myself and join with the music.

What do these moments prove? They prove that your mind can escape the confines of the body and join with something, no matter how far away in space and/or time that thing is. They prove that your mind is not really confined to the body. You can escape it anytime you choose, wherever you are, without going anywhere. You don't even need to have an out-of-body experience. You can simply realize that the body never contained you in the first place.

> In these instants of release from physical restrictions, you experience much of what happens in the holy instant; the lifting of the barriers of time and space, the sudden experience of peace and joy, and, above all, the <u>lack</u> of awareness of the body, and [the lack] of the questioning <u>whether or not all this is possible</u>.

When Jesus says that "in these instants...you experience much of what happens in the holy instant," he is clearly saying that these are not exactly what he means by a holy instant. We can therefore call them "quasi-holy instants." What they show us is that we have the capacity for genuine holy instants. We have the ability to lose awareness of time, to feel peace and joy as we mentally join with something, and to forget about our body. And notice: We do all this without questioning whether any of it is possible. That last point is true, isn't it? If we can do this with something as mundane as Led Zeppelin, why can't we do it with God, or with the holiness in our brother?

> 14. It <u>is</u> possible <u>because you want it</u>. The sudden <u>expansion</u> of awareness that takes place with your <u>desire</u> for it is the irresistible appeal the holy instant holds. It calls to you to be yourself, within its safe embrace. There are the laws of limit lifted <u>for</u> you, to welcome you to openness of mind and freedom. Come to this place of refuge, where you can be yourself in peace. <u>Not</u> through destruction, <u>not</u> through a breaking out [Ur: "breaking out"], but merely by a quiet melting in [Ur: "melting in"]. For peace will join you there, simply because <u>you</u> have been willing to let go the limits <u>you</u> have placed upon love, and <u>joined</u> it where it is and where it led you, in answer to its gentle call to be at peace.

The message I get from this section is this: I don't have to see the body as my prison. And I don't have to use it to act out my fantasies. If I do those things, I will inevitably heap on the body the guilt for making me separate and making me sinful. Instead, I can just realize that the body never had the power I have seen in it. It cannot make me separate and it cannot turn me into an attacker.

To be free of the body, I don't need to somehow escape its prison cell. To join with others, I don't need to somehow break out of the body. I can simply let my mind expand to join with the object of my love. I can join with my brother. I can join with God. I can choose to have a holy instant. This experience represents what I really want—to take refuge in expanded awareness, to escape the laws of limit and be welcomed into openness of mind and freedom. I experience tastes of this freedom in quasi-holy instants. Why not, then, choose the real thing?

VII. I Need Do Nothing
Commentary by Robert Perry

This brief section, one of my favorites, was taken down as a personal message for Helen Schucman. It was taken down during the dictation of chapter 22 and later moved to chapter 18. It was not part of the Urtext, but of what is called the Special Messages (which is why I have identified insertions of the original dictation with "SM" for Special Messages, rather than the usual "Ur"). Ken Wapnick describes the circumstances of its dictation:

> On May 31, 1967, Helen was in the midst of another crisis, and Jesus' answer to her was a special message....
>
> Helen's crisis, which on an external level was literally a non-event, revolved around a threatened union strike that would have involved the elevator operators in Helen's building. She and Louis lived on the 16th floor, and Helen's fear was that the strike would begin at a time when she and Louis would be separated, one of them in the apartment and the other down below. Since in Helen's mind walking up or down the sixteen flights of stairs meant instant cardiac arrest, for either her or Louis, she was beside herself at the imminent threat of separation. Having thus defined the problem, her solution was obvious and logical: she and Louis would move to a near-by hotel. They did, where they remained for a week, never knowing that the strike was called off even before it had begun. (*Absence from Felicity*, pp. 325-326)

1. You still have too much faith in the body as a source of strength. What plans do you make that do <u>not</u> involve its comfort or protection or enjoyment in some way? This makes the body an end and not a means in your interpretation, and this <u>always</u> means <u>you still find sin attractive</u>. No one accepts Atonement for himself who still accepts sin as his goal. You have thus not met your *one* responsibility. Atonement is not welcomed by those who <u>prefer</u> pain and destruction.

This was written to Helen, but applies equally well to us. Think about your plans. Don't they all involve your body's "comfort or protection or enjoyment in some way"? This means we regard the body as an end. No debate there. And this means we regard sin as an end. Sin, rather than Atonement, is our real aim, which means that even though we think we want comfort, protection, and enjoyment, we are actually going after pain and destruction.

Can this be true? When I pursue my body's pleasure, I am really trying to convince myself that I'm a sinner, so that I can justifiably punish myself with pain and destruction? Am I really that ill? There is evidence, however, for this seemingly bizarre view. After a lifetime of pouring attention into one's body, how does one feel? Selfish, self-absorbed, narcissistic, hedonistic. Like a sinner. Could that have been the underlying goal all along?

> 2. [SM: You have made much progress, and are really trying to make still more, but] There is one thing that you have never done; you have not [SM: not for one instant have you] utterly forgotten the body. It has perhaps faded at times from your sight, but it has not yet <u>completely disappeared</u>. You are not asked to let this happen for more than an instant, yet it is in this instant that the miracle of Atonement happens. Afterwards you will see the body again, but never quite the same. And every instant that you spend <u>without</u> awareness of it gives you a different view of it when you return.

In the midst of all our plans to make sure we have our favorite chocolates and mineral water, to guarantee that we don't get too much sun, or too much cold, and to ensure that our back won't act up, if we could take just *one* instant and forget our body—totally—we would experience a holy instant. In this instant, the miracle of Atonement would come to us, and nothing would be the same again. When this instant was over, the body wouldn't look the same. It would have quietly stepped off its pedestal—perhaps only onto a lower pedestal, but on its way to being off all pedestals and a mere servant.

> 3. At no <u>single</u> instant does the body exist at all. It is always remembered or anticipated, but <u>never</u> experienced just *now*. Only its past and future make it seem real. Time controls it entirely, for sin is never wholly in the present [SM: For sin is never present]. In any <u>single</u> instant the attraction of guilt would be experienced as pain and nothing else,

and would be avoided. <u>It has no attraction *now.*</u> Its whole attraction is imaginary, and therefore <u>must</u> be thought of in [SM: from] the past or in the future.

I have never fully understood this paragraph (though not for lack of trying). Here is my best shot for now. The body and sin are inherently linked. Sin is about attacking for the sake of my personal ends. The body is the perfect symbol of this. It is the instrument with which I attack, and it contains many of the ends *for* which I attack. The body is the symbol of the separate, selfish me.

The body is also much like the coffee cup in Workbook Lesson 7. That lesson says that we don't really see the cup now. Rather, we are merely reviewing our past experiences of the cup. The same with the body. It exists in our minds not as the handful of scattered sensations that it's giving me right now, but as an overall concept built up of innumerable past experiences and future goals. Based only on the present moment, we would have in mind the same body that a one-month-old baby has: none. It takes many weeks for a baby to figure out that those hands waving in front of it and banging into its face are actually its own.

Sin is similarly dependent on time. Sin is all about "I got screwed in the past and oh will it feel good when I turn the tables in the future." The enjoyment of sin is not the enjoyment of the moment, but of the *story.* This story, like all great myths, has the power to blind us to the present suffering that it causes. With sin, that present suffering comes in the form of guilt. While I fantasize about settling the score, underneath it all I am simply feeling guilty for being so mean-spirited.

Now here is the key point: *Desiring the story of sin is what hooks us in to the story of the body.* Without sin's story of "I lost in the past but will win in the future," the body's story of its past and future is completely uninteresting and will actually vanish from our mind:

> The body disappears, because you have no need of it except the need the Holy Spirit sees. For this, the body will appear as useful form for what the mind must do. (W-pI.199.4:3-4)

> 4. It is impossible to accept the holy instant <u>without reservation</u> unless, <u>just for an instant,</u> you are willing to see no past or future. You cannot <u>prepare</u> for it without placing it in the <u>future</u>. Release is given you

> the <u>instant</u> you desire it. Many have spent a lifetime in preparation, and have indeed achieved their instants of success. This course does not attempt to teach more than they learned in time, but it does aim at <u>saving</u> time. You may be [SM: You are] attempting to follow a very long road to the goal you have accepted. It is extremely difficult to reach Atonement by fighting against sin. Enormous effort is expended in the attempt to make holy what is hated and despised. Nor is a lifetime of contemplation and long periods of meditation aimed at <u>detachment</u> from the body necessary. All such attempts will ultimately succeed because of their purpose. Yet the means are tedious and very time consuming, for all of them <u>look to the future</u> for release from a state of present unworthiness and inadequacy.

After decades of serving our body, for some of us the guilt becomes too much. We become sick of being so self-centered and tired of feeling so guilty. We want to be holy. We set out on the spiritual path, in an effort to redeem ourselves. Perhaps we take the traditional Western route, and fight against our sinful bodily impulses. We try to wrestle this rotten self to the ground and make it obey God, make it holy. For Helen, this was the more familiar route, as she was deeply attracted to Catholicism.

Or perhaps we take the more Eastern route, in which we spend hours at a crack meditating. Jesus doesn't seem as negative about this way as about the other, but notice the phrase "aimed at *detachment* from the body." Remember, the body is the seat of sin. Trying to detach ourselves from the thing that makes us sin is ultimately not so different from trying to fight off its sinful impulses. That plus the length of time spent meditating implies an unconscious attempt to make oneself holy.

Both routes, therefore, smack of what the "Little Willingness" (18. IV) section spoke of: trying to make yourself holy so that one day you'll be worthy of holy instants. This ultimately does succeed, says Jesus, but it takes a very long time. Its implicit statement "I'm not worthy of holy instants now" becomes a self-fulfilling prophecy.

> 5. Your way will be different, <u>not</u> in purpose but in means. <u>A holy relationship is a means of saving time</u>. One instant spent <u>together</u> with your brother [SM: One instant spent *together*] restores the universe to <u>both</u> of you. You *are* prepared. Now you need but to remember <u>you need do nothing</u>. It would be <u>far</u> more profitable now merely to concentrate on this than to consider what you <u>should</u> do. When peace comes at last

to those who wrestle with temptation and fight against the giving in to sin; when the light comes at last into the mind given to contemplation; or when the goal is finally achieved by anyone, it <u>always</u> comes with just <u>one</u> happy realization; "*I need do nothing.*"

6. Here is the ultimate release which everyone will one day find in his own way, at his own time. You [SM: We] do not need this time. Time has been <u>saved</u> for you because you and your brother [SM: because you] are together. This is the special means this course is using to save you time. You are not making use of the course if you insist on using means which have served others well, neglecting what was made for *you*. Save time for me by only this one preparation, and practice doing <u>nothing else</u>. "I need do nothing" is a statement of allegiance, a truly undivided loyalty. Believe it for just one instant, and you will accomplish more than is given to a century of contemplation, or of struggle against temptation.

Now Jesus sets the Course's way in contrast to the traditional Western and Eastern ways. It has the same goal: the realization of holiness through holy instants. But its means is very different. We can see that means as composed of three aspects:

The first aspect is the holy relationship. "A holy relationship is a means of saving time." "Time has been saved for you because you and your brother are together." Notice how both Western and Eastern journeys were solitary journeys. Yet as Jesus says elsewhere, "The lonely journey fails because it has excluded what it would find" (14.X.10:7).

The second aspect is joint holy instants. Here, the two holy relationship partners experience holy instants together. "One instant spent together restores the universe to *both* of you." With Helen and Bill, this, of course, is how their holy relationship was born. Their "better way" experience was a joint holy instant (also called a holy encounter).

The third aspect is practicing "I need do nothing." The way of the world says, "I need to do something to meet my needs, so that I can be filled, whole." The pursuit of holiness says, "I need to do something to make myself holy, so that I can be worthy of God." The Course's way says, "I don't need to do anything to make myself whole or holy. God created me whole and holy." This thought is the present gateway into the holy instant, where we experience our eternal wholeness and holiness.

"I need do nothing" is the thought that the sin-wrestlers and champion meditators reach at the end. After all their toil up a summit they felt they did not deserve, they realize in astonishment, "It was mine all along!" We can save immense time if this is the thought that *propels* the journey, rather than the startling surprise at the *end* of the journey.

This, then, is the Course's special means—experiencing joint holy instants within the holy relationship, by practicing the realization that we are worthy of them *now*. Now note this line, which sounds ominous in our climate of spiritual eclecticism, yet which makes perfect sense: "You are not making use of the course if you insist on using means which have served others well, neglecting what was made for *you*."

> 7. To <u>do</u> anything involves the body. And if you recognize you <u>need</u> do nothing, you <u>have</u> withdrawn the body's value from your mind. Here is the quick and open door through which you slip past centuries of effort, and <u>escape</u> from time. This is the way in which sin loses <u>all</u> attraction *right now*. For here is time denied, and past and future gone. Who needs do nothing has no need for time.

You need do nothing because you have everything already. The reality of this automatically wipes away the story of the body and the story of sin. Both stories become completely useless. Even the story of holiness—"If I do this now, I will become holy in the future"—becomes useless. Indeed, all stories lose their value, for stories consist of time, and if you have everything now, then the whole notion of gradual gain over time misses the point. Imagine someone saying to Bill Gates, "I have this great plan whereby, if you work hard and scrimp and save, in thirty years you could become a *millionaire*!" What value would this story have to him?

> To do nothing is to rest, and make a place within you where the activity of the body ceases to demand attention. Into this place the Holy Spirit comes, and there abides. He will remain when you forget, and the body's activities return to occupy your conscious mind.
> 8. Yet there will always be this place of rest to which you can return. And you will be more aware of this quiet center of the storm than all its raging activity. This quiet center, <u>in which you do nothing</u>, will remain with you, giving you rest in the midst of every busy doing on which you are sent. For <u>from</u> this center will you be directed how to use the body sinlessly. It is this center, from which the body is <u>absent</u>, that will keep it so in your awareness of it.

These final sentences sketch the process we go through. First, we make a place of stillness in us, in which we aren't planning our next move on the chess board of the world. This is a place of rest, rest from bodily doing, and rest from the thought that we must acquire what we do not have. For just a moment, we have forgotten the chess board, and the piece we move across it. Into this place of rest, the Holy Spirit comes, giving us a holy instant, giving us the miracle of Atonement.

A moment later, it's over. We open our eyes and once again we occupy our mind with our next chess moves. The Holy Spirit now may not be our focus, but He has not left our mind. He is still there in that deep place of stillness within. We may have left it, but He has not. However, we have not left it entirely. The final paragraph suggests that we will maintain a dual awareness, and uses the image of a hurricane to describe this. While our body is caught up in the raging storm of doing, our mind will be resting in the stillness of the eye of the storm, *doing nothing*. Since we can't deal with the storm without being conscious of it, we will clearly be maintaining a kind of split-level awareness, dealing *with* the storm while at the same time resting *from* the storm. This is what the great saints enjoy: peace and stillness in the midst of action.

These two levels of experience are definitely not disconnected. The One we are resting with in the quiet center is also the One Who is also directing our actions in the storm. We still use the body, of course, but we no longer use it as an engine of sin. Now it is the tool of the Holy Spirit. He sends us on one "busy doing" after another, not in service of our plans, but in service of His. Now we use the body *sinlessly*, for it is no longer our end, our goal. Indeed, in that quiet center within us, it does not even exist.

Application: Let's apply this section to our version of Helen's crisis. Think of a situation in your life in which you are wondering what to do. Perhaps you are wondering how to respond to what looks like a crisis. Perhaps you are wondering where to go with a relationship, or a job, or a move. Name this situation by filling in the blank: "What should I do about _____?"

In pondering what to do in this situation, do bodily considerations arise? Please list specific considerations about your body's comfort, safety and pleasure. What are you concerned will happen to threaten your body's ...:

Comfort _____

Safety _____

Pleasure _____

Realize that the body is a thing of time. Its purpose is to do things in time, to get things for you in time. By fixating on the body, you chain yourself to time. See that, while thinking about this situation, you are caught up in time. Notice how far back the situation goes in your perception, and how far forward you are thinking while dwelling on it. Try to put dates to the situation's beginning in the past and end in the future, according to how you see it.

Beginning: _____

End: _____

See also that you have a goal in mind—some ideal outcome for the situation, which you are shooting for. What you have to do in the present may not be pleasant—you may be working hard to wade through difficult circumstances. But you consider it worth it in order to achieve your projected goal. You may even want to write down this goal:

_____

_____

_____

Now see the situation as a whole: It is an arena of time in which the body acts, trying to acquire a future happiness and safety, to a large degree for itself. Can you see all this operating in your picture of the situation?

Realize that this overall picture—of your body moving in time to meet the needs of your separate, bodily self—is another way of saying that your goal is sin. For you are trying to satisfy a bodily identity, a separate self. This amounts to worshipping your separate self, and doing so at the expense (or at least the disregard) of others, at least to some degree. If this is who you are, this person who constantly grabs after his or her own needs, doesn't that imply that you are a sinner?

Consider the possibility that your unconscious goal all along was to prove to yourself that you are sinful. According to the Course, this was your actual projected goal all along, underneath the goal you had on the surface. And this is shown by the fact that you never really achieve your surface goal of safety and happiness, but you *do* achieve the goal of feeling selfish and guilty.

What you really need is not to figure out what to do in this situation, but to drop this whole perspective in which your body acts in time to procure happiness for your separate self. Rather than trying to figure out what to do, you need a holy instant. Don't make the mistake, however, of trying to clean yourself up so you are worthy of it. Many try to escape the guilt of grubbing for their needs by trying to purify themselves in order to earn a holy instant. Unfortunately, this affirms that they are truly guilty and have to wait for holy instants until they have made themselves worthy.

Let's repeat these lines as a way of accepting, rather than earning, the holy instant:

> *I will forget my body, and its needs, just for an instant.*
> *I will let it disappear from my awareness.*
> *I see myself only as a mind, afloat in an endless field of spirit.*
> *I am willing, just for an instant, to see no past or future.*
> *The past is over. It can touch me not.*
> *I place the future in the Hands of God.*
> *I take this very instant, now, and think of it as all there is of time.*
> *I will forget the outer situation, too. I do not know what it means.*
> *I need do nothing to acquire happiness or earn holiness.*
> *I can be happy now. God has given me everything.*
> *I am holy now. God has made His holiness an eternal part of me.*
> *I need do nothing.*

(Say this last line over and over again.)

I make a place of rest within me.
In this place I need do nothing.
This place of rest invites the Holy Spirit to come and abide in me.
The storm may rage outside, but in this center, all is quiet, all is
rest.
In this center, I need do nothing.
I need do nothing.

Spend a moment repeating this last line. You can open your eyes when you are ready.

Now realize that, if you established this quiet center, if you had a holy instant, you will look out on your puzzling situation from a new vantage point. You will act from a new purpose. "For from this center you will be directed how to use the body sinlessly" (T-18.VII.8:4). Instead of using it to meet the needs of your separate self, you will use it to awaken your brothers.

Ask the Holy Spirit, abiding in your quiet center, "How can I use my body in this situation to extend the holy instant to the entire situation? How can I use my body to draw everyone involved into a holy instant?" Write down any impressions or words or pictures you receive.

VIII. The Little Garden
Commentary by Robert Perry

1. It is only the awareness of the body that makes love seem limited. For the body *is* a limit on love. The belief in limited love was its origin, and it was <u>made</u> to limit the <u>un</u>limited. Think not that this is merely allegorical, for it was made to limit *you*. Can you who see yourself <u>within</u> a body know yourself <u>as an idea</u>? Everything you recognize you identify with [Ur: by] <u>externals</u>, something <u>outside</u> itself. You cannot even think of <u>God</u> without a body, or in some form you think you recognize.

The body was made to limit our love, and it has done a good job at it. After all the care and feeding we give it, all the bathing and resting, how much love do we have left over for others? If we are tempted to think this is some kind of metaphor or allegory, Jesus assures us it is not. The body was literally made to limit *us*, to make us seem finite and tiny. And it has done a good job at that, too. While in this body, we cannot think of ourselves as a pure, formless idea. Indeed, we cannot think of anything without a form, even God. Even if we picture Him as a vast light, that is still a form. The body has warped all of our thinking around itself. It is like an anchor attached to every thought in our mind, dragging them all down with it.

2. The body cannot <u>know</u>. And while you limit your awareness to its tiny senses, you will not see the grandeur that surrounds you. God cannot come into a body, nor can you join Him there. Limits on love will <u>always</u> seem to shut Him out, and keep you <u>apart</u> from Him. The body is a tiny fence around a little part of a glorious and complete [Ur: completely limitless] idea. It draws a circle, infinitely small, around a very little segment of Heaven, splintered from the whole, proclaiming that within it is <u>your</u> kingdom, where God can enter not.
3. Within this kingdom the ego rules, and cruelly. And to defend this little speck of dust it bids you fight against the universe.

Based on the description here, I picture the body as a sea wall, completely surrounding a tiny island that is slightly below sea level. This sea wall shuts out the vast ocean of our Self and of God. Unfortunately, this sea wall is leakproof—no ocean water gets in. The wall does have windows in it, but they have a special tinted glass that actually filters out anything blue. Thus, through them, you cannot see the ocean. You can only see other adjacent sea walls. Looking through them, you get the impression that reality is nothing but a vast expanse of little sea walls.

Inside this wall, the ego rules like a tyrant chieftain, commanding you to wage constant war against the universe in order to preserve your little plot of sand.

> This fragment of your mind is such a tiny part of it that, could you but appreciate the whole, you would see instantly that it is like the smallest sunbeam [Ur: is] to the sun, or like the faintest ripple on the surface of the ocean. In its amazing arrogance, this tiny sunbeam has decided it is the sun; this almost imperceptible ripple hails itself as the ocean. Think how alone and frightened is this little thought, this infinitesimal illusion, holding itself apart against the universe. The sun becomes the sunbeam's "enemy" that would devour it, and the ocean terrifies the little ripple and wants [Ur: "wants"] to swallow it.

Now Jesus begins an extended metaphor—actually, two metaphors—about the relationship between this part of our mind (the part within the body's fence) and the whole of our mind (our true Self). In one metaphor, our little fenced-off mind is a ripple and our Self is the ocean. In the other, our mind is a sunbeam and our Self is the sun. What follows is a kind of dark comedy based on the ripple and sunbeam's wrong perspective. The ripple says, "I'm the whole ocean," and the sunbeam says, "I'm the sun," just as we say, "This mind is the whole of me." Now we relate to the rest of the whole as the vast and frightening unknown. And as this unknown lovingly beckons us to rejoin it, we interpret that as it trying to devour us.

> 4. Yet neither sun nor ocean is even aware of all this strange and meaningless activity. They merely continue, unaware that they are feared and hated by a tiny segment of themselves. Even that segment is not lost to them, for it could not survive apart from them. And what it thinks it is in no way changes its total dependence on them for its being. Its whole existence still remains in them. Without the sun the sunbeam would be gone; the ripple without the ocean is inconceivable.

The comedy continues. While the ripple and sunbeam are desperately trying to preserve their existence in the face of the devouring ocean and sun, the ocean and sun are completely oblivious to their tiny, furious campaign. "They [ocean and sun] merely continue, unaware that they are feared and hated by a tiny segment of themselves." From their standpoint, the ripple and sunbeam are still a continuous part of them. Indeed, whereas the ripple and sunbeam think that their existence rests on staying separate from the greater whole, the fact is that their existence rests on their *oneness* with that whole.

> 5. Such is the strange position in which those in a world inhabited by bodies seem to be. Each body seems to house a <u>separate</u> mind, a <u>disconnected</u> thought, living alone and in no way joined to the Thought by which it was created. Each tiny fragment seems to be self-contained, needing another for <u>some</u> things, but by no means <u>totally</u> dependent on its [Ur: their] one Creator for <u>everything</u>; [Ur: And] needing the whole to give it <u>any</u> meaning, for by itself it does [Ur: by themselves they *do*] mean nothing. Nor has it [Ur: Nor *have* they] any life apart and by itself [Ur: themselves].

Now Jesus decodes the metaphor for us. (He will frequently do this—present a metaphor and then interpret it for us, leaving no doubt as to its meaning.) We in this world are in the same strange, darkly comedic position as the ripple and sunbeam. Doesn't his description capture how we experience ourselves—as a separate mind, living alone in our little house of clay? True, we are dependent on others for some things, but we are clearly not dependent on God for our very being. The existence of a God would be a help, but whether God existed or not, *we* would still exist—or so we think.

> 6. [Ur: Yet] Like to the sun and ocean your Self continues, unmindful that this tiny part regards <u>itself</u> as you. It is not missing; it could not <u>exist</u> if it were separate, nor would the whole <u>be</u> whole without it. It is not a separate kingdom, ruled by an <u>idea</u> of separation from the rest. Nor does a fence surround it, preventing it from <u>joining</u> with the rest, and keeping it apart from its Creator. This little aspect is <u>no different</u> from the whole, being continuous with it and at one with it. It leads no separate life, because its life *is* the oneness in which its being was created.

He is still decoding his metaphor: "Like to the sun and ocean (metaphor) your Self continues (application of metaphor)." To really take in the meaning of this discussion, we need to contrast it with our view. From our perspective, we are inside this wall of flesh. It surrounds us. It cuts us off from everything else, so that we can only have contact with the outside through it. Because of it, we are self-contained—more like a car than a lamp. Like a car, we just need to acquire fuel from outside us, and we can go wherever we want. Unlike the lamp, we have no electrical cord that ties us to a source, such that when the cord is unplugged, our lights go out.

Jesus is saying that this is all a complete illusion. It is all false, and because of one thing: the body isn't there. We have an experientially convincing *experience* of a being in a body, but that body does not exist. From the inside, we seem to be in it. From the perspective of our Self, however, there is no body to be seen. Try to picture your body as not actually there. It is an imaginary fence. It is a dream body. It does not wall in your mind. Your mind is continuous with the limitlessness of your true Self and God.

> 7. Do not accept this little, fenced-off aspect as yourself. The sun and ocean are as nothing beside what <u>you</u> are. The sunbeam sparkles only in the sunlight, and the ripple dances as it rests upon the ocean. Yet in neither sun nor ocean is the power that rests in you. Would you remain <u>within</u> your tiny kingdom, a sorry king, a bitter ruler of all that he surveys, who looks on nothing yet who would still die to <u>defend</u> it? This little self is <u>not</u> your kingdom. Arched high above it and surrounding it with love is the glorious whole, which offers all its happiness and deep content to <u>every</u> part. The little aspect that you think you set apart is no exception.

Application. Repeat to yourself:

I refuse to accept this little, fenced-off aspect as myself.
This tiny mind is like a ripple on the ocean.
Yet the literal ocean is nothing compared to the ocean of my Self.

The image of the king within his tiny kingdom is saturated with irony. We are familiar with the image of the glorious king who is the "ruler of all that he surveys." We are also familiar with the self-sacrificing patriot, who loves his country so much that he is willing to "die to defend it" against the incursion of evil. Yet, characteristically, Jesus has taken these familiar images and twisted them. Now, there is no glorious kingdom surrounded by evil foes. Instead, it is a joke of a kingdom. The king is no stately monarch, but rather a "sorry king" who rules a tiny, worthless tract of desert (as we will soon see). He is, therefore, "a *bitter* ruler of all that he surveys" (my italics). His willingness to die in defense of his kingdom is deeply misguided, because, given the kingdom's worthlessness, he is dying for "nothing." Further, the "threat" that surrounds his kingdom is heavenly love. In short, the king is totally insane.

We are that king.

> 8. Love knows no bodies, and reaches to everything created like itself. Its total lack of limit *is* its meaning. It is <u>completely</u> impartial in its giving, encompassing <u>only</u> to preserve and <u>keep complete</u> what it would give. In your tiny kingdom you have so little! Should it not, then, be there that you would call on love to enter? Look at the desert—dry and unproductive, scorched and joyless—that makes up your little kingdom. And realize the life and joy that love would bring to it from where <u>it</u> comes, and where it would return <u>with</u> you.

As I said, the "foe" that surrounds our kingdom and would surmount the walls is love. This love does not regard the limit erected by our body. It just wants to give to us. And why wouldn't we want its gifts? The kingdom enclosed by the body is the kingdom of our mind, the little fenced-off mind we call our own. What kind of place is it? Is it a lush, green place with cool, life-giving water? Or is it more like a desert, scorched by the hot glare of hate and starved for the water of life, with nothing but stingy, prickly thoughts growing in its barren soil?

We *are* like that king, you know. We are depressed by what a tiny, worthless desert our mind is, and yet at the same time we would rather die than see its borders breached, even if the "breach" is the entry of life-giving love into this "dry and unproductive, scorched and joyless" place.

Application: Can you see your mind as a desert? Can you see the appropriateness of the image? Then why are you so defensive about it?

Why do you patrol its borders so vigilantly? Realize that, in regard to this kingdom, you are that crazy king, "a bitter ruler of all that he surveys, who looks on nothing yet who would still die to defend it." Then say:

> *I invite love into the desert of my mind.*
> *I want the life and joy that it would bring.*
> *I want my mind to be a green and life-giving place.*
> *I give no power to the wall of dust that seems to surround my*
>   *mind.*
> *And love itself knows no limits.*
> *I invite love in.*
> *I invite love in.*

Spend some time repeating "I invite love in," holding your mind still and quiet, expecting love to answer.

9. The Thought of God surrounds your little kingdom [your mind], waiting at the barrier you built [your body] to come inside and shine upon the barren ground. See how life springs up everywhere! The desert becomes a garden, green and deep and quiet, offering rest to those who lost their way and wander in the dust. Give them a place of refuge, prepared by love for them where once a desert was. And everyone you welcome will bring love with him from Heaven for you. They enter one by one into this holy place, but they will not depart as they had come, alone. The love they <u>brought</u> with them will <u>stay</u> with them, as it will stay with <u>you</u>. And under its beneficence your little garden will expand, and reach out to everyone who thirsts for living water, but has grown too weary to go on alone.

At last, the king has a moment of lucidity. Love has been knocking at the gate of his tiny desert plot (we won't call it a kingdom) for so long, but this time instead of shouting, "Go away or I'll shoot," he says quietly, "Okay, come in." And then everything changes. Love comes flooding in and "life springs up everywhere!" The desolate kingdom has become "a garden, green and deep and quiet," and its "no trespassing" sign has been replaced by one that says "everyone welcome." Now it becomes an oasis, a shelter for all those who have lost their way in the desert, wandering half-crazed from heatstroke and dehydration. They enter one by one, but they leave two by two, each one carrying plantings for their own new garden. In this way, the original garden expands and slowly begins to carpet the desert.

This is a lovely paragraph, yet if the kingdom/garden is our mind, how do people come *into* it and take shelter there? I have always equated this with what Jesus scholar Marcus Borg has said about people being inside the "zone" or "Buddha field" that exists around enlightened figures:

> Within the Buddhist tradition, people speak of a "Buddha field" which could be felt not only around Buddha, but also around other enlightened figures who came after him. Within the Christian tradition, a similar "zone" was felt around St. Francis, as well as around other figures. (*Jesus: A New Vision*, p. 144)

10. Go out and <u>find</u> them, for they bring your Self with them. And lead them gently to your quiet garden, and receive their blessing there. So will it grow and stretch across the desert, leaving no lonely little kingdoms locked away from love, and leaving <u>you</u> inside. And you will <u>recognize</u> yourself, and see your little garden gently transformed into the Kingdom of Heaven, with all the love of its Creator shining upon it.

This is such a beautiful image of service. Once we allow love into our mind's kingdom, we must give our lives to the service of our brothers. In this paragraph, we not only invite the thirsty wanderers into our garden, we actually go out on search and rescue missions to find them. We thus not only save them, but we also receive their blessing. They are the messengers of our greater Self, and when they enter our garden, It enters with them.

Application: Ask the Holy Spirit, "Is there someone I know who is wandering in the desert, and whom I need to invite into the garden of my love, to receive their blessing there?"

11. The holy instant is your invitation to love to enter into your bleak and joyless kingdom, and to transform it into a garden of peace and welcome. Love's answer is inevitable. It will come because you came <u>without</u> the body, and interposed no barriers to [Ur: which would]

<u>interfere</u> with its glad coming. In the holy instant, you ask of love only what it offers everyone, neither less nor more. Asking for <u>everything</u>, you will <u>receive</u> it. And your shining Self will lift the tiny aspect that you tried to hide from Heaven straight to Heaven. No part of love calls on the whole in vain. No Son of God remains <u>outside</u> His Fatherhood.

How do we invite love into our "bleak and joyless kingdom"? By forgetting our body and accepting a holy instant. We shouldn't be shy about asking for this. We are not being greedy. We are asking "of love only what it offers everyone." Yet in doing so, we are asking for everything, and we will receive it. We cannot call on God in vain.

12. Be sure of this; love has entered your special relationship, and entered fully at your weak request. You do <u>not</u> recognize that love has come, because you have not yet let go of <u>all</u> the barriers you hold against your brother [Ur: against *each other*]. And you and he will <u>not</u> be able to give love welcome separately. You could no more know God alone than He knows <u>you</u> without your brother. But <u>together</u> you could no more be <u>unaware</u> of love than love could know you not, or fail to recognize <u>itself</u> in you.

Jesus is again addressing Helen and Bill's relationship. He is telling them that they *have* experienced the holy instant; love *has* entered their desert kingdom. This is a reference to their joining in a better way. But the full effects of love have not manifested, he says. They aren't yet seeing life spring up everywhere. Why? Because they are shutting each other out, and thereby shutting love out. They have to welcome God together. They have to knock down the walls between their two kingdoms. Once they do that, it will be impossible for them not to recognize and celebrate love's presence in their midst.

13. You have reached the end of an ancient journey, not realizing yet that it is over. You are still worn and tired, and the desert's dust still seems to cloud your eyes and keep you sightless. Yet He Whom you welcomed has come to you, and would welcome <u>you</u>. He has waited long to give you this. Receive it now of Him, for He would have you <u>know</u> Him. Only a little wall of dust [the body] still stands between you and your brother [Ur: between you]. Blow on it lightly and with happy laughter, and it will fall away. And walk into the garden love has prepared for <u>both</u> of you.

What a poignant closing paragraph. Helen and Bill had been wandering in the desert since ancient times, worn and tired and hopeless. Finally, they found each other. By joining with each other, they invited love into the desert. A garden sprang up right next to them. They had reached the oasis. At last their ancient journey was over.

But they can't see this. Their eyes are still blinded by the desert's dust, and so they still retain the mindset of the wanderer in desperate straits. The dust that blinds them is the body. It is the wall of dust that encircles them and keeps each one alone in a private world. By walling them off from each other, it also walls them off from the oasis that has sprung up next to them. The body is what keeps them blind to the joyous fact that they have made it.

More specifically, it is their *investment* in the body. The investment in this wall is what keeps them from investing in each other. This is what fills their relationship with blind anger. Looking at the animosity between them, things can appear quite dire. Yet remember, they've reached their destination. It is time to celebrate. All they need do is blow on this barrier of dust "lightly and with happy laughter, and it will fall away." That's it. If we could only approach the bitter separateness within our relationships in this spirit—as fragile walls of dust to be blown on lightly and with happy laughter—we too could walk into the garden love has prepared for both of us.

Application: Is there a relationship in your life that is burdened with separateness? Picture this separateness as a wall between you. Ask within, "What is the name of this wall?" Then see that name appear on the wall. Now realize that this is just a wall of *dust*, nothing more. Realize how much bigger and stronger your true unity is than this thin, fragile wall. Then blow on the wall of dust, lightly and with happy laughter. And embrace the shining person on the other side.

IX. The Two Worlds
Commentary by Robert Perry

1. You have been told to bring the darkness to the light, and guilt to holiness. And you have also been told that error must be corrected at its source. Therefore, it is the tiny part of yourself [Ur: your self], the little thought that seems split off and separate, the Holy Spirit needs. The rest is fully in God's keeping, and needs no guide. Yet this wild and delusional thought needs help because, in its delusions, it thinks it is the Son of God, whole and omnipotent, sole ruler of the kingdom it set apart to tyrannize by madness into obedience and slavery. This is the little part [Ur: of you] you think you stole from Heaven. Give it back to Heaven. Heaven has not lost it, but *you* have lost sight of Heaven. Let the Holy Spirit remove it from the withered kingdom in which you set it off, surrounded by darkness, guarded by attack and reinforced by hate. Within its barricades is still a tiny segment of the Son of God, complete and holy, serene and unaware of what you think surrounds it.

To bring darkness to light, to correct error at its source, means to give this little part of our self—the part we think is all of it—back to Heaven. The error lies in thinking that this part is outside of Heaven, thinking that it's surrounded by the body and living in a world of bodies. In fact (as we saw in "The Little Garden"), this part is not actually contained in the body. It is still a seamless part of the whole. This tiny part we call ourselves remains a tiny segment of the Son of God. *It* is not an error; the error is the circle we have drawn around it.

2. Be you not separate, for the One Who <u>does</u> surround it has brought union to you, returning your little offering of darkness to the eternal light. How is this done? It is extremely simple, being based on what this little kingdom really <u>is</u>. The barren sands, the darkness and the lifelessness, are seen only through the body's eyes. Its bleak sight [Ur: *Its* vision] <u>is</u> distorted, and the messages <u>it</u> transmits to you who <u>made</u> it to limit your awareness <u>are</u> little and limited, and so fragmented they are meaningless.

The way this little part is returned to Heaven is very simple, for it is not really apart from Heaven now. Its separateness is an illusion conjured up by the body's eyes. Those eyes (along with the other senses) are what show us a picture in which we are surrounded first by the body, and then by a world of bodies. Think about it: Isn't it the information given you by the body that defines for you what reality is and what you are? What if all this information is false? What if you designed the body in order to give you a false picture? What if right now you are surrounded not by bodies, but only by God?

> 3. From the world of bodies, <u>made</u> by insanity, insane messages seem to be returned to the mind that made it. And these messages bear witness to this world, pronouncing it as true. For <u>you</u> sent forth these messengers [the senses] to bring this <u>back</u> to you. Everything these messages relay to you is quite external. There are <u>no</u> messages that speak of what lies underneath, for it is <u>not</u> the body that could speak of this. Its eyes perceive it not; its senses remain quite <u>unaware</u> of it; its tongue cannot relay <u>its</u> messages.

All insane systems rest on control of information. They dole out only the information that supports the system's insane view of reality, while acting like the information is unbiased and uncensored. That is what we have done to ourselves. We first made a false world and we then made a body that reports on this false world, making sure that these are the only reports we get. We never get reports of what is real—the realm of spirit beneath the phony world of bodies. We are living in a state in which the government (our ego) has perfect and absolute control of the media.

> Yet God can bring you there, if you are willing to follow the Holy Spirit through seeming terror, trusting Him not to abandon you and <u>leave</u> you there. For it is not <u>His</u> purpose to frighten you, but only <u>yours</u>. <u>You</u> are severely tempted to abandon <u>Him</u> at the outside ring of fear, but <u>He</u> would lead you safely through and <u>far</u> beyond.
> 4. The circle of fear lies just below the level the body sees, and <u>seems</u> to be the whole foundation on which the world is based. Here are all the illusions, all the twisted thoughts, all the insane attacks, the fury, the vengeance and betrayal that were made to keep the guilt in place, so that the world could <u>rise</u> from it and keep <u>it</u> hidden.

In the above sentences, we have a series of levels, which we need to

70

understand if this section is to make sense:

1. The level of the body and the physical world.
2. The circle of fear. This is the realm, just below consciousness, of all the thoughts that make us feel guilty—all the twisted thoughts of attack, fury, and vengeance that we are terrified of facing.
3. The guilt. This is fueled and kept in place by the circle of fear.
4. Heaven, the domain of spirit.

To get to 4, we have to let the Holy Spirit lead us below 1 and through 2. We need to let Him show us our hatred, so that we can let it go. Once it is gone, 3 goes with it, and then we are in 4. Our fear, however, is that as soon as we enter the circle of fear, He will abandon us, and we'll be stuck there, having to stare at our vicious hatred forever. But He won't leave us. Rather, He'll lead us "safely through and far beyond." Ironically, the real danger is that *we'll* abandon *Him*.

> Its [guilt's] <u>shadow</u> rises to the surface [the physical world], enough to hold its [guilt's] most external manifestations [the physical world] in darkness, and to bring despair and loneliness to it [the physical world] and keep it [the physical world] joyless. Yet its [guilt's] <u>intensity</u> is veiled by its [guilt's] heavy coverings [the physical world], and kept <u>apart</u> from what was made [the physical world] to keep it [guilt] hidden. The body cannot see this [guilt], for the body <u>arose</u> from this [guilt] for its [guilt] protection, which depends [Ur: which must *always* depend] on keeping it [guilt] <u>not</u> seen. The body's eyes will <u>never</u> look on it [guilt]. Yet they will <u>see</u> what it [guilt] dictates.

The remainder of paragraph 4 is a pronoun nightmare. However, it is extremely important. It describes the relationship between levels 1 (the physical world) and 3 (the guilt). To understand the concept presented, imagine that you are sitting in a theater. In front of the stage hangs a thin burlap curtain. Behind the curtain is a monstrous presence, a massive and hideously deformed man. Behind the man is a bright light, which casts the man's shadow onto the curtain, filling the curtain with darkness. This, therefore, is what you in the audience see—the man's shadow on the curtain. You don't see the true extent of his hideousness, for the shadow is two-dimensional and its outline is indistinct. But you can tell enough. You read in your program that the curtain was actually erected by the man, both to keep himself hidden and to show you his shadow.

The man is guilt and the curtain/shadow is the physical world. The physical world was erected by guilt, both in order to keep guilt *hidden* and to *show us* guilt's shadow. That shadow lies across the entire world. It is all the sickness, suffering, attack, war, starvation, separation, isolation, and death that so dominate this world.

It is a grisly image, one that has no counterpart in today's thinking, where both science and religion agree that the physical universe is a wondrous miracle. Yet it explains a lot about what it's actually like to be here.

> 5. The body will remain guilt's messenger, and will act as it [guilt] directs as long as <u>you</u> believe that guilt is real. For the <u>reality</u> of guilt is the illusion that seems to make it [the body] heavy and opaque, impenetrable, and a <u>real</u> foundation for the ego's thought system. Its [the body's] thinness and transparency are not apparent until you see the light <u>behind</u> it. And then you see it as a fragile veil before the light.

The body is guilt's messenger boy. Why? Because all it does is bring us messages from the world that guilt made for us to see. Indeed, guilt is what makes the body—and the world of bodies—seem solid. Think about my shadow-on-the-curtain metaphor. If you didn't know where the shadow came from, you might think the curtain was a solid wall with a dark shape painted onto it. Now, however, imagine that the man moves out of the way, and you see just the light, shining brightly behind the curtain. Now you realize that the curtain is just "a fragile veil before the light." And that is what you will realize about the body, and the world of bodies, when guilt is out of the way and you see only the light.

> 6. This heavy-seeming barrier, this artificial floor that looks like rock, is like a bank of low dark clouds that seem to be a solid wall before the sun. Its impenetrable appearance is <u>wholly</u> an illusion. It gives way softly to the mountain tops that rise above it, and has no power at all to hold back anyone willing to climb above it and see the sun. It is not strong enough to stop a button's fall, nor hold a feather. Nothing can rest upon it, for it is but an <u>illusion</u> of a foundation. Try but to touch it and it disappears; attempt to grasp it and your hands hold nothing.

Now Jesus gives us another one of his metaphors. This body, this heavy barrier that seems as solid as rock, is really like a bank of clouds. Clouds look so solid, but of course they are just mist. When we apply this to the body, the implications are dramatic. The body isn't solid. Since all we see are bodies, nothing that we see is solid. It is all just mist.

I realize that you are probably thinking that you've heard this before, from modern physics. However, what the Course is really saying about that mist is quite different than what physics is saying. We'll get to that in a bit.

> 7. Yet in this cloud bank [the literal cloud bank he is using to make his point] it is easy to see a whole world rising. A solid mountain range, a lake, a city, all rise in your imagination, and <u>from</u> the clouds the messengers of your perception return to you, assuring you that it is <u>there</u>. Figures stand out and move about, actions seem real, and forms appear and shift from loveliness to the grotesque. And back and forth they go, as long as you would play the game of children's make-believe [Ur: "make believe"]. Yet however long you play it, and regardless of how much imagination you bring to it, you do <u>not</u> confuse it with the world below, nor seek to make it real.

Everything we see around us is just shapes in a cloud bank. We are like children lying on our backs on a hillside, looking at the clouds and playing make-believe. "Ooh, look, I see a horse." "I see a car." "Look there—I see a person's face." We are so good at this game that in the clouds we "see a whole world rising." We see mountains, lakes, and cities. We see figures stand up, move about, change shape, and vanish. Our eyes assure us it's all there, for just as they see vaporous clouds as solid, so they are designed to see unreal bodies as real.

All the forms and all the actions we see, even right this instant, are a result of our playing make-believe with clouds.

> 8. So should it be with the dark clouds of guilt, no more impenetrable and no more substantial. You will <u>not</u> bruise yourself against them in traveling through. Let your Guide <u>teach</u> you their <u>unsubstantial</u> nature as He leads you <u>past</u> them, for <u>beneath</u> them is a world of light whereon they cast no shadows. Their shadows lie upon the world <u>beyond</u> them, still <u>further</u> from the light. Yet from them <u>to</u> the light their shadows <u>cannot</u> fall.

Now, just as in "The Little Garden," Jesus decodes his metaphor. Just as you know that clouds are not solid, and that the cities and people you see arising from them aren't real, he says, "So should it be with the dark clouds of guilt." The dizzying dance of subatomic particles described by modern physics is really just a manifestation of the mists of guilt. The Course agrees with physics that the objects we see are not solid, but physicists tend to see what underlies those objects—subatomic particles, energy—as being quite real. The Course is saying that what underlies all of it—including things at the subatomic level—is really the dark emotion of guilt. This guilt is the invisible substance of the physical world. The very fabric of the world, then, is a kind of gravitational pull that drags everything down towards punishment and death. Again, this explains a lot.

In the final four sentences, Jesus briefly sketches an image that uses his cloud metaphor to summarize the various levels. Let me try to draw this image out. Imagine a huge thunderhead cloud hovering above the horizon at sunrise. The sun is peeking just over the horizon and is shining there in a strip of clear sky. Above this strip is the billowing cloud, piled high in the sky. Here is how the levels figure in:

1. On the very top of the cloud you see a cloud city, with cloud figures moving about in it. This city, however, lies in shadow, the shadow cast by the cloud itself.

2. As we know from the fourth paragraph, just below this city is the circle of fear—all of the attack thoughts that generate the guilt that is the substance of the cloud.

3. Then below this circle is the vast bulk of the cloud, the guilt of which the city is just a surface manifestation.

4. Then below the cloud is that strip of clear, lit-up sky. This is the real world—a new level that was not present in the earlier description from paragraphs 3 and 4.

5. Then below that is the sun, the source of light. That is Heaven.

Trusting that the clouds are just clouds, just vapor, we need to let the Holy Spirit lead us through them, starting at the city, where all of our attention is now, down through the circle of fear, then through the raw, unadulterated guilt, and finally into the clear light of the real world below. That is the journey on which the Course takes us.

> 9. This world of light, this circle of brightness is the real world, where guilt meets with forgiveness. Here the world <u>outside</u> is seen anew, <u>without</u> the shadow of guilt upon it. Here are <u>you</u> forgiven, for here you have forgiven everyone. Here is the new perception, where everything is bright and shining with innocence, washed in the waters of forgiveness, and cleansed of every evil thought you laid upon it. Here there is no attack upon the Son of God, and <u>you</u> are welcome. Here is your innocence, waiting to clothe you and protect you, and make you ready for the final step in the journey inward. Here are the dark and heavy garments of guilt laid by, and gently replaced by purity and love.

When you reach the real world, the "circle of brightness," you are out of the clouds, which means you are out of *guilt*. You know you are forgiven. You shed "the dark and heavy garments of guilt" you've been wearing and become clothed in innocence. From here, you look back on that city and you see it no longer wreathed in the shadow of guilt, but bathed in light. You look at the figures in the city, and you see them no longer saturated with guilt, but shining with purity. You have forgiven them. Now, wearing your new robes of purity, you are made ready for the final step—disappearing into the Source of light.

> 10. Yet even forgiveness is not the end. Forgiveness <u>does</u> make lovely, but it does <u>not</u> create. It <u>is</u> the source of healing, but it is the <u>messenger</u> of love and not its Source. Here you are led, that God Himself can take the final step unhindered, for here does nothing <u>interfere</u> with love, letting it be itself. A step <u>beyond</u> this holy place of forgiveness, a step still further inward but the one *you* cannot [Ur: you *cannot*] take, transports you to something <u>completely</u> different. Here is the Source of light; nothing perceived, forgiven nor transformed. But merely <u>known</u>.

The state of perfect forgiveness is a very lofty state. That is what Jesus achieved in his life. Yet even this state, as beautiful and sublime as it is, is not the end. Achieving this state does not mean that you have realized love. You have merely removed all *interference* to love. And now you are ready for God's final step. Reaching the real world, the world of forgiveness, then, is your job; the final step is His. He will transport "you to something completely different," beyond perception, beyond transformation, beyond forgiveness. Here, and only here, you know the meaning of love.

> 11. This course will <u>lead</u> to knowledge, but knowledge itself is still beyond the scope of our curriculum. Nor is there any need for us to try to speak of what must forever lie beyond words. We need remember only that whoever attains the real world, beyond which learning cannot go, <u>will</u> go beyond it, but in a different way. Where learning ends there God begins, for learning ends before Him Who is complete where He begins, and where there *is* no end. It is not for us to dwell on what cannot <u>be</u> attained. There is too much to learn. The readiness for knowledge still must be attained.

We love talking about Heaven, that mystical realm where all limits and boundaries pass away, and where words fail. Many paths put their primary focus there, and delight in paradoxical statements like "Him Who is complete where He begins, and where there *is* no end." While the Course obviously contains such statements, they are not its primary focus. "There is too much to learn," it says. "The *readiness* for knowledge [Heaven] still must be attained" (italics mine).

It's as if we live out in the countryside and, to get to some distant destination, we must first walk to the airport. Once we get to the airport, our labors are done and we will be flown to our exotic destination without further effort. Many teachings put their major focus on that exotic destination. The Course, however, is all about *walking to the airport.* You can talk about the destination forever, and you'll feel good doing so, but if you never actually get off the couch and start walking, you'll never catch that plane, and you'll never get there.

> 12. Love is not learned. Its meaning lies within itself. And learning ends when you have recognized all it is *not.* That is the <u>interference</u>; that is what needs to be undone. Love is not learned, because there never <u>was</u> a time in which you knew it not. Learning is useless in the Presence of your Creator, Whose <u>acknowledgment</u> of you <u>and yours of Him</u> so <u>far</u> transcend <u>all</u> learning that <u>everything</u> you learned is meaningless, replaced forever by the knowledge of love and its one meaning.

When you learn something, you approach it from the outside and gradually enter into an understanding of it, usually by seeing its similarity to things you already understand. Love is not like that. "Its meaning lies within itself." You can't approach it from the outside and get to know it gradually. You either know it, totally, or you don't know it at all. The good news, though, is that we have always known what love is. We just need to remember that knowledge.

That is what the entire spiritual journey is about—readying ourselves for the memory of love. We make that journey through forgiveness. Forgiveness, quite simply, is *the letting go of all that interferes with love*. And when that letting go is complete, we are ready for the final step. Then, suddenly, we stand in the Presence of our Creator, and He acknowledges us, and we acknowledge Him. And finally, at last, we know what love means.

> 13. Your relationship with your brother [Ur: Your relationship] has been uprooted from the world of shadows, and its unholy purpose has been safely brought through the barriers of guilt, washed with forgiveness, and set shining and firmly rooted in the world of light. From there it calls to you to follow the course it took, lifted high above the darkness and gently placed before the gates of Heaven. The holy instant in which you and your brother were united is but the messenger of love, sent from <u>beyond</u> forgiveness to <u>remind</u> you of all that lies beyond it. Yet it is <u>through</u> forgiveness that it will <u>be</u> remembered.

This again is speaking to Helen and Bill about their relationship. The holy instant in which they joined was a messenger sent from Heaven. This messenger came, and in that instant, took their relationship on the very journey that paragraph 8 outlined for us. It was uprooted from that cloud city and brought down through the clouds of guilt, all the way to the world of light below. Clearly, this happened to some deep, unconscious element in the relationship, for on the surface the relationship was still plagued by specialness. Now, Helen and Bill are being asked to *consciously* follow the course it took.

> 14. And when the memory of God has come to you in the holy place of forgiveness [the real world, the circle of brightness beneath the clouds of guilt] you will remember nothing else, and memory will be as useless as learning, for your <u>only</u> purpose will be creating [in Heaven]. Yet this

you cannot know until every perception has been cleansed and purified [through forgiveness], and finally removed forever. Forgiveness removes only the untrue, lifting the shadows [of guilt] from the world and carrying it, safe and sure within its gentleness, to the bright world of new and clean perception [the real world]. There is your purpose *now* [your purpose is reaching the real world, not Heaven]. And it is there that peace awaits you.

Most of my clarification of this paragraph is in the brackets I inserted, because if you understood the previous paragraphs, this one is clear. What really strikes me, though, about this paragraph is the idea that, once we're awake in Heaven, we won't have memory anymore. Think of that. Both the process of remembering past events and of acquiring future learning will be useless, for we will be totally absorbed in extending What Is, in adding to the Kingdom through our creating.

This sounds wonderful, yet if we really want to reach this lofty place, we need to busy ourselves with the mundane task of cleansing and purifying every single perception through forgiveness. If someone tells you there is a more direct route—and many will—ask yourself if it actually gets you to that airport I spoke of earlier, or if it just amounts to sitting on the couch and dreaming about the exotic destination of Heaven.

Commentaries on Chapter 19

THE ATTAINMENT OF PEACE

I. Healing and Faith
Commentary by Robert Perry

1. We said before [17.VI.5:2] that when a situation has been dedicated wholly to truth, peace is inevitable. Its attainment is the criterion by which the wholeness of the dedication can be safely assumed. Yet we also said [17.VI.6:1] that peace without faith will never be attained, for what is [Ur: *wholly*] dedicated to truth as its only goal is brought to truth *by* faith. This faith encompasses everyone involved [in the situation], for only thus the situation is perceived as meaningful and as a whole. And everyone must be involved in it [the situation], or else your faith is limited and your dedication incomplete.

This refers back to the holy relationship discussions in "Setting the Goal" (17.VI), which said that if we dedicate a situation in advance to the goal of truth, its outcome will be truth, and with truth will come peace. However, to actually reach the goal of truth, we need *faith*, faith that we can really get there. This faith must include faith in our holy relationship partner. If the two of us will only get there together, then we can't believe that we ourselves will get there unless we have faith that the other person will, too.

It's a stretch to have faith in this one person (to say the least), but let's be realistic—there are other people involved in our situation. If we are to have faith in reaching our goal, then we must have faith in them too, right? This seems like too much, but at least we don't have to have faith in *everyone*. Well, hold on. Where do we draw the line regarding who is involved in this situation and who is not? No matter where we would draw the line, we can make a case for including someone that is just on the *other side* of that line. Ultimately, says Jesus, everyone is involved in our situation, literally everyone. We, then, must have faith in everyone.

2. Every situation, properly perceived, becomes an opportunity to heal the Son of God. And he is healed *because* you offered faith to him, giving him to the Holy Spirit and releasing him from every demand your ego would make of him. Thus do you see him free, and in this vision does the Holy Spirit share. And since He shares it He has given

it, and so He heals <u>through you</u>. It is this <u>joining</u> Him in a <u>united</u> purpose that <u>makes</u> this purpose real, because <u>you</u> make it <u>whole</u>. And this *is* healing. The <u>body</u> is healed <u>because you came without it</u>, and joined the Mind in which all healing rests.

Each situation we find ourselves in is an opportunity to extend healing. Our normal statement to others is, "You exist to serve my demands, but we know you'll screw that up, don't we?" We heal by saying just the opposite: "I release you from serving my goals. I have faith in you to serve God's goal." By seeing this person as freed from our demands, we join the Holy Spirit's vision of this person. And by joining with His vision, we also join with His purpose. Only when we join with Him does our own dedication become truly whole. And because we are joining "the Mind in which all healing rests," we are healed. Even the body is healed, because we forgot it, *because we came without it*. How ironic.

> 3. The body cannot heal, because it cannot <u>make itself sick</u>. It *needs* no healing. Its health or sickness depends <u>entirely</u> on how the mind perceives it, and the purpose that the mind would use it <u>for</u>. It <u>is</u> obvious that a segment of the mind <u>can</u> see itself as <u>separated</u> from the Universal Purpose. When this occurs the body becomes its weapon, used <u>against</u> this Purpose, to <u>demonstrate</u> the "fact" that separation <u>has</u> occurred. The body thus becomes the instrument of illusion, acting accordingly; <u>seeing</u> what is not there, <u>hearing</u> what truth has never said and <u>behaving insanely</u>, being imprisoned *by* insanity.

Whatever sicknesses your body is carrying—and all bodies carry a bunch—they do not come from the bodily level, from germs, genes, or diet. That's hard to believe, isn't it? Instead, they come from what you *use the body for*. This includes using it as proof that you are separate, shut up within its tiny cell; using it as a witness (through its senses) to the "reality" of an unreal world; and using its behavior to serve insane ends. It's not what you (or germs or vitamins) do *to* the body that makes it sick or healthy, but what you do *with* it, what purpose you use it for. That's what needs to be healed. A very different approach to health, isn't it?

> 4. Do not overlook our earlier statement that faithlessness leads straight to illusions [17.VII.5:5-6]. For faithlessness <u>is</u> the perception of a brother <u>as</u> a body, and the body <u>cannot</u> be used for purposes of union. If,

then, you <u>see</u> your brother as a body, <u>you</u> have established a condition in which <u>uniting</u> with him becomes impossible. Your <u>faithlessness</u> to him has separated you <u>from</u> him, and kept you <u>both</u> apart from being healed. Your faithlessness has thus <u>opposed</u> the Holy Spirit's purpose, and brought illusions, <u>centered on the body</u>, to stand <u>between</u> you. And the body <u>will</u> seem to be sick, for you have made of it an "enemy" of healing and the <u>opposite</u> of truth.

Why does seeing someone as a body mean that you have no faith in him? Faith in him is faith in his innate goodness, and in his ability to reunite with that goodness and with you, and with all of reality. If he is a body, then this kind of faith is simply not justified. If he is a body, then first of all, he is driven by the body's inherently selfish drives, and second, he is fundamentally separate from everyone and everything. He therefore cannot join with you. Joining is not a series of prescribed actions performed by bodies. It is something that happens between two *minds*.

Seeing your brother as a body, then, keeps him separate from you and condemns him to rot in his fleshy prison cell. This keeps both of you apart from healing, and apparently even causes your body to be sick.

5. It <u>cannot</u> be difficult to realize that faith <u>must</u> be the opposite of faith<u>less</u>ness. Yet the difference in how they operate is less apparent, though it follows directly from the fundamental difference in what they <u>are</u>. Faithlessness would always <u>limit and attack</u>; faith would remove <u>all</u> limitations and <u>make whole</u>. Faithlessness would destroy and <u>separate</u>; faith would unite and <u>heal</u>. Faithlessness would interpose illusions between the Son of God and his Creator; faith would remove <u>all</u> obstacles that <u>seem</u> to rise between them. Faithlessness is wholly dedicated to illusions; faith wholly to truth. <u>Partial dedication is impossible</u>. Truth is the <u>absence</u> of illusion; illusion the <u>absence</u> of truth. Both cannot <u>be</u> together, nor perceived in the <u>same place</u>. To dedicate yourself to <u>both</u> is to set up a goal forever impossible to attain, for <u>part</u> of it is sought through the body, <u>thought of</u> as a means for seeking out reality through <u>attack</u>. [Ur: While] The <u>other</u> part would <u>heal</u>, and therefore calls upon the mind and <u>not</u> the body.

Even though it's obvious that faith and faithlessness are opposite, what is not so obvious is the stark difference in how they operate. In the following table (loosely inspired by sentences 3-6), I've tried to capture the opposite statements that faithlessness and faith make to our brother:

Faithlessness	Faith
"You are of the body and its lower nature. How can I count on you to reach a spiritual goal with me?"	"You are not confined to that body, and thus you are whole. You'll get there with me."
"You are just that lump of clay, separate from me. How can we genuinely join?"	"Your true vastness could never be contained in that body. How can we *not* join?"
"You are a body, driven by its instincts and needs. And for that, you deserve to be punished."	"Since the body is not your reality, you never really did those things your body did. That is why you deserve to be healed. And that is why you deserve my faith in you."
"There is so much between you and God that you might as well forget about uniting with Him."	"I truly believe that all that seems to lie between you and God is pure illusion, nothing more."
"I believe in your darkest illusions about yourself."	"I believe in the radiant truth in you, and I want my belief to strengthen yours."

Application: Choose someone in your life, especially someone you are counting on to reach a holy goal with you. First, imagine saying the statements in the left column out loud to this person's face. How does that feel?

Second, say the statements in the right column to this person right now, in your mind. Do your best to mean them. How does that feel?

Now realize that the left column represents your dedication to illusions, while the right represents your dedication to the goal of truth. Further realize that you have been trying to hold on to both sets of statements, yet that this is impossible. They completely contradict each other. "To dedicate yourself to both is to set up a goal forever impossible to attain."

Could it be that setting this unattainable goal is where your sense of failure comes from?

> 6. The <u>inevitable</u> compromise is the belief that the <u>body</u> must be healed, and <u>not</u> the mind. For this divided goal [see 5:10] has given both an <u>equal</u> reality, which could [Ur: and can *seem* to] be possible only if the mind is limited <u>to</u> the body and divided into little parts of <u>seeming</u> wholeness, but <u>without connection</u>. This will <u>not</u> harm the body, but it *will* keep the delusional thought system <u>in the mind</u>. Here, then, is healing needed. And it is here that healing *is*. For God gave healing not <u>apart</u> from sickness, nor established remedy where sickness <u>cannot</u> be. They <u>are</u> together, and when they are <u>seen</u> together, <u>all</u> attempts to <u>keep</u> both truth <u>and</u> illusion in the mind, where both <u>must</u> be, are recognized as <u>dedication to illusion</u>; and <u>given up</u> when <u>brought</u> to truth, and seen as totally <u>unreconcilable</u> with truth, in <u>any</u> respect [Ur: aspect] or in any <u>way</u>.

The section began by saying that only by having faith can we be wholly dedicated to the goal of truth. In this section, this primarily means faith in the other people involved in our pursuit of the goal of truth. Then we were told that faith sees our brothers as unseparated minds, while faithlessness sees them as separate bodies. Finally, we were told that we are trying to see our brothers both through the eyes of faith and the eyes of faithlessness.

Now we are told that holding onto both actually warps our idea of what healing is. We meld faith (focused on minds) and faithlessness (focused on bodies) together and get this: "Okay, my brother and I are little pieces of mind stuck inside bodies. Both mind and body are essential aspects of us. I believe in healing, but what needs to be healed is our bodies. That's what is giving us all the trouble." Healing is really of the mind, but we have melded mind and body together, so out comes this belief that healing means healing the body.

What really needs healing is this very attempt to join two incompatible realms. We are trying to pursue both truth (mind) and illusion (body). This must be "recognized as *dedication to illusion*; and *given up* when *brought* to truth, and seen as totally *unreconcilable* with truth, in *any* aspect or in any *way*."

Application: Think of a situation which you feel has been genuinely dedicated in advance to the goal of truth, at least by you, perhaps by others involved.

Now write down the names of three people who will need to play their part if the goal is to be achieved.

1.
2.
3.

Now, in relation to each one, ask yourself, "How much faith do I have that this person will play his/her part (the part they have been given as their contribution to the goal) perfectly?"

Write down a number from one to ten after each name, signifying your level of faith in relation to that person.

Now repeat these lines in relation to each person:

> *I can have faith in you, [name], because you are a Son of God.*
> *I can have faith in you, [name], because you are not your body.*
> *I can have faith in you, [name], because beyond your body, you and I are one.*
> *I can have faith in you, [name], because I release you from my demands and give you to the Holy Spirit.*

7. Truth and illusion <u>have</u> no connection. This will remain <u>forever</u> true, however much <u>you</u> seek to connect them. But <u>illusions</u> are <u>always</u> connected, <u>as is truth</u>. Each is united, a <u>complete</u> thought system, but totally <u>disconnected</u> to <u>each other</u>. [Ur: Where there is *no* overlap, there separation *must* be complete.] And to perceive <u>this</u> is to recognize where separation <u>is</u>, and <u>where it must be healed</u>. The <u>result</u> of an idea is <u>never</u> separate from its source. The <u>idea</u> of separation <u>produced</u> the body and remains connected <u>to</u> it, <u>making</u> it sick because of the mind's identification <u>with</u> it. You <u>think</u> you are <u>protecting</u> the body by <u>hiding</u> this connection, for this concealment <u>seems</u> to keep your identification safe from the "attack" of truth.

As we've seen, we try to join the goal of truth—which has to do with the mind—with the goal of illusions—which has to do with the body. This leads to a kind of hybrid goal: the healing of the body. This paragraph lays the real facts on the table: Truth and illusion are totally disconnected from each other. Any attempt to weave them together is doomed.

Separation is not a fact proven to us by the body. It is an idea in the mind, and so that is where it must be healed—in the mind. This idea not only produced the body, but also makes the body sick, because it is a sick idea. We, however, have a great investment in keeping this real story hidden. Why? Because we are afraid that if we realize that the body is being produced by a sick idea, and then let that idea go, the body will go with it.

8. If you but understood how much this strange concealment has hurt your mind, and how confused your own identification has become because of it! You do not see how great the devastation wrought by your faithlessness, for faithlessness is an attack that seems to be justified by its results. For by withholding faith you see what is unworthy of it, and cannot look beyond the barrier to what is joined with you.

By concealing the fact that a sick idea in our mind has produced the body, we have deeply hurt our mind. For as long as that fact is concealed, the body seems to be an objective fact. It seems to be who we are.

For a Son of God to view himself as a tiny, fragile hunk of meat is a lack of faith in himself. It is an attack on himself. Yet this faithlessness is also a self-fulfilling prophecy, for it makes the body really seem to be his reality. Now, being a body, he seems truly unworthy of faith, as well as truly separate from his brother.

9. To have faith is to heal. It is the sign that you have accepted the Atonement for yourself, and would therefore share it. By faith, you offer the gift of freedom from the past, which you received. You do not use anything your brother has done before to condemn him now. You freely choose to overlook his errors, looking past all barriers between yourself and him, and seeing them as one. And in that one you see your faith is fully justified. There is no justification for faithlessness, but faith is always justified.

Application: Think of someone whom you have more or less given up on. Then say this to him or her:

I have faith in you, [name].
I have faith in your nature as God's Son.
What you have done in the past is irrelevant.
It cannot compromise my faith in you.
I do not use anything you have done before to condemn you now.
I freely choose to overlook your errors.
I look past everything that would separate us, including our bodies.
I see the two of us as one.
And in that one, I see that my faith in you is fully justified.

10. Faith is the opposite of fear, as much a part of love as fear is of attack. Faith is the acknowledgment of union. It is the gracious acknowledgment of everyone as a Son of your most loving Father, loved by Him like you, and therefore loved by you as yourself. It is His Love that joins you and your brother, and for His Love you would keep no one separate from yours. Each one appears just as he is perceived in the holy instant, united in your purpose to be released from guilt. You see [Ur: saw] the Christ in him, and he is [Ur: was] healed because you look on what makes faith forever justified in everyone.

Application: Thinking of this same person, say the following:

In my faith in you, [name], I have no fear of what you will do.
My faith in you is an acknowledgment that you are a Son of my most loving Father.
You are loved by Him as I am, and therefore loved by me as myself.
It is His Love that joins us.
And for the sake of His Love, I would not keep you separate from my love.
I see you only according to how you look now, in the holy instant.
I see the Christ in you.
And thus I look on what makes faith forever justified in everyone.

Realize that if you say and really *mean* these lines, this person will be healed by your faith.

11. Faith is the gift of God, through Him Whom God has <u>given</u> you. Faithlessness looks upon the Son of God, and judges him <u>unworthy</u> of forgiveness. But through the eyes of faith, the Son of God is seen <u>already</u> forgiven, free of all the guilt he laid upon himself. Faith sees him only *now* because it looks not to the past to judge him, but would see in him <u>only</u> what it would see in <u>you</u>. It sees <u>not</u> through the body's eyes, nor looks to bodies for its justification. It is the messenger of the <u>new</u> perception, sent forth to gather witnesses unto its coming, and to return their messages to <u>you</u>.

Sometimes it seems as if to have faith in someone, we would need to overlook everything he has done; we would need to overlook everything our eyes have seen of him. And that is true. A different way to say this is that we need to see him through the eyes of faith. This is not denial. It is a new perception, which doesn't use our physical eyes. It sees more deeply than that, seeing past everything the other person's body has done. It sees only the pure Son of God in him, abiding in the eternal present.

12. Faith is as easily exchanged for knowledge as is the real world. For faith <u>arises</u> from the Holy Spirit's perception, and is the sign you share it <u>with</u> Him. Faith is a gift you offer to the Son of God <u>through</u> Him [the Holy Spirit], and <u>wholly</u> acceptable to his Father as to Him. And therefore offered <u>you</u>. Your holy relationship, with its <u>new</u> purpose, offers you faith to give unto your brother [Ur: *each other*]. Your faithlessness has driven you and him [Ur: had driven you] <u>apart</u>, and so you do [Ur: did] not <u>recognize</u> salvation in him. Yet [Ur: But] faith <u>unites</u> you in the holiness you see, <u>not</u> through the body's eyes, but in the sight of Him Who joined you, and in Whom <u>you</u> are united.

This faith is not blind faith inspired by emotionalism, showing us a fantasy world seen through wishful thinking. Rather, this faith is part of a higher perception, part of *true* perception. It is a gift from the Holy Spirit, through which we see the *real* world, a world more real than what our physical eyes see before us.

As the previous section said (18.IX), when Helen and Bill joined, their relationship was in some sense taken through the clouds of guilt, purified, and planted in the real world. Now it rests there as a source of healing and power in their minds, radiating its gifts. One of those gifts is faith. Their faithlessness in each other had driven them apart, but now they have the chance, if they take hold of this new faith, to see each other through different eyes, and to undo their separateness by joining.

> 13. Grace is not given to a <u>body</u>, but to a <u>mind</u>. And the mind that <u>receives</u> it looks <u>instantly</u> beyond the body, and sees the holy place where <u>it</u> was healed. <u>There</u> is the altar where the grace was given, in which <u>it</u> [the mind] stands. Do you, then, offer grace and <u>blessing</u> to your brother [Ur: each other], for you stand at the <u>same</u> altar where grace was laid for <u>both</u> of you. And be you healed by grace <u>together,</u> that <u>you</u> may heal through faith.

Jesus is saying that in the holy instant in which Helen and Bill joined, they came before a holy altar, where grace was laid for both of them. All they needed to do was accept this gift and they would be healed. Apparently, the way they were to accept the gift of grace was to offer it to each other. Now we can understand the meaning of his instruction (not a question), "Do you, then, offer grace and blessing to each other." What does it mean to offer grace to another person? One meaning of grace is "a capacity to tolerate, accommodate, or forgive people" (from Microsoft Word's internal dictionary). Offering our brother grace, then, means saying to him, "Your slate is wiped clean. Your sins are forgiven."

> 14. In the holy instant, you and your brother stand before the altar God has raised unto Himself and <u>both</u> of you. Lay faithlessness aside, and come to it <u>together</u>. There will you see the miracle of your relationship as it was <u>made again</u> through faith. And there it is that you will realize that there is <u>nothing</u> faith can<u>not</u> forgive. <u>No</u> error <u>interferes</u> with its calm sight, which brings the miracle of healing with equal ease to <u>all</u> of them. For what the messengers of love are sent to do <u>they do,</u> returning the glad tidings that it was done [Ur: done,] [returning these glad tidings] to you and your brother who stand together before the altar from which they were sent forth [Ur: sent forth, *together*].

Remember "I Need Do Nothing" (18.VII), which told us that joint holy instants within a holy relationship are the Course's special means for saving us time? This paragraph is talking about the same thing. It is asking Helen and Bill to enter holy instants together. The image is of them coming before an altar, an altar raised not by them to God, but by God to them and to Himself. This altar represents that deep place in their minds where their relationship is already holy, where nothing is beyond being healed, where all is already forgiven and they are already united, where complete faith in each other is already theirs.

They came to this altar in their original holy instant, when they joined in demonstrating a better way. Now Jesus is asking them to come to it again.

The messengers of love are hard to define. They seem to be miraculous perception going forth from us, doing miracles out there, and then returning to us with news about those miracles. The messengers are our perception, in other words, in that our perception does go out into the world and then bring reports back to us about the world. But, being miraculous perception, these messengers don't just report about change; they make change happen. We will encounter them again in a few sections.

> 15. As faithlessness will keep your little kingdoms barren and separate, so will faith help the Holy Spirit prepare the ground for the most holy garden that He would make of it. For faith brings peace, and so it calls on truth to enter and make lovely what has already been prepared for loveliness. Truth follows faith and peace, completing the process of making lovely that they begin. For faith is still a learning goal, no longer needed when the lesson has been learned. Yet truth will stay forever.

Helen and Bill's faithlessness will keep them apart, locked in their tiny desert kingdoms, each playing the role of that crazy king, the bitter ruler of all that he surveys (18.VIII.7:5). Faith in each other, however, will give them the very holy instants Jesus talked about in that same section, the holy instants that would let them walk into the garden that love had prepared for both of them (18.VIII.13:8). Their faith, then, will pave the way for truth, for faith brings the experience of peace, and peace is the condition for the coming of truth. This truth will stay forever, long after faith, having fulfilled its purpose, has passed away.

The bottom line: If you want healing in your relationship, have faith in the other person, and count on this faith to bring about joint holy instants—holy encounters in which the two of you experience healing.

> 16. Let, then, your dedication be to the eternal [the truth, which stays forever], and learn how not to interfere with it and make it slave to time

[don't turn truth into bodies and what they do]. For what you think you do to the eternal you do to *you* [you'll seem to turn yourself into a body]. Whom God created as His Son [you] is slave to nothing, being lord of all, along with his Creator. You <u>can</u> enslave a body, but an <u>idea</u> is free, <u>incapable</u> of being kept in prison or limited in <u>any</u> way <u>except by the mind that thought it</u>. For it remains <u>joined</u> to its source, which is its jailer or its liberator, according to which it chooses as <u>its</u> purpose <u>for itself</u>.

"Let, then, your dedication be to the eternal" summarizes the entire section. The section, if you remember, began with a discussion about "when a situation has been dedicated wholly to truth." It then talked about how this dedication can only take place through faith, especially faith in our brother, faith that his nature transcends his body. Seeing him as a body is an expression of lack of faith in him. The whole section, then, is saying, "If you want to be truly dedicated to the goal of truth, have faith in your brother to get there with you. Have faith that he is not that separate, sinning body, but that he is God's holy Son. This will heal him, and allow the two of you to enter into holy encounters (joint holy instants) in which you briefly stand together before God's altar, upon which your relationship is already perfectly healed."

This final paragraph emphasizes that if we see the truth in our brother as his body, we will see the truth in ourselves as our body, and will thus enslave ourselves to time. Yet, in fact, we are lord of all, along with God. True, our body can be enslaved, but if the body is only an idea in the mind, then it is only the mind that can really imprison it. And the mind does this according to the purpose it gives that idea (the body), which is based on the purpose the mind gives *itself*. I think this is the meaning of the last two sentences. The principle in them is not hard to understand, but what that principle is being applied to is hard to discern.

II. Sin versus Error
Commentary by Robert Perry

1. It is <u>essential</u> that error be not confused with sin [Ur: "sin"], and it is this distinction that makes salvation possible. For error can be corrected, and the wrong made right. But sin, were it possible, <u>would</u> be irreversible. The belief in sin is necessarily based on the firm conviction that minds, <u>not</u> bodies, can attack. And thus the mind <u>is</u> guilty, and will forever so remain unless a mind <u>not</u> part of it can give it absolution. Sin calls for punishment as error for correction, and the belief that punishment *is* correction is clearly insane.

The opening paragraph of this crucial two-section discussion announces many of the themes we will see as we go along. Sin and error are really two different interpretations of attack. One says, "No big deal. Your attack was only an error, merely a mistake. It can be corrected." The other says, "Your mind actually attacked and damaged another mind. Now you have turned your mind into something sinful. You deserve only to be punished—except on the unlikely chance that your victim will absolve you."

Notice his closing remark about "the belief that punishment *is* correction is clearly insane." Being uncomfortable with punishment, we like to call it correction. "It's not about making them pay for what they did," we say. "It's about making sure they don't do it again." Not only should we question the sincerity of this statement, but Jesus is implying that punishment doesn't actually succeed in correcting.

2. Sin is not an error, for sin entails an arrogance which the idea of error lacks. To sin would be to violate reality, <u>and to succeed</u>. Sin is the proclamation that attack is real and guilt is <u>justified</u>. It assumes the Son of God <u>is</u> guilty, and has thus <u>succeeded</u> in losing his innocence and making himself what God created <u>not</u>. Thus is creation seen as <u>not</u> eternal, and the Will of God open to opposition <u>and defeat</u>. Sin is the grand illusion [Ur: "grand illusion"] underlying <u>all</u> the ego's grandiosity. For <u>by</u> it God <u>Himself</u> is changed, and rendered incomplete.

The interpretation of an attack as a sin, as Jesus points out, is an incredibly arrogant interpretation. Do you really think your attack was so real that it succeeded in actually violating reality? Do you really believe it could change your nature, causing you to lose your innocence and become genuinely guilty? If you can thus corrupt your nature as God created it, then think what that implies. It means that God's creative act can be changed, opposed, and defeated. It means that God Himself can be changed and rendered incomplete. Do you really think you have this kind of power? Might this not be simply a delusion of grandiosity? Might not sin be nothing more than a grand illusion?

> 3. The Son of God <u>can</u> be mistaken; he <u>can</u> deceive himself; he can even turn the power of his mind <u>against</u> himself. But he cannot sin [Ur: can *not*]. There is <u>nothing</u> he can do that would <u>really</u> change his reality in <u>any</u> way, nor make him <u>really</u> guilty. That is what sin <u>would</u> do, for such is its <u>purpose</u>. Yet for all the wild insanity inherent in the whole <u>idea</u> of sin, <u>it is impossible</u>. For the wages of sin *is* death, and how can the immortal die?

Yes, we can make errors. We can make mistakes. We can engage in self-deception, fall into insanity, and use our power to attack ourselves. But we cannot change who we are, and that is what sin purports to do. It purports to change us from innocent and deserving of life to evil, guilty, and deserving only of death. But can it really pull this off? How can it make us deserving of death when we cannot die?

This sounds very abstract, but this is the central issue of our existence. In each moment we observe ourselves attacking, if only in little ways, if only by failing to reach out more lovingly and generously. With each small attack, we assume that we have actually changed our identity, rendering ourselves less innocent and less deserving. What if that "natural," perfectly human assumption is actually the height of arrogance?

> 4. A <u>major</u> tenet in the ego's insane religion is that sin is <u>not</u> error but <u>truth</u>, and it is <u>innocence</u> that would deceive. <u>Purity</u> is seen as arrogance, and the acceptance of the self <u>as sinful</u> is perceived as holiness. And it is this doctrine that <u>replaces</u> the reality of the Son of God as his Father created him, and willed that he be forever. Is this <u>humility</u>? Or is it, rather, an attempt to wrest creation <u>away</u> from truth, and keep it separate?

"The ego's insane religion" sounds a lot like traditional religion! In that context, to announce, "I am pure" is seen as arrogant and sinful, whereas to admit, "I am sinful" is seen as holy. I just found this quote on a Baha'i website: "Those that claim to be holy and righteous are the greatest perverters and offenders in the sight of God!"

Besides the odd combination of "I am sinful" = "I am holy," Jesus asks if it is humble to claim that you are not as God created you and willed you to be forever. Is it humble to claim that you have managed to wrest yourself away from God by making yourself irreconcilable with His Holiness?

> 5. <u>Any</u> attempt to reinterpret sin as error is always indefensible to the ego. The <u>idea</u> of sin is <u>wholly</u> sacrosanct to its thought system, and quite unapproachable except with reverence and awe. It is the most "holy" concept in the ego's system; lovely and powerful, wholly true, and <u>necessarily</u> protected with every defense at its disposal. For here lies its "best" defense, which all the others serve. Here is its armor, its protection, and the fundamental <u>purpose</u> of the special relationship in its interpretation.

Jesus is talking about the ego's thought system as a religion, and subtly implying that it is the religion within conventional religion. In this strange religion, the most holy and sacred idea of all is sin, to be approached with the same reverence and awe that one should approach God. In this religion, the slightest questioning of the concept of sin is the most unforgivable heresy (something you can observe if you have ever read conservative Christian commentators critique the Course). The idea of sin is so heavily defended simply because it is itself the ego's best defense. Everything the ego has us engage in, including the special relationship, is designed to reinforce the "reality" of sin.

And lest we look down on those in traditional religion, we need to remember that we are card-carrying members of the ego's religion, too. We may have our doubts about the faith, as it were, but we are still attending the ego's black mass every day.

> 6. It can indeed be said the ego <u>made</u> its world on sin. Only in such a world <u>could</u> everything be upside down. This <u>is</u> the strange illusion that makes the clouds of guilt seem heavy and impenetrable. The solidness that this world's foundation <u>seems</u> to have is <u>found</u> in this. For sin

has changed creation from an Idea of God to an <u>ideal</u> the <u>ego</u> wants; a world <u>it</u> rules, made up of bodies, mindless and capable of <u>complete</u> corruption and decay.

The ego (not God) made the world, and built it all on the concept of sin. Sin says that every mind is separate and driven to do evil, thereby corrupting itself and making itself deserving of death. Look around at this world. Everywhere you look you see a physical representation of this. You see *bodies* that are separate, driven to do evil, and doomed to corruption, decay, and finally death. Here we have sin incarnate as an entire universe. Even now, without our belief in this idea, the world would not even seem solid, but would be recognized as nothing but clouds, nothing but mist.

> If this is a <u>mistake</u>, it can be undone easily by truth. <u>Any</u> mistake can be corrected, if <u>truth</u> be left to judge it. But if the mistake is given the <u>status</u> of truth, to what <u>can</u> it be brought? The "holiness" of sin is kept in place by just this strange device. As <u>truth</u> it <u>is</u> inviolate, and everything is brought to *it* for judgment. As a <u>mistake</u>, *it* must be brought to truth. It is impossible to have faith in sin, for sin <u>is</u> faithlessness. Yet it <u>is</u> possible to have faith that a <u>mistake</u> can be corrected.

Minds like to latch onto a single unquestioned idea that everything else is referred to. For conservative Christians, that idea is the notion that Jesus died for our sins. For post-9/11 Americans, that idea is that our nation and way of life are threatened by terrorists. For everyone who believes in the ego, that idea is sin. We *know* that idea is true; it's pointless to question it. And so we refer everything to it. We judge everything against it.

Sometimes, those central, unquestioned ideas are revealed to be a house of cards as soon as you start really questioning them. And that is what we must do with the idea of sin. Rather than judging everything against it, we need to judge it against a higher standard, the standard of real truth. If we do that, we can undo the idea of sin and everything it made, including the physical world.

> 7. There is no stone in all the ego's embattled citadel that is more heavily defended than the idea that sin is real; the <u>natural</u> expression of what the Son of God has <u>made</u> himself to be, <u>and what he is</u>. To the

ego, <u>this is no mistake</u>. For this <u>is</u> its reality; this is the "truth" from which escape will <u>always</u> be impossible. This is his past, his present and his future. For he has somehow managed to corrupt his Father, and change His Mind <u>completely</u>. Mourn, then, the death of God, Whom sin has killed! And this <u>would</u> be the ego's wish, which in its madness it believes it has <u>accomplished</u>.

At the very heart of the ego's temple, inside its holy of holies, is the sacred notion of sin. Yet this temple is a fortress, designed with one end in mind: to keep God from breaching the walls. When the outer walls come tumbling down, the ego retreats to the next wall, and then the next. The very last place that the "enemy" will reach is that holy of holies, the inner sanctum of sin.

The foundational nature of sin can be seen in our unquestioned assumptions about ourselves. Our view of ourselves is much like that of a self-hating vampire: compelled to prey on others, loathing ourselves for it, yet nonetheless unable to stop it. We believe, therefore, that we have corrupted the nature that God gave us, and this amounts to a belief that we have overthrown God, even killed Him. It sounds arrogant, but this is what we believe every time we feel a pang of guilt over something we regret having done.

> 8. Would you not <u>rather</u> that all this be nothing more than a <u>mistake</u>, <u>entirely</u> correctable, and so easily escaped from that its whole correction is like walking through a mist into the sun? For that is all it <u>is</u>. Perhaps you would be tempted to <u>agree</u> with the ego that it is far better to be sinful than mistaken. Yet think you carefully before you allow yourself to make this choice. Approach it not lightly, for it <u>is</u> the choice of hell or Heaven.

There is a strange attraction in the idea of being sinful. It means that we define ourselves. It means that since our attacks are real, the loot we get from them is real, too. But at what a cost! For the sake of these "benefits" we are willing to walk into hell. Wouldn't we prefer Heaven? Wouldn't we rather see our attacks as mere mistakes, entirely correctable? There is nothing worse than a mistake of ours that can never be corrected. Wouldn't it be wondrous, miraculous, then, if the whole mythology of sin was just a fantasy, which can be corrected as easily as "walking through a mist into the sun"?

Application: Think of some recent thing you did that left you feeling guilty—guilt that you were definitely conscious of. Look into your feeling of guilt. Does it not include the idea that you damaged something, something real? Does it not include the idea that you corrupted yourself? If you think of yourself before this deed, didn't you seem cleaner before, and dirtier, more tarnished afterwards? Don't you also feel that your sin makes you worthy of punishment, of some kind of payment? For instance, if the person you believe you wronged expressed anger towards you, wouldn't you feel that you had to internalize that anger, take it in as your just deserts?

Now focus on these lines:

> *It is arrogant to think that I can damage the reality that God created.*
>
> *It is arrogant to think that I can lose my innocence and make myself what God created not.*
>
> *It is grandiose to think that I can defeat the Will of God, which declares me innocent.*
>
> *It is grandiose to think that I can tear myself away from God (by making myself sinful).*
>
> *It is arrogant to think that I can deserve to die, for I live forever.*

III. The Unreality of Sin
Commentary by Robert Perry

1. The attraction of guilt is found in sin, <u>not</u> error. Sin will be repeated <u>because</u> of this attraction. Fear can become so acute that the sin is denied the acting out. But while the guilt <u>remains</u> attractive the mind will suffer, and not let go of the <u>idea</u> of sin. For guilt still calls to it, and the mind hears it and yearns for it, making itself a willing captive to its sick appeal. Sin is an idea of evil that cannot <u>be</u> corrected, and yet will be forever <u>desirable</u>. As an <u>essential</u> part of what the ego thinks you <u>are</u>, you will <u>always</u> want it. And only an <u>avenger</u>, with a mind <u>unlike</u> your own, could stamp it out through <u>fear</u>.

Is there any of us who doesn't feel the compulsion to do certain things we know we shouldn't? Yes, these things make us feel guilty, but in doing them, we chase a payoff so precious that the guilt seems worth it, an unfortunate side effect that we can live with. The desire for this payoff is so strong that it seems impossible to let it go. Even if we don't act out the desire because of fear of punishment, the urge remains. We feel deprived and the pressure builds. Surely this scenario is familiar to all of us.

This paragraph addresses this same scenario, and gives it an entirely different explanation. According to it, guilt is not an unfortunate side effect that we can live with because of how attractive the real payoff is. Guilt *is* the payoff. Guilt is what we are attracted to. This is the desire that, when denied, simply builds, until it can be resisted no longer.

Application: Think of a behavior that you feel you shouldn't do, but feel compelled to do. Then ask yourself two questions:

Do I feel guilty for this?
Could that guilt be what I am really attracted to here?

2. The ego does not think it possible that love, <u>not</u> fear, is really called upon by sin, *and always answers*. For the ego brings sin to <u>fear</u>,

demanding punishment. Yet punishment is but another form of guilt's <u>protection</u>, for what is <u>deserving</u> punishment must have been <u>really done</u>. Punishment is always the great <u>preserver</u> of sin, treating it with respect and honoring its enormity. What must be punished, <u>must be true</u>. And what is true <u>must</u> be eternal, and will be repeated endlessly. For what you think is real <u>you want</u>, and will <u>not</u> let it go.

When we "sin," we are trying to prove to ourselves the idea "I am evil" (see 1:6). That's the attraction, however sick it is. How can punishment get rid of this? Punishment just reinforces it. Punishment says, "You really did this, and what you did was huge, enormous. It defines you. You really are evil." Punishment is like a religious ritual that grants honor and hallowed respect to the "sacred" claim "I am evil." And if evil is our reality, and reality is permanent, then we must repeat this evil, continually, forever.

3. An <u>error</u>, on the other hand, is <u>not</u> attractive. What you see clearly <u>as a mistake</u> you <u>want</u> corrected. Sometimes a sin can be repeated over and over, with <u>obviously</u> distressing results, but <u>without</u> the loss of its appeal. And suddenly, you change its status from a sin to a <u>mistake</u>. Now you will <u>not</u> repeat it; you will merely stop and let it go, <u>unless the guilt remains</u>. For then you will but change the <u>form</u> of sin, granting that it was an error, but <u>keeping it uncorrectable</u>. This is not really a change in your perception, for it is <u>sin</u> that calls for punishment, <u>not</u> error.

A "sin" may be evil, but it is an evil that you want. It is thus (seen as) an expression of who you are. How can you, then, let it go, no matter how distressing its results? A mistake, on the other hand, implies that you wanted something else but you got this instead. The result, in other words, was not what you wanted. It was not an expression of who you are. Therefore, the only thing you want at this point is to correct it.

The key, then, is to change the status of a sin to that of a mistake. However, this must be done sincerely. If you call it a mistake but still feel guilty and assume it can't be corrected, you are still seeing it as a sin, no matter what you call it.

Application: Use that same example you used in the first paragraph's application, and say,

III. The Unreality of Sin

This is not a sin.
It is just a mistake.
It is not an expression of who I am.
It is not what I really want.
Therefore, it is entirely correctable.
There is no need for me to feel guilty about it.

4. The Holy Spirit <u>cannot</u> punish sin. Mistakes He recognizes, and would correct them all as God entrusted Him to do. But <u>sin</u> He knows not, nor can He <u>recognize</u> mistakes that cannot be corrected. For a mistake that cannot be corrected is <u>meaningless</u> to Him. Mistakes are *for* correction, and they call for <u>nothing else</u>. What calls for punishment must call for <u>nothing</u>. Every mistake *must* be a call for love. What, then, is sin? What <u>could</u> it be but a mistake you would keep hidden; a call for help that you would keep <u>unheard</u> and thus <u>unanswered</u>?

In the entire history of the world, the Holy Spirit has never seen a sin. He has seen countless attacks, but He immediately recognized all of them as mere mistakes. A mistake is an outcome that does not reflect what we really want. These outcomes naturally call for correction. Since this correction must come from beyond the mindset that made the mistake, they also call for *help*. And since what must be corrected is this mind's notion that it is unlovable, they also call for *love*.

Why are we so compelled to interpret these mistakes as sins? It is because we don't want them corrected. We don't want the Holy Spirit to help us out of them.

5. In time, the Holy Spirit <u>clearly</u> sees the Son of God can make mistakes. On this you <u>share</u> His vision. Yet you do <u>not</u> share His recognition of the difference between time and eternity. And when correction is completed, time *is* eternity.

I love the subtle humor of the first two sentences: "In time, the Holy Spirit clearly sees that people can screw things up. On this particular point, you quite agree with Him." But what you don't realize is that time is not real, and so the things done in time are also not real.

[Ur: Time is like a downward spiral that seems to travel down from a long, unbroken line, along another plane, but which in no way *breaks* the line, or interferes with its smooth continuousness. Along the spiral, it *seems* as if the line *must* have been broken, but, at the *line*, its wholeness is apparent. Everything seen from the spiral is misperceived. But, as you approach the line, you realize that *it* was not affected by the drop into another plane at all. But, *from* this plane, the *line* seems discontinuous. And this is but an error in perception, which can be easily corrected *in the mind*, although the body's eyes will see no change. The eyes see many things the mind corrects, and *you* respond, *not* to the eyes' illusions, *but to the mind's corrections*. You *see* the line as broken, and as you shift to different aspects of the spiral, the line looks different. Yet in your mind is One Who *knows* it is unbroken, and forever changeless.]

Ken Wapnick says that, in the editing process he undertook with Helen, Jesus asked that this passage be removed, for reasons which he never understood. The passage contains a great image of the relationship between time and eternity. Eternity is pictured as an unbroken line. At some point along this line, however, another line branches off from it, spiraling downward. This is the spiral of time. We are perched on this spiral, and as we look up from there at the original line of eternity, it looks like that line was broken at the point where the spiral begins, that the line of eternity snapped there and followed the spiral downward, rather than continuing on as it was. It looks like our detour into time actually dragged the eternal down into time, so that our eternal innocence was really changed into a bubbling pot of sin. If true, this would make time itself, along with everything we do in time, into a real sin.

But the Holy Spirit knows that the line of eternity is unbroken and forever changeless. We have not fractured Heaven, and so our "sins" are just harmless mistakes. With His help, we can see this. Even though our eyes present to us a picture of Heaven's formless spirit changed into separate, corruptible bodies, we can mentally correct for that, in the same way that we mentally correct for the illusion of a stick that "bends" as it enters the water.

The Holy Spirit [Ur: This One] can teach you how to look on time differently and see <u>beyond</u> it, but <u>not</u> while you believe in sin. In error, yes, for this <u>can</u> be corrected by the mind. But sin is the belief that <u>your</u> perception is <u>unchangeable,</u> and that the <u>mind</u> must <u>accept as true</u> what it is told <u>through</u> it. If it does not obey, the <u>mind</u> is judged insane. The only power that could change perception is thus kept impotent, held to the body by the fear of changed perception which its Teacher, Who is one with it, would bring.

The Holy Spirit can only teach us to correct for the illusions presented by our eyes if we let go of the belief in sin. For sin says, "It is my nature to see through narrowed, spiteful eyes. I can't change who I am." If we persist in trying to change our perception, our ego will tell us that we are trying to go against our nature, that we have gone bonkers and floated off into la-la land. This self-ridicule is a powerful motivator which usually keeps our mind well tethered to the status quo of sin.

> 6. When you are tempted to believe that sin is real, remember this: If sin is real, both God and you are not. If creation is extension, the Creator must have extended Himself, and it is impossible that what is part of Him is totally unlike the rest. If sin is real, God must be at war with Himself [Ur: *within Himself*]. He must be split, and torn between good and evil; partly sane and partially insane. For He must have created what wills to destroy Him, and has the power to do so. Is it not easier to believe that you have been mistaken than to believe in this?

If you believe in sin, you are implicitly accepting the following argument:

> God creates by extending Himself. Whatever He creates is an extension of Him.
> He created a being that is evil and in conflict with Him—that wills to destroy Him and has power to do so.
> Therefore, there must be something *within God* that is evil and in conflict with Himself.
> God must be split into warring parts, one good and one evil.
> God is therefore a mixture of totally incompatible ideas. He is an inherent contradiction.
> You and God together are an inherent contradiction.
> Both you and God cannot be real.

Are we really prepared to believe this? As Jesus says, "Is it not easier to believe that you have been mistaken than to believe in this?"

7. While you believe that your reality or your brother's is bounded by a body, you will believe in sin. While you believe that bodies can unite, you will find guilt attractive and believe that sin is precious. For the belief that bodies limit mind leads to a perception of the world in which the proof of separation seems to be everywhere. And God and His creation seem to be split apart and overthrown. For sin would prove what God created holy could not prevail against it, nor remain itself before the power of sin. Sin is perceived as mightier than God, before which God <u>Himself</u> must bow, and offer His creation to its conqueror. Is this humility or madness?

As long as we believe that bodies are real, that bodies really encase minds, then sin will be real to us. We will look out and see a world "in which the proof of separation seems to be everywhere." We will see a world in which the power of sin has overthrown God, grabbing reality away from Him. Having done so, it has then carved into little pieces the limitless spirit He created, and then shut each piece away in a lockbox made of meat. That is what we see all around us right now, the "proof" that sin has won and God has lost. We need to ask ourselves, "Is this humility or madness?"

8. If sin is real, it must forever be beyond the hope of healing. For there would be a power <u>beyond</u> God's, capable of making another will that could attack His Will and <u>overcome</u> it; and give His Son a will <u>apart</u> from His, and <u>stronger</u>. And each part of God's fragmented creation would have a <u>different</u> will, <u>opposed</u> to His, and in eternal opposition to Him <u>and to each other</u>. Your holy relationship has, as its purpose now, the goal of proving <u>this</u> is impossible. Heaven has smiled upon it, and the belief in sin has been uprooted in its smile of love. You <u>see</u> it still, because you do not realize that its <u>foundation</u> has gone. Its <u>source</u> has been removed, and so it can be cherished but a little while before it vanishes. Only the habit of <u>looking</u> for it still remains.

Imagine a Heaven in perfect harmony, with God and His Son sharing one Will and therefore abiding in a state of absolute peace. Then imagine that a power beyond God's enters. It possesses the Son and gives him a will in opposition to God's, and stronger. Then this power gives each individual Son his own separate will, so that the Sons are now in ceaseless war with each other, as well as with God. This power has turned Heaven into total chaos. (Indeed, this picture will be revisited in "The Laws of Chaos.") What could possibly overcome this power? For it has roundly defeated what was the ultimate power—God Himself.

Each holy relationship has the goal of proving that this whole picture is false. For at the heart of each holy relationship, that power of sin—which is really just a belief—has been uprooted. True, the two people still look for sin out in the world. But this looking is a habit whose driving force has been removed. The looking is like the reflexes of an insect that are still moving, even though the insect has just died. It is only a matter of time before those reflexes die down as well.

> 9. And yet you look with Heaven's smile upon <u>your</u> lips, and Heaven's blessing on your sight. You will <u>not</u> see sin long. For in the <u>new</u> perception the mind <u>corrects</u> it when it <u>seems</u> to be seen, and it becomes invisible. Errors [Ur: But *errors*] are quickly recognized and quickly given to correction, to be healed, <u>not</u> hidden [see 4:9]. <u>You</u> will be healed of sin and all its ravages the <u>instant</u> that you give it no power over your brother [Ur: *each other*]. And you will help him [Ur: *help* each other] overcome <u>mistakes</u> by joyously <u>releasing</u> him [Ur: one another] from the belief in sin.

Even though the habit of looking for sin remains, "you look with Heaven's smile upon your lips, and Heaven's blessing on your sight." And because of this, your mind corrects the perception of sin quickly once it's seen. You realize that seeing it is really just an error, to be quickly given to the Holy Spirit, rather than hidden from Him. From this place, when you see your holy relationship partner temporarily caught in the trap of sin, rather than punishing him for it, you can think, "He's trying to prove to himself that he is evil. I can release him from this belief with my love." This gift of release is what will really cause sin to lose the power it had over you.

Application: Think of someone close to you, and then think of a time that he or she saw sin in you. Then say to this person,

> *I see what you are doing.*
> *You are trying to prove to yourself that you are evil.*
> *But I know better.*

*I look on you with Heaven's smile on my lips, and Heaven's
blessing on my sight.
You are the Son my Father loves.*

10. In the holy instant, you will see the smile of Heaven shining on both you and your brother [Ur: on *both* of you]. And you will shine upon him [Ur: each other], in glad acknowledgment of the grace that has been <u>given</u> you [see I.13]. For sin will <u>not</u> prevail against a union Heaven has smiled upon. Your perception was <u>healed</u> in the holy instant Heaven gave you. Forget what you <u>have</u> seen [sin], and raise your eyes in faith to what you now <u>can</u> see [the smile of Heaven shining on both of you]. The barriers to Heaven will disappear before your holy sight, for you who were sightless have been <u>given</u> vision, and you <u>can</u> see. Look not for what has been <u>removed,</u> but for the glory that has been <u>restored</u> for you to see.

Again, Jesus is asking us to enter into joint holy instants with our holy relationship partner. In these holy instants, we will see Heaven smiling on both of us, and in the joy of that, we will shine on each other. Bathed in the light of this grace, it will be clear to us that the "power" of sin could never prevail over reality, or over our relationship.

It was an instant like this in which our holy relationship was born. In that instant, our belief in sin was uprooted and we were given vision to see. Now we face a choice: Will we continue looking for what has been removed—sin—or will we use the vision that was given us, to look upon the real world?

11. Look upon your Redeemer, and behold what He would show you in your brother, and let not sin arise again to blind your eyes. For sin would keep you separate from him, but your Redeemer would have you look upon your brother as yourself. Your relationship is now a temple of healing; a place where all the weary ones can come and rest. Here is the rest that waits for all, after the journey. And it is brought *nearer* to all by your relationship.

It's as if we've been living in a dark room, filled with a dense mist that blinds us. At last, however, we found a door in this room, opened it, and discovered a beautiful world just outside, full of swaying trees, lush meadows, and dancing brooks. Now we stand in the doorway, and Jesus is saying to us, "I know the temptation is strong, but don't go back in that room."

That is the situation Helen and Bill were in. In their holy instant, they left the room, and there in the meadow outside they saw a temple of healing—their relationship—a place "where all the weary ones can come and rest," a place just like the little garden. The question now was, would they walk to that temple hand in hand and start welcoming the weary ones, or would they look at it, sigh happily at its beauty, and walk back into the room?

IV. The Obstacles to Peace
Commentary by Robert Perry

"The Obstacles to Peace" is the longest and probably the most important section in the Text. Allen Watson has called it "the core presentation" of the Course. Its concluding image—that of standing before, lifting, and passing beyond the veil before the face of Christ—is perhaps the Course's central image. Ideas that this section grounds (especially the fear of God) are referred to again and again throughout the Text, Workbook, and Manual. It is easily the section most referenced in later sections in the Course.

This section is a series of arresting discussions about a long list of key Course topics, and it is easy to approach it as that—as a series of pieces. What is far more difficult is to see how all of these pieces fit together into a single whole. Unfortunately, this whole has remained invisible to both students and commentators. As Greg and I go through this section, therefore, we will be trying to explain the pieces, but also trying to explain how they fit into the whole.

The whole is organized around the holy relationship. It is specifically about that relationship's process—the process of holiness gradually replacing sin in a relationship in which two people have joined. In this process, holiness first enters the relationship and plants itself deep in the relationship, thus displacing the relationship's previous goal of sin. Then that holiness, which is also peace, goes through a process of flowing over several obstacles erected by what remains of the goal of sin. This process culminates in the two partners forgiving each other and joining, and thereby passing beyond the final veil and uniting with God.

1. [Ur: Your relationship is now a temple of healing, a place where all the weary ones can come and find rest. Here is the rest {peace} that waits for all, after the journey. And it is brought *nearer* to all, by your relationship.] As [Ur: this] peace extends [Ur: expands] from deep inside yourself [Ur: yourselves] to embrace <u>all</u> the Sonship and give it rest, it will encounter many obstacles. Some of them <u>you</u> will try to impose [Ur: interpose]. Others will seem to arise from elsewhere; from

your brothers, and from various aspects of the world <u>outside</u>. Yet peace will gently cover them, extending past <u>completely</u> unencumbered [Ur: unhindered]. The extension of the Holy Spirit's purpose from <u>your</u> relationship to others, to bring them gently <u>in</u>, [Ur: has already begun. This] is the way in which He will bring means and goal in line. The peace He lay [Ur: laid], deep within you and your brother [Ur: within *both* of you], will quietly extend to <u>every</u> aspect of your life [Ur: lives], surrounding you and your brother [Ur: both of you] with glowing happiness and the calm awareness of <u>complete</u> protection. And you will carry its message of love and safety and freedom to everyone who draws nigh unto your temple, where healing waits for him. You will <u>not</u> wait to give him this, for you will <u>call</u> to him and he will answer you, <u>recognizing</u> in your call the Call for God. And you will draw him in and give him rest, as it was given <u>you</u>.

I have included at the beginning the three sentences that ended yesterday's section simply because the original dictation began with them. They just happened to end up at the end of the previous section through the editing process.

In order to understand the section as a whole, it is crucial to grasp this first paragraph. It lays out an entire process:

First, Helen and Bill joined in their goal of demonstrating a better way.

This allowed the Holy Spirit to enter and lay peace deep within their relationship. This peace, in other words, was shared by them, but at an unconscious level.

This peace then seeks to expand beyond its dwelling place in the unconscious, in two movements: first surrounding Helen and Bill and every aspect of their lives, and then expanding further to embrace all the Sonship.

To accomplish this, this peace will have to flow over two kinds of obstacles, corresponding to the two movements mentioned above. The first kind of obstacles are those arising from within Helen and Bill. These are the ones covered by "The Obstacles to Peace." The second kind of obstacles are those arising from others and from the world, as the peace seeks to encompass them. These obstacles are not covered in this section.

This second movement of the peace, from Helen and Bill to the whole

Sonship, is pictured in beautiful terms as their relationship becoming a temple of healing, which takes in all the weary travelers and gives them rest—peace.

> 2. All this will you do. Yet the peace that already lies deeply within must first expand, and <u>flow across</u> the obstacles <u>you</u> placed before it. This will you do [Ur: *This it will do*], for nothing undertaken <u>with</u> the Holy Spirit remains unfinished. You can indeed be sure of <u>nothing</u> you see <u>outside</u> you, but of this ["this" refers to the previous sentence] you *can* be sure [in the Urtext, there was no colon here, but a paragraph break]: The Holy Spirit asks that you offer Him a resting place where <u>you</u> will rest in Him. He answered you, and entered your relationship. Would you not now <u>return</u> His graciousness, and enter into a relationship with Him? For it is <u>He</u> who offered <u>your</u> relationship the gift of holiness, without which it would have been forever impossible to appreciate your brother [Ur: each other].

Before the peace that is deep within can flow out and give those weary travelers rest, it must *first* flow across the obstacles the two people placed before it. This may seem like an impossible condition, but it's not. That peace *will do this*. This is more sure than anything you see outside you, including the rising and setting of the sun.

But you are going to have to cooperate in this process. And you do so by entering into a relationship with the Holy Spirit, by offering Him a resting place inside you, where you rest with Him. This is only logical, since He has already graced you with His presence and entered into a relationship with you. He has already established a resting place deep within you, where He waits to give you the peace that dwells there like stored electricity, waiting to flow out and power your life.

> 3. The gratitude you owe to Him He asks but that you receive for Him. And when you look with gentle graciousness upon your brother [Ur: each other], you are beholding Him. For you are looking where He is, and not apart from Him [Ur: you]. You cannot see the Holy Spirit, but you can see your brothers truly. And the light in them will show you all that you need to see. When the peace in you has been extended to encompass everyone, the Holy Spirit's function here will be accomplished. What need is there for seeing, then? When God has taken the last step Himself, the Holy Spirit will gather all the thanks

and gratitude that you have offered Him, and lay them gently before His Creator in the name of His most holy Son. And the Father will <u>accept</u> them in <u>His</u> Name. What need is there of seeing, in the presence of <u>His</u> gratitude?

We owe the Holy Spirit so much gratitude for entering our relationship and guiding us home. We cannot see Him, but when we see our brothers truly, through the eyes of gentle graciousness, we *are* seeing Him.

When that peace within has arisen to encompass not only the two of us, but the entire Sonship, the Holy Spirit's purpose will be done. And then He will take all the gratitude we have offered Him and make it an offering to God, where it will then become God's gratitude to us. This gratitude is no fleeting human emotion that pertains only to the realm of time. Instead, this gratitude is so transcendent that it belongs only to the realm of knowledge, beyond all form. In the presence of this ineffable gratitude, "what need is there of seeing?"

A. The First Obstacle: The Desire to Get Rid of It

1. The first obstacle that peace must flow across is <u>your</u> desire to get <u>rid</u> of it. For it cannot extend <u>unless</u> you keep it. <u>You</u> are the center from which it radiates outward, to call the others <u>in</u>. You are its home; its tranquil dwelling place from which it gently reaches out, but <u>never</u> leaving <u>you</u>. If <u>you</u> would make it homeless, how can it abide within the Son of God? If it would spread across the whole creation, it <u>must</u> begin with you, and <u>from</u> you reach to everyone who calls, and bring him rest by <u>joining</u> you.

Remember the big picture. When Helen and Bill joined, the Holy Spirit planted peace deep within their relationship, uprooting and replacing the belief in sin that had been the relationship's foundation (see III.8-9). Now that peace wants to flow out from the two of them and embrace the entire Sonship. They, then, are meant to be the center, the home, from which this peace "would spread across the whole creation."

Yet, as we saw, before it can do this, it has to surmount the obstacles within *them*. And now we encounter the first of these: the "desire to get rid of it." This sounds bizarre, yet we can understand it in this way. Imagine that one day Hitler is fooling around with an "Angelic Ouija

Board," and through this he inadvertently invites an angelic presence into him. This presence takes up residence deep within him, but clearly wants to expand and encompass all of him. Now he feels like he's been invaded by a foreign presence that wants to take him over. He feels like he's the victim of "angelic possession." Being Hitler, wouldn't he want to "get rid of" this presence?

Yet we probably don't need this metaphor to understand the principle. We've all probably had times when God or the Holy Spirit felt like an invading presence that wanted to occupy way too much of our inner territory.

> 2. Why would you want peace homeless? What do you think that it must dispossess to dwell with you? What seems to be the cost you are so unwilling to pay? The little barrier [Ur: barriers] of sand [the body] still stands [Ur: stand] between you and your brother [Ur: between you] [see 18.VIII.13:6]. Would you reinforce it [Ur: them] now? You are not asked to let it [Ur: them] go for yourself [Ur: yourselves] alone. Christ asks it of you for Himself. He would bring peace to everyone, and how can He do this except through you? Would you let a little bank of sand, a wall of dust, a tiny seeming barrier, stand between your brothers and salvation? And yet, this little remnant of attack you cherish still against your brother *is* the first obstacle the peace in you encounters in its going forth. This little wall of hatred would <u>still</u> oppose the Will of God [represented by the flow of peace outward], and keep it limited.

You want to kick peace out because you think it's trying to kick out something that you hold dear. That something is the *body*, "the little barrier of sand," the "wall of dust," that stands between you and your brothers. Let's face it. Our lives are to a large degree oriented around our bodies. When a spiritual impulse enters our lives, we want to know if it is going to get in the way of that primary dedication. We immediately wonder, "Is this going to compromise my comfort, my pleasure, or my safety?" We often suspect that it will compromise all three, and this makes us want to get rid of it. This makes perfect sense to us, since we already used this same reasoning to get rid of our brothers. We long ago made a choice that, when it comes down to it, catering to this wall of sand matters more to us than joining with our brothers.

The problem is not the body itself, but our attachment to it as an *end* in itself. This attachment is the same thing as our dedication to sin. This dedication was uprooted when we joined with our holy relationship partner (see III.8:5), but a tiny vestige of it still remains. This is the "little remnant of attack" mentioned here, as well as the "little feather" we will see later.

> 3. The Holy Spirit's purpose rests in peace within you. Yet you are <u>still</u> unwilling to let it <u>join</u> you wholly. You still oppose the Will of God, just by a little. And that little <u>is</u> a limit you would place upon the whole. God's Will is one, <u>not</u> many. It <u>has</u> no opposition, for there is none <u>beside</u> it. What you would still contain behind your little barrier and keep <u>separate</u> from your brother [Ur: each other] seems [Ur: is] mightier than the universe, for it would <u>hold back</u> the universe <u>and its Creator</u>. This little wall would hide the purpose of Heaven, and keep it *from* Heaven.

The Holy Spirit's purpose/peace rests deep inside you, and would flow out through you. But you still eye it warily. You still view your body as a needed containment wall that would hold back the Will of God as it seeks to flow through you to your brother. In the end, then, this wall seems mightier than Heaven itself.

(I must confess that, as worded, I don't understand sentence 7. It says that what is contained behind the wall—which should be the Holy Spirit's peace—seems mightier than the universe. Yet the thought in this entire discussion is that the wall is what blocks God's Will, and thus you would expect the wall itself to be what appears to be mightier than the universe. I can't help but suspect that something has gone wrong in the wording here, even though the Urtext rendering of it doesn't really provide any help. So I don't know.)

> 4. Would you thrust salvation <u>away</u> from the <u>giver</u> of salvation? For such have <u>you</u> become. Peace could no more <u>depart</u> from you than from God. Fear not this little obstacle. It can<u>not</u> contain the Will of God. Peace <u>will</u> flow across it, and join you <u>without</u> hindrance. Salvation cannot <u>be</u> withheld from you. It <u>is</u> your purpose. You <u>cannot</u> choose [Ur: will] <u>apart</u> from this. You <u>have</u> no purpose apart from your brother [Ur: each other], nor apart from the one you asked the Holy Spirit to <u>share</u> with you. The little wall will fall away so quietly beneath the wings of peace [Ur: peace!]. For peace will send its messengers from you to all the world, and barriers [that the world puts up] will fall

113

away before their coming as easily as those that <u>you</u> interpose will be surmounted.

In this contest between the peace planted deep inside and our attachment to the wall of sand, it's clear which one we see as the underdog. Yet Jesus sees it the other way around. Nothing can really stand in the way of this peace, nor could this peace be kicked out of us. The obstacle is the underdog; the peace is the favorite which, in fact, cannot lose.

Application: You probably realize that there is a spiritual presence deep within you that is trying to occupy your whole mind and every aspect of your life, and extend through you to all your brothers. And you probably sense that your devotion to your body's comfort, pleasure, and safety blocks this from happening. Moreover, you probably see that block as being the stronger force in this contest.

> Now close your eyes and visualize your body as a stone wall that surrounds your mind.
> The stones of this wall are held together by the mortar of your attachment to the body.
> In the middle of the enclosed patch of ground, the earth has actually cracked open.
> Way down deep inside this crack is a glowing light—a spiritual presence that wants to come up to the surface and get through that stone wall, so it can reach the world.
> You assume that it hasn't got a chance. The wall is too strong, too thick.
> Then something completely unexpected happens.
> You see a massive flock of white doves flying up out of the crack.
> Rather than trying to go through the wall, they fly right over it.
> And as they do, the wall turns to sand, and collapses in a silent heap,
> while the doves fly out in all directions to the horizon.

5. To overcome the world is no more difficult than to surmount your little wall. For in the miracle of <u>your</u> holy relationship, <u>without</u> this barrier, is <u>every</u> miracle contained. There is no order of difficulty

in miracles, for they <u>are</u> all the same. Each is a gentle <u>winning over</u> from the appeal of guilt to the appeal of love. How can this <u>fail</u> to be accomplished, <u>wherever</u> it is undertaken? Guilt can raise no <u>real</u> barriers against it. And all that seems to stand between you and your brother <u>must</u> fall away because of the appeal <u>you</u> answered. From you who answered, He Who answered you would call. His home is in your holy relationship. Do not attempt to stand <u>between</u> Him and His holy purpose, for it <u>is</u> yours. But let Him quietly <u>extend</u> the miracle of your relationship to everyone <u>contained</u> in it as it was given.

We simply don't realize the power of what was planted deep in our relationship. Every possible miracle is contained in it, to the point where it can surmount with equal ease the barriers we raise as well as all the ones the world raises. For deep within our relationship is the Holy Spirit Himself, Who carries with Him the power of God and the power of love. In response to the appeal of this love, all that those barriers can offer is the appeal of guilt. And who would choose the misery of guilt over the joy of love?

6. There is a hush in Heaven, a happy expectancy, a little pause of gladness in acknowledgment of the journey's end. For Heaven knows you well, as you know Heaven. No illusions stand between you and your brother now. Look not upon the little wall of shadows. The sun has risen <u>over</u> it. How can a shadow <u>keep</u> you from the sun? No more can <u>you</u> be kept by shadows from the light in which illusions end. <u>Every</u> miracle is but the end of an illusion. Such was the journey [an illusion]; such its ending [a miracle?]. And in the goal of truth which you <u>accepted</u> must <u>all</u> illusions end.

Despite our lack of confidence in the presence within us to surmount the barrier of our attachment to the body, Heaven looks down on us and sees that our journey is, for all intents and purposes, over. It is so quietly certain of this that "there is a hush in Heaven, a happy expectancy, a little pause of gladness in acknowledgment of the journey's end." For while we are staring in despair at the wall, Heaven sees that the sun has risen over it. We no longer sit in shadow. The light has come.

This reminds me of a great scene in the movie *The Aviator*, about Howard Hughes. There is a U.S. senator who is ruining the reputation of Hughes, who has a controlling interest in TWA. This senator is also pushing through a bill that will make the rival airline—Pan Am—the only airlines that can fly internationally. Hughes, who seems utterly defeated, as well as lost in paranoid delusions, manages to rouse himself, comes to the hearings that this senator is holding, and turns the tables on him. Before the nation, he reveals the senator to be the puppet of Juan Trippe, the head of rival Pan Am. And then Hughes gets up and walks out. At that point, Juan Trippe, who has been watching the proceedings on TV, tells someone to switch it off. The man says, "But the hearings aren't over." Trippe responds, "The hearings *are* over. The airline bill will be defeated in the Senate. TWA will begin flights from New York to Paris...then on to Moscow, to Japan, to Hawaii, to Los Angeles...to New York."

Even though the hearings would go on, and would be followed some time later by a vote in the Senate, Trippe knew that, in that moment, the whole thing was over. And that is exactly how Heaven looks at our journey the instant that we join with our brother and allow the Holy Spirit into the relationship. It may appear as if the story still goes on, but in fact, it is over.

> 7. The little insane wish to get rid of Him Whom you invited <u>in</u> and push Him <u>out</u> *must* produce conflict. As you look upon the world, this little wish, uprooted and floating aimlessly, can land and settle briefly upon <u>anything</u>, for it <u>has</u> no purpose now. <u>Before</u> the Holy Spirit entered to abide with you it <u>seemed</u> to have a <u>mighty</u> purpose; the fixed and unchangeable dedication to sin and its results. Now it is aimless, wandering pointlessly, causing no more than tiny interruptions in love's appeal.
> 8. This feather of a wish, this tiny illusion, this microscopic remnant of the belief in sin, is all that remains of what once <u>seemed</u> to be the world. It is no longer an unrelenting barrier to peace. Its pointless wandering makes its results <u>appear</u> to be more erratic and unpredictable than before. Yet what <u>could</u> be more unstable than a tightly organized delusional system? Its <u>seeming</u> stability is its pervasive <u>weakness,</u> which extends to <u>everything</u>. The <u>variability</u> the little remnant induces merely indicates its <u>limited</u> results.
> 9. How mighty can a little feather be before the great wings of truth? Can it oppose an eagle's flight, or hinder the advance of summer? Can it interfere with the <u>effects</u> of summer's sun upon a garden covered by the snow? See but how easily this little wisp is lifted up and carried away, never to return, and part with it in gladness, not regret. For it is

nothing in itself, and stood for nothing when you had greater faith in its protection. Would you not rather greet the summer sun than fix your gaze upon a disappearing snowflake, and shiver in remembrance of the winter's cold?

Your dedication to sin is the essence of a whole host of things: your desire to get rid of the peace that entered, your attachment to the body, and your perception of sin in others—your judgment of them. This dedication to sin used to be the bedrock of your life, the ground on which you stood. But when the Holy Spirit entered, He uprooted this belief (III.8:5). Now it is no longer your foundation, and it is no longer the solid rock that it used to be. It is merely a tiny feather, floating around erratically and settling randomly on various things—which means your condemnation landing on various things.

Because it is so erratic and unpredictable, it seems even worse than before. You find yourself condemning people and things in ways that seem so bizarre and ungoverned that you feel as if you are crazier than before. Jesus is trying to correct this mistaken impression. He is saying, "Look, this belief in sin used to be your whole foundation and used to be a net you threw over everything. Now, its erratic nature shows that it is no longer rooted; it has been uprooted. And the fact that it jumps from thing to thing shows that it no longer covers everything—its results are limited."

Jesus had made virtually the same point to Helen during the dictation of chapter 4:

> The reason for the fear reaction is quite apparent. You have not yet been able to *suspend* judgment, and have merely succeeded in weakening your *control* over it. Since you have an unfortunate tendency to be self-punishing, you believe that control of judgment is a *self-preserving* function, and therefore require it as a *necessary* defense of your self. Weakening this defense delivery is thus perceived as dangerous vulnerability, which frightens you. (*Absence from Felicity*, p. 288)

Helen, in other words, had managed to partially let go of judgment (condemnation), but this took the form of simply weakening her control over it. Now it was waving around uncontrollably, randomly slapping people in the face, so to speak. It was as if she had acquired mental

Tourette's syndrome. Yet Jesus is saying that this is actually a sign of progress, for it means that she has weakened her hold on judgment, a step toward letting it go altogether.

Application: Think about your drive to see sin out in the world, to judge and condemn others, to look for their faults and mistakes. Realize that this drive is the same impulse as your wish to get rid of the Holy Spirit, to get rid of the peace He would bring you. And that this impulse is the same one as all your resistance to God, to the spiritual path, to the Course, to forgiveness.

Now imagine that this drive, this resistance, has become nothing more than a tiny feather, now that the Holy Spirit has come into your life.

> "As you look upon the world, this little wish, uprooted and floating aimlessly,
> Can land and settle briefly on anything, for it has no purpose now."

See it landing on this person or that, accusing them of sin, judging their mistakes.

> "Before the Holy Spirit entered to abide with you, it seemed to have a mighty purpose;
> the fixed and unchangeable dedication to sin.
> Now it is aimless, wandering pointlessly,
> Causing no more than tiny interruptions in love's appeal."

Continue to see this feather float around, landing on this thing and condemning it, and now landing on that.

Now picture the feather floating in mid-air, right in the path of an eagle's flight.

> "How mighty can a little feather be before the great wings of truth?
> Can it oppose an eagle's flight?"

See the wings of the eagle fly right through the space in which the feather floated, without any hindrance whatsoever.

And realize that in just this way the truth is coming into your life and cannot be stopped by the feather of your resistance.

Now picture a garden covered by winter snow.

See your little feather of resistance resting on top of one of the mounds of snow.

> "Can it interfere with the effects of summer's sun upon a garden covered by snow?"

See the sun shine upon the garden. See its inevitable effect upon the snow.

Can your feather stop the shining of the sun of truth upon your mind and the inevitable melting of your icy condition?

Now picture a light breeze blowing through your garden.

> "See but how easily this little wisp is lifted up and carried away, never to return,
> and part with it in gladness, not regret."

Now reflect on your tendency to think that your resistance to God, your desire to look for sin in others, will carry the day,
That it will always shut out God and your happiness and freedom,
That you will never make it to God.
Now look back at your garden, where the snow has nearly melted.
There is just one snowflake left.
And realize that, by seeing things from the despairing standpoint of your resistance,
you are living in the past, in a winter that was replaced by spring and now by summer.
And hear Jesus ask you this question:

> "Would you not rather greet the summer sun than fix your gaze upon a disappearing snowflake, and shiver in remembrance of the winter's cold?"

i. The Attraction of Guilt

Because the "big picture" of this section is so important, let's review what we have seen thus far. It begins with two people whose relationship is dedicated to sin. But they experience a holy instant of joining. In this instant, the Holy Spirit enters their relationship and uproots their belief in sin. It is no longer the operative foundation of their relationship. There in its place, He lays His peace. That peace is now the relationship's unconscious foundation, and this peace seeks to rise up to the surface, where it will first wrap the two partners in its tranquility, and then extend beyond them to embrace the entire Sonship.

However, a remnant of their dedication to sin still remains. And this remnant desperately puts up obstacles to the rising up of this peace. The first obstacle is the simple desire to get rid of the peace, to uproot *it*. For this peace threatens the status quo, which is largely focused on the two people catering to their bodies, that most sacred "wall of dust."

One form that this remnant of the belief in sin takes is looking for sin in the world, which the two partners still do. They may even find that the habit of looking for something to condemn has become even more wild and unpredictable than before. This leads them to wonder if their ego is even more in control than it was. Jesus, however, clarifies that this is how rootless things behave—erratically. The erratic nature of their judgments, therefore, is evidence that their belief in sin really *has* been uprooted. Its days are numbered.

However, this does not mean that the habit of looking for sin in the world should not be attended to and reined in. The rest of the discussion of the first obstacle, a sub-subsection entitled "The Attraction of Guilt," lays before us a choice: Will we look for evidence of a sinful world or for evidence of kind world?

> 10. The attraction of guilt produces fear of love, for love would <u>never</u> look on guilt at all. It is the <u>nature</u> of love to look upon <u>only</u> the truth, for there it sees itself, with which it would unite in holy union and completion. As love must look past fear, so must fear see love not. For love contains the <u>end</u> of guilt, as surely as fear <u>depends</u> on it. Love is attracted <u>only</u> to love. Overlooking guilt completely, <u>it sees no fear</u>. Being wholly without attack, it <u>could</u> not be afraid. Fear is attracted to what love sees <u>not</u>, and each believes that what the other looks upon does not exist. Fear looks on guilt with just the same devotion that love looks on itself. And each has messengers which it sends forth, and which return to it with messages written in the language in which their going forth was asked.

This paragraph introduces the main theme of the rest of this subsection: the messengers of perception. We normally assume perception works like a window, where information about the outside world simply streams in, unfiltered, through the window. Yet in fact, perception works more like a blatantly biased newspaper, which sends out messengers into the world to seek only for news which supports the paper's agenda.

These messengers are not just our senses, but the way in which we use those senses. They are patterns of attention, patterns of seeking for certain kinds of information. For our senses do not attend to everything equally. They seek for what we consider important and attend to that. This paragraph speaks of two systems of messengers.

One system is that of fear. The emotion of fear is fed by guilt—if you see guilty people out in the world, you will feel afraid of what they might do to you. So fear is attracted to seeing guilt. It sends its messengers out to return with word of guilt and evil out there.

The other system is that of love. Love is attracted to seeing love. So it sends its messengers out to bring back reports about love. It completely overlooks guilt. For this reason, fear is afraid of it.

> 11. Love's messengers are gently sent, and return with messages of love and gentleness. The messengers of fear are harshly ordered to seek out guilt, and cherish every scrap of evil and of sin that they can find, losing none of them on pain of death, and laying them respectfully before their lord and master. Perception cannot obey two masters, each asking for messages of different things in different languages. What fear would feed upon, love overlooks. What fear demands, love cannot even see. The fierce attraction that guilt holds for fear is wholly absent from love's gentle perception. What love would look upon is meaningless to fear, and quite invisible.
>
> 12. Relationships in this world are the result of how the world is seen. And this depends on which emotion was called on to send its messengers to look upon it, and return with word of what they saw. Fear's messengers are trained through terror, and they tremble when their master calls on them to serve him. For fear is merciless even to its friends. Its messengers steal guiltily away in hungry search of guilt, for they are kept cold and starving and made very vicious by their master, who allows them to feast only upon what they return to him. No little shred of guilt escapes their hungry eyes. And in their savage search for sin they pounce on any living thing they see, and carry it screaming to

121

their master, to be devoured.

13. Send not these savage messengers into the world, to feast upon it and to prey upon reality. For they will bring you word of bones and skin and flesh. They have been taught to seek for the corruptible, and to return with gorges filled with things decayed and rotted. To them such things are beautiful, because they seem to allay their savage pangs of hunger. For they are frantic with the pain of fear, and would avert the punishment of him who sends them forth by offering him what <u>they</u> hold dear.

Because these three paragraphs are a single discussion, I'm going to deal with them all together. This discussion is drawing on a conventional image, that of the upper-class gentleman with his hunting dogs. Jesus, however, has severely twisted this image.

The master in this case is a bit of a faceless monster, who is merciless even to his friends. He is incredibly cruel to his dogs. He trains them through terror. He keeps them cold and starving. He harshly orders them on their hunts. He will kill them if they lose even a scrap of game upon returning. He lets them eat only what they bring to him. This has turned the dogs into vicious, merciless creatures who, unlike real hunting dogs, hunt totally indiscriminately, pouncing on anything, living or dead. They find rotting flesh beautiful because they see in it relief from hunger and from their master's punishment. They therefore bring it eagerly to him, in the simple-minded thought that if they give him what they love he won't punish them. As twisted as this is, it does remind one of the sick relationship dogs can get into with cruel masters, where they relate to their masters with a mixture of fear and eager submissiveness, and then turn around and face the world with snarling viciousness.

But what does the image mean? The master is fear (which is virtually synonymous with the ego). The hunting dogs are our patterns of perception. They are the way in which our senses selectively seek for certain things—*hunt* for certain things. What these dogs hunt for are guilt and flesh. This is what they bring back to be devoured by fear. This is what *feeds* our fear.

To put this more literally, as we look at our world, our eyes are directed by the fear within us, by our dark master, the ego. Under its direction, our eyes are like obedient dogs, hunting for evidence of sin. They find this in bodies. Why bodies? As we saw in "The Unreality of Sin" (19.

III.7:3), bodies are constant "proof" that sin has overpowered the unity of Heaven. Our eyes don't just hunt for bodies, though. They primarily hunt for bodies *sinning*, bodies *misbehaving*. Let's admit that Jesus has us on this one. We are well trained in looking for evidence of sin in others. Once we find this, our eyes bring this evidence back to our mind, where it feeds our fear, where it makes us afraid. After all, this evidence shows us a world ruled by the awful power of sin. What else would such a world do but scare us?

Our patterns of perceptual seeking, like the dogs, are driven by our own fear of our lord and master, the ego. We are afraid of all the labels the ego will slap on us if we look for only the good. We are afraid that it will call us a bliss ninny, an unrealistic dreamer, a doormat, an empty-headed fool. Like the dogs, we are afraid of the punishment that the ego will visit on us if we don't use our eyes to rip the world to shreds.

Application: Now let's apply this powerful image. See, in your mind's eye, someone you dislike or have resentments toward enter the room. See this person begin to talk, to behave. Notice how you are actively looking for the faults in this person's speech, behavior, and character. You are looking for evidence of sin. Your eyes are on the hunt.

Visualize your act of looking for sin as your sending forth hungry hunting dogs from your mind, maybe even from your eyes. You control their behavior, and under your control they leap out to attack anything sinful they see in this person and drag it back to your mind. Maybe they pounce on this person's lying tongue, and rip it out. Maybe they tear out this person's hateful eyes. Maybe they pounce on this person's whole sinful body. Just watch for a bit and see what they do.

Then watch them carry their prey—whatever it is—back to your mind. There, they lay it before a dark, hooded figure—their master. He picks up the meat they have brought him and starts eating. And as he does, he grows in size and power. Now realize that he is fear. He is *your* fear. *You* are not being fed by this act of looking for sin in others; your *fear* is being fed. Try to feel this within yourself. Feel how your fear level rises as you observe the sin in the other person and expect it to attack you or in some way negatively impact you. With sin in front of you, you feel unsafe.

Realize also that what the dogs bring back is not this person as he or she really is. It is an unfair caricature, made for the specific purpose of feeding your fear. It is not reality at all. It is a figment of your imagination.

Now the master kicks the dogs and sends them off again, to look for more sin. The dogs, as we said, are your process of visual hunting, and now you realize that your hunting for sin is not the act of a free person. Your natural impulse is to love, but instead you look for something to hate because you are obeying a foreign presence in you. You are yielding to the coercion of the dark master. You fear that if you see this other person more charitably, in a kinder, more loving light, you will experience a torrent of backlash thoughts. You will accuse yourself of ulterior motives. You will tell yourself that you are a naïve fool. You will tell yourself that you are stupidly leaving yourself open to attack. These thoughts are designed to short-circuit your lofty aspirations and drag you back down to your normal unloving state. But they are not your thoughts. They are the thoughts of the dark master, whispered into your mind. They are designed to punish you into submission, so that you hunt only for him, and see the world only as he would have you see it.

But there is another way of looking at the world.

14. The Holy Spirit has given you love's messengers to send <u>instead</u> of those <u>you</u> trained through fear. <u>They</u> are as eager to return to you what they hold dear as are the others. If you send <u>them</u> forth, they will see only the blameless and the beautiful, the gentle and the kind. They will be as careful to let no little act of charity, no tiny expression of forgiveness, no little breath of love escape their notice. And they will return with all the happy things they found, to share them lovingly with you. Be not <u>afraid</u> of them. They offer you salvation. Theirs are the messages of <u>safety</u>, for <u>they</u> see the world as kind.

15. If you send forth <u>only</u> the messengers the Holy Spirit gives you, <u>wanting</u> no messages but theirs, you will see fear no more. The world will be transformed before your sight, cleansed of all guilt and softly brushed with beauty. The world contains no fear that <u>you</u> laid not upon it. And none you cannot ask love's messengers to <u>remove</u> from it, and see it still. The Holy Spirit has given you <u>His</u> messengers to send to your brother and return to you with what love sees. They have been given to <u>replace</u> the hungry dogs of fear you sent instead. And they go forth to signify the <u>end</u> of fear.

Here we have the other way of seeing, in which we send love's messengers. They are not given a concrete image, like the "dogs of fear." But they are called the Holy Spirit's messengers, and the traditional image for that, of course, is angels.

The contrast with the other way of seeing couldn't be more total. Rather than the whole process being guided by the fear in us, it is guided by the love in us. Rather than sending out vicious hunting dogs, we send out heavenly angels. These messengers are just "as eager to return to you what they hold dear as are the others." Yet whereas the others were eager to find sinning bodies, these ones are eager to find the opposite: expressions of charity, forgiveness, and love. They are so eager to find these that they bring back even *little* acts of charity, even *tiny* expressions of forgiveness, even *little* breaths of love. Based on the news they bring us, the world we see is kind, rather than sinful. Seeing a kind world instinctively inspires love in us, and that is the point. This whole process is designed to bring back news of a kind world that would reinforce the love in us, just as the other process brought back news of a scary world that fed the fear in us.

Can you see just how different this way is than the other way? What would your life be like if you saw the world in this way, if your eyes were like angels that spent all their time gathering evidence of a kind world?

> 16. Love, too, would set a feast before you, on a table covered with a spotless cloth, set in a quiet garden where no sound but singing and a softly joyous whispering is ever heard. This is a feast that honors your holy relationship, and at which everyone is welcomed as an honored guest. And in a holy instant grace is said by everyone together, as they join in gentleness before the table of communion. And I will join you there, as long ago I promised and promise still. For in your new relationship am I made welcome. And where I am made welcome, there I <u>am</u>.

This achingly beautiful paragraph—one of my favorites in the Course—depicts the result of sending out the messengers of love. I asked before what life would be like if we did only that. Here is the answer. This is what life would be like. For just as the dogs of fear laid before us a feast of fear, composed of rotting, sinning flesh, so the angels of love lay before us a feast of love, composed of all the news they brought us of a world filled with kindness.

With this paragraph, then, Jesus is saying, "This is what your life can be like. It can be like a joyous feast in a sacred garden. It can be an ongoing feast to celebrate your holy relationship, a feast where no one is excluded, and where each person is an honored guest. At this feast, all of you together will repeatedly join in a holy instant, a moment of grace, where together you experience true communion. And I will attend this feast as well, for I promised you long ago that wherever two people join in a holy purpose, there I am."

Try to imagine your life being like this feast of love. Isn't this what all of us want? All it takes is to be willing to get our news only from the angels of love, not the dogs of fear.

> 17. I am made welcome in the state of grace [the holy instant], which means you have at last forgiven me. For I became the symbol of your sin, and so I had to die instead of you. To the ego sin means death, and so atonement is achieved through murder. Salvation is looked upon as a way by which the Son of God was killed instead of you. Yet would I offer you my body, you whom I love, *knowing* its littleness? Or would I teach that bodies cannot keep us apart? Mine was of no greater value than yours; no better means for communication of salvation, but not its Source. No one can die for anyone, and death does not atone for sin. But you can live to show it is not real. The body does appear to be the symbol of sin while you believe that it can get you what you want. While you believe that it can give you pleasure, you will also believe that it can bring you pain. To think you could be satisfied and happy with so little is to hurt yourself, [Ur: yourself. And] and to limit the happiness that you would have calls upon pain to fill your meager store and make your life complete. This is completion as the ego sees it. For guilt creeps in where happiness has been removed, and substitutes for it. Communion [communion of the mind] is another kind of completion, which goes beyond guilt, because it goes beyond the body.

The previous paragraph was an alternative image of communion. This is obvious when you notice that people are joining in prayerful silence before "the table of communion." Now, in this new paragraph, Jesus criticizes traditional communion, from top to bottom.

The first problem is that communion is a celebration of Jesus dying for our sins. This notion, he implies, depicts him as our scapegoat, who had to be murdered so that we ourselves could get off the hook. And do you ever really love the scapegoat? Further, in the ritual of communion, we take his sacrifice into ourselves by symbolically eating and drinking his body and blood. (This sounds a lot like the dogs of fear devouring bodies that are symbols of sin, doesn't it?) Jesus points out that communion implies that his body was some kind of uniquely valuable repository of salvation, which it wasn't. His body wasn't any more valuable than ours!

Finally, seeing salvation as coming from consuming Jesus' body supports the whole notion that salvation is *of the body*. And when we seek salvation through the body, all we get are crumbs. We voluntarily limit our happiness, and then experience the guilt of self-betrayal. Real communion isn't about the body and doesn't bring guilt. "It goes beyond the body" and joins with other minds in that beautiful garden of love.

In summary, this section is all about a single choice: Will we let the tiny remnant of the belief in sin guide our eyes, so that we see a sinful, fearful world? Or will we let love guide our eyes, so that we see a kind world, one that inspires even more love in us? The first will make our lives into a feast of fear, in which we feed on dead bodies soaked with sin. The second will make our lives into a feast of love, in which we join with our brothers in holy instants in our little garden. The first approach is reflected in traditional communion, while the second is *true* communion, the holy joining of minds.

Application: Now visualize the same person you used with the dogs exercise, or perhaps someone else you have had difficulty with recently. Think over this person's behavior in your life. But this time picture the presence of love directing your eyes, guiding your attention in what to focus on. Visualize this as angels flying from your mind, or even from your eyes. Rather than looking for evidence of sin, they are looking for evidence of underlying holiness, no matter how tiny the clues may be. "They will see only the blameless and the beautiful, the gentle and the kind. They will be as careful to let no little act of charity, no tiny expression of forgiveness, no little breath of love escape their notice."

See them searching single-mindedly to find only the love. Now see them flying back to you and whispering in your ear what they found in this person. Perhaps they saw things you had never noticed. Perhaps they saw a caring for you, a commitment to you, a fondness of you that had been overlooked by the dogs you sent out before. Perhaps they saw little moments of conscientiousness or loving concern. Perhaps they noticed small favors or major acts of devotion that seemed insignificant to you before. Realize that all of these things are concrete evidence that beneath this person's misbehaving exterior lies a holy being, a true Son of God. Notice that now you don't feel so afraid in this person's presence anymore. Rather, you feel safe.

Now send these holy messengers out to search the entire world for loving thoughts and words and deeds and qualities. They search the lives of friends and loved ones, the lives of strangers, the lives of distant cities and villages. Picture them flying back with what they found: mounds and mounds of nothing but love and holiness, people lifting their minds toward God and making contact, people forgiving things you didn't know that anyone could forgive, acts of true nobility and selflessness that will never make it to the evening news. The messengers fly into a quiet, sacred garden to deposit their treasure. They lay it on a long table covered with a spotless cloth, and there it takes the form of the most incredible feast you have ever seen.

Just looking at this feast makes you feel full in your heart. You realize you live in a kind world, where you are safe. You realize this world deserves nothing but your heartfelt love. You can't understand why you felt so afraid before, why the world looked so dangerous and sinful. Now you literally live in a different world. Now your heart is overflowing with love.

You see people streaming into this garden to join you, to celebrate with you your newfound love. You see your closest friends as well as people who, in your old mode, you would have considered strangers. All of them are here to celebrate and partake in your new vision of the world. You feel privileged by the presence of each one; you consider each one your honored guest. Once everyone has gathered around the table, a silence falls, and all of you join together at this altar in a moment of grace, a holy instant in which everyone's mind unites as one.

You open your eyes and a hush falls over the crowd, as Jesus walks into the garden, smiling. With his arrival, the entire event has been transported into a whole new level of significance. You realize that he too is here to celebrate your new vision of the world. Long ago he promised he would attend this feast and he has been waiting literally for centuries to make good on that promise. He takes his seat beside you and smiles knowingly into your eyes. The feast begins and everyone starts partaking in the joyous news of a different world brought back by love's messengers. In that instant, you could not feel more complete. Everything is perfect. You feel a beautiful sense of communion with everyone there, and you think, "So this is the real world."

B. The Second Obstacle: The Belief the Body Is Valuable for What It Offers

Let's review once again. When Helen and Bill joined in a holy relationship, the Holy Spirit entered their relationship, uprooting the dedication to sin that had been its foundation, and replacing that with peace. Now this peace seeks to rise up and out, first surrounding the two of them, and then embracing the entire Sonship. It is essential to realize that the peace is trying to get *out*, not trying to get *in*.

However, a tiny remnant of that dedication to sin is still there, and it erects obstacles to the peace that wants to flow from its home deep in their relationship. The first obstacle it erects is the desire to get rid of the peace. We want to conduct a kind of exorcism, not of the demonic but of the holy. The simple reason is that the tiny remnant of sin wants its old home back. One way in which this manifests is our habit of looking for sin out in the world. Our mind sends out the hungry dogs of fear to hunt for the slightest evidence of sin in others, which is then brought back to feed our fear.

Now we come to the second obstacle, which has already been mentioned in Jesus' discussion of the first.

> 1. We said that peace must first surmount the obstacle of your desire to get rid of it. Where the attraction of guilt holds sway, peace is <u>not wanted</u>. The second obstacle that peace must flow across, and closely related to the first, is the belief that the body is valuable <u>for what it offers</u>. For here is the attraction of guilt <u>made manifest</u> in the body, and <u>seen</u> in it.

This brief paragraph lays out a structure for understanding the relationship of the first two obstacles. We want to get rid of the peace that entered because it threatens the former status quo: our "dedication to sin and its results" (A.7:3). Since guilt is one of sin's results, wanting those results means wanting *guilt*, being *attracted* to guilt. Our attraction to guilt, then, is another way of talking about what makes us want to throw away the peace that entered.

However, that is not how it seems. It seems as if we want to throw the peace out because it asks us to sacrifice all the wonderful things that the body has to offer. And this is true—we do value what the body offers, and we do see God's peace as a threat to that. What we don't realize, though, is that our attraction to the body's offerings is really the attraction of guilt in disguise. We think we want the pleasure the body gives, but we really want the *guilt* that comes with the pleasure. The guilt, you could say, is the "pleasure" within the pleasure.

So the first obstacle arises as a consequence of the second, and *both* arise as a consequence of the attraction of guilt. It is the real story behind both.

> 2. <u>This</u> is the value that you think peace would <u>rob</u> you of. This is what you believe that it would dispossess, and leave <u>you</u> homeless. And it is this for which <u>you</u> would deny a home to peace. This "sacrifice" you feel to be too great to make, too much to ask of you. Is it a <u>sacrifice</u>, or a <u>release</u>? What has the body <u>really</u> given you that justifies your strange belief that in it lies salvation? Do you not see that this is the belief in <u>death</u>? Here is the focus of the perception of Atonement as murder [see (A).17:3]. Here is the <u>source</u> of the idea that love is fear.

This paragraph makes it absolutely clear that we want to throw away the peace because it threatens our love affair with the body. This is especially clear when you realize this paragraph answers three questions posed in the discussion of the first obstacle:

Questions from first obstacle	Answers in second obstacle
"What seems to be the cost you are so unwilling to pay?" (A.2:3)	"This is the value that you think peace would rob you of [the cost it would make you pay]."
"What do you think that it must dispossess to dwell with you?" (A.2:2)	"This is what you believe that it would dispossess, and leave you homeless." *Table continued*

Questions from first obstacle	Answers in second obstacle
"Why would you want peace homeless?" (A.2:1)	"And it is this for which you would deny a home to peace."

Each question asks, "Why do you want the first obstacle (to get rid of peace)?" And each answer states, "For the sake of the second obstacle (the body's valuable offerings)." This, of course, is the exact same answer we were given after those questions were asked the first time. There, the answer was our attachment to the barrier of sand, the wall of dust, that separates us from our brother—the body.

However, the real meaning of "this" in those answers ("*This* is the value that you think peace would rob you of") is what paragraph 1 refers to: "the attraction of guilt *made manifest* in the body." In other words, we want to get rid of peace because we are attracted to what our body offers, but the real offering we seek is guilt.

If we understand that, the rest of the paragraph makes perfect sense. Would giving up the "payoff" of guilt be a sacrifice or a release? Has our experience been that the body's gifts really save us, or just saddle us with more guilt? The more we think the body's pleasures save us, the more guilty we feel, and then the only way to be made clean, to be saved, is to accept our punishment, which ultimately amounts to getting the death sentence.

Application: Think for a minute about giving the Holy Spirit free rein to come into your life and do whatever He wants, all for the sake of getting you to Heaven as fast as possible.

Then ask yourself, "What bodily comforts, pleasures, safeties, freedoms, routines, habits am I afraid of having to give up?"

Realize that your answers to this question are the second obstacle to peace.

Then realize that your real attraction to those things is the payoff of guilt. Unbeknownst to you, guilt is the "pleasure" within those pleasures. Does this make those things look any different?

3. The Holy Spirit's messengers are sent far beyond the body, calling the mind to join in holy communion and be at peace. Such is the

message that I gave them for you [Ur: them, for *you*]. It is only the messengers of <u>fear</u> that see the body, for they look for what can suffer. Is it a sacrifice to be <u>removed</u> from what can suffer? The Holy Spirit does not <u>demand</u> you sacrifice the hope of the body's pleasure; it *has* no hope of pleasure. But neither can it bring you fear of pain. Pain is the <u>only</u> "sacrifice" the Holy Spirit asks, and this He *would* remove.

The messengers of fear (those dogs again) only bring back news of bodies, for they look only for what can suffer. The Holy Spirit's messengers, however, overlook the body. They want to lift our mind above what can suffer, above the body. Is this so horrible? We keep thinking the body can make us incredibly happy, but in the end, our love affair with it makes us feel shallow, base, and self-absorbed—*guilty*. The Holy Spirit wants to save us from this. The only "sacrifice" He asks is the pain of this. Those pleasures we're so afraid to give up are always empty promises. They never deliver what we hope for.

4. Peace is extended from you only to the eternal, and it reaches out <u>from</u> the eternal in <u>you</u>. It flows across all else. The second obstacle is no more solid than the first. For you want neither to get rid of peace [first obstacle] nor <u>limit</u> it [behind the wall of the body—the second obstacle]. What are these obstacles that you would interpose between peace and its going forth but barriers you place between your will and its accomplishment? You <u>want</u> communion, <u>not</u> the feast of fear. You <u>want</u> salvation, <u>not</u> the pain of guilt. <u>And you want your Father, not</u> a little mound of clay [the body], to be your home.

When the Spirit enters our lives, after the initial inspiration has worn off, we usually get morbidly focused on what we have to give up, which has a lot to do with the body. In the process, we tend to lose sight of all the priceless treasures that await us.

This is what has happened to Helen and Bill. Peace has set up a home deep within them. Now it wants to rise up and enfold them in pure bliss. But all they can think of is how they want to get rid of it, how it threatens their bodily status quo. It's as if Jesus came knocking at the front door, and we said, "Can you come back later? Wrestling is on TV and I've still got half of my Big Mac to finish."

What we forget is that his arrival at the door is what we want; this is our will. We want that beautiful communion in the sacred garden, not the feast of fear that those vicious dogs drag in. We want God to be our home, not this malfunctioning mound of clay. As a gift to ourselves, we need to turn off the TV, chuck the Big Mac, and *run* to answer the door.

> In your holy relationship is your Father's Son. He [the Son] has <u>not</u> lost communion with Him [the Father], <u>nor with himself</u>. When you agreed to join your brother, you acknowledged this is so. This has <u>no</u> cost, but it <u>has</u> release from cost.
> 5. You have paid very dearly for your illusions, and <u>nothing</u> you have paid for brought you peace. Are you not <u>glad</u> that Heaven cannot <u>be</u> sacrificed, and sacrifice cannot <u>be</u> asked of you?

In your holy relationship lies your true Self. This is the Son of God, who abides in perfect communion with His Father. Establishing a holy relationship was an acknowledgment of this, an acknowledgment that costs you absolutely nothing. Instead, it releases you from cost. And who doesn't need that? We have all paid dearly for our illusions, more than we could afford, and as soon as we got them home they broke. We're so afraid that the holy relationship is going to cost us, yet its whole purpose is to release us from all cost. What a priceless gift that would be!

> There <u>is</u> no obstacle that you can place before our union, for in your holy relationship I am there <u>already</u>. We will surmount all obstacles <u>together</u>, for we stand <u>within</u> the gates and not outside. How easily the gates are opened from within, to let peace through to bless the tired world! Can it be difficult for us to walk past barriers together, when you have <u>joined</u> the limitless? The end of guilt is in your hands to give. Would you stop now to <u>look</u> for guilt in your brother [Ur: each other]?

There are two opposite images of the spiritual journey. In one, we are on the outside of God's peace, and that peace is surrounded by walls and gates. Standing on the outside, we knock on the gates, but no one's answering, and we aren't strong enough to force the gates open. Have you ever felt that way?

In the other image, we are actually on the inside of the walls, already there with God's peace. And Jesus is there with us. Our job now is to let peace out through the gates, to bless the tired world. Gates, of course, are designed to be opened from the inside, and Jesus is there to help us. How hard, then, can it be to open these gates? Nothing is stopping us. We could open the gates right now and let the peace of guiltlessness flow out to our brother. Why on earth, then, would we decide instead to condemn him and make him feel even guiltier than before?

> 6. Let me be to you the symbol of the <u>end</u> of guilt, and look upon your brother as you would look on me. Forgive me all the sins you think the Son of God committed. And in the light of your forgiveness he will remember who he is, and forget what never was. I ask for your forgiveness, for if <u>you</u> are guilty, so must I be. But if I surmounted guilt and overcame the world, you were <u>with</u> me. Would you see in me the symbol of guilt or of the <u>end</u> of guilt, remembering that what I signify to you you see within <u>yourself</u>?

This somewhat confusing paragraph contains two totally different ways of seeing Jesus. First, you can see him as the symbol of everyone's sins, which of course is how history has seen him, since all of our sins killed him. Seeing him this way, however, just reinforces the sin you see in your brother, which then reinforces your own sense of sinfulness.

Alternately, you can see him as a symbol of the end of guilt, a symbol of everyone's sinlessness, including your own. And then you forgive him for the sins everyone *else* committed. It sounds kind of strange, but it actually works.

Application: Think of someone you've had trouble forgiving. Now say to Jesus:

> *I forgive you for all the sins I think [name] committed.*
> *For you represent Who [name] really is.*
> *When I hold something against him/her, I hold it against you.*
> *And when I hold it against you, I hold it against myself.*

> 7. From your holy relationship truth proclaims the truth, and love looks on itself. Salvation flows from deep within the home you offered to my Father and to me. And we are there together, in the quiet communion in which the Father and the Son are joined. O come ye faithful to the holy union of the Father and the Son in <u>you</u>! And keep <u>you</u> not apart from what is offered you in gratitude for giving peace its home in Heaven. Send forth to all the world the joyous message of the end of guilt, and

all the world will answer. Think of your happiness as everyone offers you witness of the end of sin, and shows you that its power is gone forever. Where can guilt be, when the belief in sin is gone [guilt comes from sin]? And where is death, when its great advocate [guilt] is heard no more?

When Helen and Bill joined, the Christmas event occurred deep inside their relationship. There, Jesus was born, in quiet communion with the Father, his union with God representing the Sonship's union with God. In this context, "O come, all ye faithful" does not mean come to Bethlehem to adore the baby Jesus. It means come to that holy place within you, to adore "the holy union of the Father and Son in you."

Then, having witnessed this blessed Christmas within our relationship, we need to "go tell it on the mountain"—tell everyone the news that the end of guilt has arrived. This means giving to them the guiltlessness we have found within. It means forgiving them. This will turn everyone into witnesses that testify to us that guilt is over, that the power of sin has gone from the world. Think how joyous this would be. That power that seemed to take God's limitless creation and box it up in little packages of meat, that power that stood astride the world like an evil colossus, that power is no more. And with its passing, guilt and death have vanished from the face of the earth. Could anything be more joyous?

> 8. Forgive me your illusions, and release me from punishment for what I have not done. So will you learn the freedom that I taught by teaching freedom to your brother, and so releasing me. I am within your holy relationship, yet you would imprison me behind the obstacles you raise to freedom, and bar my way to you. Yet it is not possible to keep away One Who is there already. And in Him it is possible that our communion, where we are joined already, will be the focus of the new perception that will bring light to all the world, contained in you.

Jesus keeps asking us to forgive him, which raises the question: Why do we resent him? I think the most conscious reason is that he has become a symbol of guilt, a symbol of condemnation on the human race. We see him as a judgmental presence that would come in and take all our fun away. This is why the obstacles to peace are also obstacles that bar Jesus' way to us. We see both of them—Jesus and peace—as forces that want to invade our pleasant routines and take our fun away.

His answer is this: "Forgive me for being that figure you made up, that imaginary frowning figure that symbolizes the reality of everyone's sins. When you let that image of me go, you will then be able to forgive everyone. And when you do, you will release me. Right now, I am imprisoned behind the barriers you have raised to hold back peace. They hold me back, too, for I abide in that same place that peace does, deep within you. The Holy Spirit is there, too. Yet think what this means: Because I am already within you, how can you keep me out? Why not acknowledge my presence, along with the Holy Spirit's? For you yourself are there with us, already in communion with us. And if you'll just acknowledge this pre-existent communion, it can be the standpoint from which you look out upon all the world, bringing light to everyone."

Commentary by Greg Mackie

To recap: Two people have joined in a holy relationship (as Helen and Bill did). With this joining, they are no longer committed to the ego's goal of sin; instead, the Holy Spirit has entered and made peace the unconscious foundation of their relationship. This peace is meant to flow upward and outward, to reach the holy relationship partners' conscious awareness and from there extend to all the world.

But a small remnant of that old goal of sin remains, and it puts up obstacles to keep the peace within the relationship safely buried. The first obstacle is the desire to get rid of peace. We want to throw peace out in order to pursue our old goal of sin as before. One way we do this is to send out the "dogs of fear" from our minds to hunt for evidence of sin in others. They find evidence of sin and guilt—to which we are attracted— and bring it back to feed our fear.

The second obstacle is the reason why we want to get rid of peace: the belief the body is valuable for what it offers. On the surface, we're attracted to seeking pleasure (both physical and emotional) through the body; we think the Holy Spirit's peace will force us to sacrifice all our fun. But on a deeper level is the same dynamic that generates the first obstacle: That remnant of our old goal of sin causes us to be attracted to guilt (the result of sin), so we're really attracted to the guilt that results from seeking pleasure through the body. As Robert said, this is the real "pleasure" within the pleasure.

This next sub-subsection takes the process one step further: Just as the result of sin is guilt, the result of guilt is pain—the pain of punishment for our apparent sin. Underneath the search for bodily pleasure, we're really seeking bodily pain, which reinforces our belief in sin and guilt, feeding our fear even more. This is "the attraction of pain."

i. The Attraction of Pain

> 9. Your little part is but to give the Holy Spirit the whole <u>idea</u> of sacrifice. And to <u>accept</u> the peace He gives [Ur: gave] instead, <u>without</u> the limits that would hold its extension back, and so would limit <u>your</u> awareness of it. For what He gives <u>must</u> be extended if <u>you</u> would have its limitless power, and use it for the Son of God's release. It is not <u>this</u> you would be rid of, and having it you <u>cannot</u> limit it. If peace is homeless, so are you and so am I. And He Who <u>is</u> our home is homeless <u>with</u> us. Is this your wish [Ur: will]? Would you forever be a wanderer in search of peace? Would you invest your hope of peace and happiness in what <u>must</u> fail?

Again, we're convinced that the Holy Spirit's peace demands sacrifice. We think living the spiritual life means giving up all those bodily goodies, like sex and chocolate and revenge. If we're Christian, we also believe that Heaven comes at the price of the sacrifice of Jesus' body on the cross (see 19.IV(A)17). But the actual sacrifice (though not ultimately a real sacrifice) is dumping the Holy Spirit's peace for the sake of bodily pleasure. This dooms us to seek peace in a way that must fail. It blocks the extension of peace from our holy relationship, which blocks our own awareness of it. It evicts peace from its home in our minds, and thus renders ourselves, Jesus, and even God Himself, our true Home, homeless in our awareness.

Do we really want to trade the Holy Spirit's peace for a bowl of Häagen-Dazs? If we do not—and we truly do not—we must give up the whole idea of sacrifice and *accept* His peace. In simple terms, this is how we lay down the obstacles to peace, so that the peace within our holy relationship can bless us and save the world.

> 10. Faith in the eternal is <u>always</u> justified, for the eternal is forever kind, infinite in its patience and wholly loving. It will accept you wholly, and give you peace. Yet it can unite only with what <u>already</u> is at peace in you, immortal as itself. The body can bring you neither peace nor turmoil; neither joy nor pain [Ur: not pain nor joy]. It is a means, and <u>not</u> an end. It has <u>no</u> purpose of itself, but only what is <u>given</u> to it [Ur: *given* it to do]. The body will seem to <u>be</u> whatever is the means for reaching the goal that you <u>assign</u> to it. Only the mind can set a purpose, and only the mind can see the means for its accomplishment, and justify its use. Peace and guilt are both conditions of the mind, to be <u>attained</u>. And these conditions are the home of the emotion that calls [Ur: called] them forth, and therefore is <u>compatible</u> with them [Ur: it].

Right now, we place faith in the body to give us peace and happiness, but this faith is totally unjustified because the body will never give us these things. However, faith in the eternal, which abides at the heart of our holy relationship, is *always* justified. It will unite with the eternal in us (not the body) and give us the peace the body never can.

Yet the body in and of itself is not an implacable barrier to peace; the problem is our belief in *the body as an end in itself,* a belief expressed in our search for happiness through the body's pleasure. In truth, the body is a *means* rather than an end, a neutral tool that the mind can give whatever purpose it wants. We can listen to the voice of fear and use the body to seek guilt, which will bring us pain, or we can listen to the voice of love and use the body to seek peace, which will bring us joy. The choice is entirely up to us.

> 11. But think you which it is [fear or love] that is compatible with <u>you</u>. Here is your choice, and it *is* free. But all that <u>lies</u> in it <u>will</u> come with it, and what you think you are can <u>never</u> be <u>apart</u> from it. The body is the great <u>seeming</u> betrayer of faith. In it lies disillusionment and the seeds of faithlessness, but <u>only</u> if you ask [Ur: asked] of it what it <u>cannot give</u>. Can <u>yos]</u> mistake be reasonable grounds for depression and disillusionment, and for retaliative attack on what you think has failed you? Use not your <u>error</u> as the justification for your faithlessness. You have <u>not</u> sinned, but you <u>have</u> been mistaken in what is faithful. And the correction of <u>your</u> mistake will <u>give</u> you grounds for faith.

Which emotion is truly compatible with who we really are: love or fear? If we choose love, we will recognize that we are eternal and seek peace. If we choose fear, we will think we are a body and seek guilt. As we've seen throughout this section, the latter is exactly what we are doing, because of that remnant of the goal of sin.

Of course, we don't *think* we seek guilt. We think we seek peace and happiness through the body's pleasure. Yet what actually happens when we place faith in the body to bring us happiness? We are inevitably disappointed, as the body that seemed to promise so much inevitably fails us. Unconsciously, we believe that this is our punishment for the sin of seeking pleasure through the body. But then we turn around and project our guilt onto the body itself. Now, the *body* is to blame for failing to live up to its promises. This leads us to become disillusioned with the body, and to attack the body with sickness, pain, and death for its seeming betrayal.

Fortunately, none of this is real. The body has done nothing to us; it only carries out our orders. We have not sinned; our faith in the body to make us happy is only a mistake in what deserves our faith. And the correction of this mistake will give us grounds for faith in the eternal.

> 12. It is impossible to seek for pleasure through the body and <u>not</u> find pain. It is essential that this relationship be understood, for it is one the ego sees as proof of sin. It is not <u>really</u> punitive at all. It is but the inevitable result of equating yourself <u>with</u> the body, which is the <u>invitation</u> to pain. For it invites <u>fear</u> to enter and become your <u>purpose</u>. The attraction of guilt must enter with it, and <u>whatever</u> fear directs the body to do <u>is</u> therefore painful. It will share the pain of <u>all</u> illusions, and the illusion of pleasure will <u>be</u> the same as pai

This is the punch line everything has been leading up to: "It is impossible to seek for pleasure through the body and *not* find pain." This is a challenging teaching for those who (like me) still seek pleasure through the body. I don't think this means we have to give up all of our bodily pleasures cold turkey—doing so at our current level of development would probably feel like such a sacrifice that we'd end up giving up the Course—but it does mean that we have to come to recognize how much pain our search for pleasure really delivers: "It is essential that this relationship be understood."

I think the key is to remind ourselves, as this section has, that giving up pleasure-seeking for the Holy Spirit's peace is not a sacrifice, but a release. As we practice this idea and it really sinks in, we'll eventually

reach the point where asking that question Course students often ask—
"Can I still have sex/eat donuts/get a massage/(fill in favorite bodily
pleasure here)?"—will be like a fish who's learned that dangling lines
have hidden hooks asking, "Can I still have that juicy worm?" Yes, but
why on earth would you *want* it?

It isn't difficult to see that the search for happiness through bodily
pleasure ends up in pain. No matter how many pleasures we have, we all
suffer as well, and the inevitable ending is the pain of old age and death.
We all realize that we'll die, but we tell ourselves we might as well have
fun while we can. (In the checkout line at the supermarket last night, I
saw a *Cosmopolitan* magazine headline that read, "101 Sex Tricks to Try
Before You Die.")

The ego uses our inevitable pain as proof of sin—"You're being
punished for the sins of the flesh!"—but here's what is really going on.
Seeking bodily pleasure equates us with the body and invites fear to
become our goal. (If you think you're a vulnerable body, how can you
not be afraid?) Fear needs guilt to feed itself, so as long as fear is our
goal, we'll be attracted to guilt. Guilt inevitably causes us pain, so as
long as we're letting fear direct the body we'll experience pain, even if
we call it "pleasure."

> 13. Is not this inevitable? Under fear's orders the body will pursue
> guilt, serving its master whose attraction to guilt maintains the whole
> illusion of its existence. This, then, is the attraction of pain. Ruled
> by this perception the body becomes the servant of pain, seeking it
> dutifully and obeying the idea that pain is pleasure. It is this idea [pain
> is pleasure] that underlies all of the ego's heavy investment in the body.
> And it is this insane relationship that it keeps hidden, and yet feeds
> upon. To you it teaches that the body's pleasure is happiness. Yet to
> itself it whispers, "It is death."

Here we see the system laid out in all its twisted depravity. As the last
paragraph said, we have made fear our goal. Fear is attracted to guilt,
and because fear is our goal, we are attracted to guilt too. Therefore,
we pursue guilt (both through physical pleasure and through the last
subsection's method of looking for sin in the world). Guilt produces
pain, so our pursuit of guilt is also the pursuit of pain. We are attracted to
pain, just as we are attracted to guilt.

Pain is the ego's idea of a good time—pain is *pleasure* to it, which is why it loves the body so much. But of course, we don't really enjoy pain, so the ego must keep the real basis for its investment in the body hidden from us. It tells us that the body's pleasure is happiness (the second obstacle: the belief the body is valuable for what it offers). But beneath the surface, it knows that the body's pleasure actually delivers pain, including the ultimate pain of death (a foretaste of the third obstacle: the attraction of death).

The attraction of pain is a difficult idea to connect with, because on the surface we all fear pain. Yet even this fear is a twisted form of our attraction of pain: Having committed to the goal of fear, we want to feed our fear, and the fear of pain is a great way to do this. Moreover, the idea that our search for bodily pleasure is really a search for guilt, pain, fear, and death makes more sense when we realize that these things *are* what the body ultimately delivers. Given how inevitable that is, is it really that difficult to believe that something in us has been aiming for this all along?

> 14. Why should the body be <u>anything</u> to you? Certainly what it is <u>made</u> of is not precious. And just as certainly <u>it</u> has no feeling. It transmits <u>to</u> <u>you</u> the feelings that you want. Like any communication medium the body receives and sends the messages that it is given. It has <u>no</u> feeling for them. <u>All</u> of the feeling with which they are invested is given by the sender and the receiver. The ego and the Holy Spirit both recognize this, and both also recognize that here <u>the sender and receiver are the</u> <u>same</u>. The Holy Spirit <u>tells</u> you this with joy. The ego <u>hides</u> it, for it would keep you unaware of it. Who would send messages of hatred and attack if he but understood he sends them to <u>himself</u>? Who would accuse, make guilty and condemn <u>himself</u>?

We who have equated ourselves with the body regard the body as *everything* to us, but it's really nothing. In and of itself, it is just a valueless hunk of meat. (It isn't worth much even on a strictly material level—I saw a website that said the raw materials of a human body are worth about $4.50.) At best, it is simply a communication device, like a telephone, which transmits whatever messages are delivered through it. And just as a telephone doesn't say, "I'd like to share my feelings about that last call," the body feels nothing, but instead simply transmits the feelings of sender and receiver.

There is a twist here, though: *We* are both sender and receiver; we always dial our own number. The Holy Spirit gladly shares this with us, because it enables us to send out messages of love and thus receive them ourselves. The ego, though, hides this from us because it wants to convince us that attacking others is the way we will find happiness and peace. We wouldn't attack if we really realized we were attacking ourselves.

> 15. The ego's messages are <u>always</u> sent <u>away</u> from you, in the belief that for your message of attack and guilt will someone <u>other</u> than yourself suffer. And even if <u>you</u> suffer, yet someone <u>else</u> will suffer more. The great deceiver recognizes that this is not so, but as the "enemy" of peace, it urges you to <u>send out</u> all your messages of hate and free <u>yourself</u>. And to convince you this is possible, it bids the body search for pain in attack upon another, calling it pleasure and <u>offering</u> it to you as freedom *from* attack.

We've seen a couple of ways that we seek pleasure through the body in service of the goal of fear: through purely physical pleasure and through the emotional pleasure of seeking with the body's eyes for evidence of sin and guilt in the world. Here is another way: using the body to attack others by sending them messages of guilt—pointing that accusing finger. This sure seems to feel good, doesn't it? Just as with the first two ways, the ego's bait is to tell us this will bring us happiness. But the hook is the pain we *really* feel from the guilt of attacking another, the pain the ego needs to keep itself alive.

> 16. Hear not its madness, and believe not the impossible is true. Forget not that the ego has <u>dedicated</u> the body to the goal of sin, and places in it <u>all</u> its faith that this can be accomplished. Its sad disciples chant the body's praise continually, in solemn celebration of the ego's rule. Not one but <u>must</u> believe that <u>yielding</u> to the attraction of guilt is the <u>escape</u> from pain. Not one but <u>must</u> regard the body as himself, <u>without</u> which he would die, and yet <u>within</u> which is his death equally inevitable.

We all think the body is valuable for what it offers. We "chant the body's praise continually," worshiping it in numerous ways. We make sure it has enough food and drink. We pamper it. We dress it up to attract another body with which we can have sex. We exercise it and take care of it when it gets ill. We even give our bodily temple plastic surgery when it starts to crumble. And all of this is by no means confined to those people we might be tempted to call "shallow." It is universal; indeed, even in modern spiritual circles the body is generally regarded as sacred.

Jesus pleads with us: Hear not this madness! Don't believe you can find happiness by identifying with the body in any way. Pull the blinders off and look honestly at what's really going on. The ego has dedicated the body to the goal of sin, which inevitably brings with it guilt, pain, and finally death. Thinking the body is valuable for what it offers is not freedom; it is doom.

> 17. It is not given to the ego's disciples to realize that they have dedicated themselves to death. Freedom is offered them but they have not accepted it, and what is offered must also be received, to be truly given. For the Holy Spirit, too, is a communication medium, receiving from the Father and offering His messages unto the Son. Like [Ur: to] the ego, the Holy Spirit is both the sender and the receiver. For what is sent through Him returns to Him, seeking itself along the way, and finding what it seeks. So does the ego find the death it seeks, returning it to you.

Our dedication to the body is a dedication to death (the third obstacle to peace). This is perfectly logical: What else could a dedication to something that inevitably dies be *but* a dedication to death? This dedication blinds us to the freedom from death that the Holy Spirit has offered us. The ego has sought and found death, and we who are its disciples have accepted the ego's offering of death.

Fortunately, there is another option. The Holy Spirit is within us (remember the context here: the Holy Spirit entered when we joined with another in a holy relationship). He received the Father's message of freedom, and now He offers the message of freedom to us. However much we may reject it, He is both sender and receiver of His messages, and so He receives freedom *for* us. And it will be ours the moment we decide that the peace He planted at the heart of our holy relationship offers more value to us than the body's "gift" of death.

C. The Third Obstacle: The Attraction of Death

To recap: Two people have joined in a holy relationship, allowing the Holy Spirit to replace their former goal of sin with peace. This peace is now the unconscious foundation of their relationship. But a remnant of that goal of sin remains, and that remnant wants to re-establish itself as the foundation of the relationship. So, it sets up obstacles to prevent peace from flowing upward and outward, to keep that peace safely bottled up.

The obstacles are a nested system of defense in which each one is produced by the one after it. The first obstacle is the desire to get rid of peace. The second obstacle is the reason we want to get rid of peace: our belief that the body is valuable for what it offers. As we've seen, on the surface we value the body for the pleasure it offers, but underneath that we really want what the search for pleasure produces: guilt, for which we punish the body in the form of bodily pain.

The ultimate bodily punishment, of course, is death, which brings us to the third obstacle: the attraction of death. The real reason we want to get rid of peace (first obstacle) and want the offerings of the body (second obstacle) is that they bring us death (third obstacle). We want death because of that remnant of our old goal of sin. Being the ultimate punishment, death feeds our attraction to guilt, our attraction to pain, and our fear, thus keeping sin alive.

> 1. To you and your brother, in [Ur: To you, into] whose special relationship the Holy Spirit entered, it is given to release and be released from the dedication to death. For it [release] was offered you, and you accepted. Yet you must learn still more about this strange devotion, for it contains the third obstacle [Ur: the third of the obstacles] that peace must flow across. No one can die unless he chooses death. What seems to be the fear of death is really its attraction. Guilt, too, is feared and fearful. Yet it could have no hold at all except on those who are attracted to it and seek it out. And so it is with death. Made by the ego, its dark shadow falls across all living things, because the ego is the "enemy" of life.

Jesus starts his examination of our dedication to death by telling us the way out: our holy relationship. Yet before we can "release and be released from" this sick dedication, we must recognize how deep it really is. It is so deep that we actually *choose* death, because we are perversely attracted to it. We say we don't want it, but if we really choose death this can't be so, for why would we choose it if we weren't attracted to it? We do fear death on the surface, but this actually goes hand in hand with our attraction to it: Because our goal is fear (19.IV(B).12:5), we're attracted to death precisely *because* we fear it—death feeds our fear, just as sin, guilt, and pain do. Identified with the ego, the master of fear and "enemy" of life, we have joined a cult of death.

> 2. And yet a shadow cannot kill. What is a shadow to the living? They but walk past and it is gone. But what of those whose dedication is not to live; the black-draped "sinners," the ego's mournful chorus, plodding so heavily away from life, dragging their chains and marching in the slow procession that honors their grim master, lord of death? Touch any one of them with the gentle hands [Ur: hand] of forgiveness, and watch the chains fall away, along with yours. See him throw aside the black robe he was wearing to his funeral, and hear him laugh at death. The sentence sin would lay upon him he can escape through [Ur: with] your forgiveness. This is no [Ur: not] arrogance. It is the Will of God. What is impossible to you who chose His Will as yours? What is death to you? Your dedication is not to death, nor to its master. When you accepted the Holy Spirit's purpose in place of the ego's you renounced death, exchanging it for life. We know that [Ur: the *result* of] an idea leaves not its source. And death is the result of the thought we call the ego, as surely as life is the result of the Thought of God.

Now we see how the holy relationship offers freedom from death. When we joined in a common goal with another person, we renounced together our dedication to death and to the lord of death, the ego. This is another way of saying we renounced our "dedication to sin and its results" (19.IV(A).7:3), for death is the ultimate result of sin. We replaced that dedication with the Holy Spirit's goal of peace. And with this commitment to a goal that undoes the illusion of death came the means to that goal: *forgiveness*. Since death is our sentence for sins, forgiveness is the obvious remedy: "It sees there was no sin" (W-pII.1.1:3), and therefore no death penalty. The way to free our brothers and ourselves from death is to touch them with the gentle hand of forgiveness—to see them not as sinners condemned to death but as holy Sons of God blessed with eternal life.

Application: See yourself as part of the ego's mournful chorus, a dark procession of mourners in black robes, dragging chains as they trudge to their own funeral, singing a melancholy funeral dirge to their grim master, the lord of death. The other people in this procession are particular people in your own life whom you see as "sinners": people against whom you hold grievances. Is this not what your life really feels like: an inexorable march through ever-increasing pain and suffering, surrounded by people who are always misbehaving and disappointing you, to the grave that awaits you all?

But now you hear the Holy Spirit say to you: "Forgive, and you will see this differently. There is no death. The Son of God is free." He directs you to touch the person walking directly in front of you with the hand of forgiveness. As you do so, a miraculous transformation occurs. Watch this person's heavy chains fall away, and notice that your chains have fallen away as well. See him throw aside his black robe, revealing a pristine white robe underneath. See him laugh at the lord of death.

A surge of joy rises up in you, and you too throw off your black robe and join in your brother's laughter. The two of you then happily touch the rest of the members of the procession and watch them throw off their robes and chains. Now, everyone is laughing at the lord of death, and in this chorus of laughter he fades and disappears, taking the black robes and chains with him. With this, all of you join hands, gather in a circle in your white robes, and sing a joyous hymn of thanksgiving to God your Father.

i. The Incorruptible Body

> 3. From the ego came sin and guilt and death, in <u>opposition</u> to life and innocence, and to the Will of God Himself. Where can such opposition lie but in the sick minds of the insane, dedicated to madness and set <u>against</u> the peace of Heaven? One thing is sure; God, Who created neither sin nor death, wills not that you be bound by them. He knows of neither sin <u>nor</u> its results [Ur: result] [death]. The shrouded figures in the funeral procession march not in honor of their Creator, Whose Will it is they <u>live</u>. They are not <u>following</u> His Will; they are <u>opposing</u> it.

The last paragraph spoke of how releasing people from death through our forgiveness is not arrogance. It *seems* to be arrogance, because we are so steeped in the idea that death is God's Will. Death seems to be inevitable, an essential part of life, even holy. The solemnity and symbolism of our funerals reflect this. And how often have you heard someone say when a person dies (especially if the passing was sudden and unexpected), "It was God's Will"? The bottom line: We believe death comes from God.

Nonsense, says Jesus. Sin, guilt, and death come from the ego; only life and innocence come from God. Death is *never* "God's Will"; it is solely an idea in sick minds bent on *opposing* God's Will. God does not even know of sin or the death that results from it. His Will is only for life, unbound in any way.

> 4. And what is the black-draped body they would bury? A body which they dedicated to death, a symbol of corruption, a sacrifice to sin, offered to sin to feed upon and keep itself alive; a thing condemned, damned by its maker and lamented by every mourner who looks upon it as himself. You who believe you have condemned the Son of God to this *are* arrogant. But you who would release him are but honoring the Will of his Creator. The arrogance of sin, the pride of guilt, the sepulchre of separation, all are part of your unrecognized dedication to death. The glitter of guilt you laid upon the body would kill it. For what the ego loves, it kills for its obedience. But what obeys it not, it cannot kill.

Who among us does not condemn his or her body? It's never good-looking enough, healthy enough, or even light enough. It seems to inflict pain and suffering on us, especially the older we get. And of course, we know what it's going to be eventually: worm food.

All of this, we are told, is not because of anything inherent in the body, but because *we* have dedicated it to death. The image here reminds me of the earlier image of the hunting dogs bringing guilty bodies to fear to be devoured. Here, we bring *our* body to *sin* to be devoured. Identifying with the body is a dedication to sin, for which we feel guilt, for which we punish ourselves with death. The ego gives the death penalty to things that actually *obey* it—how twisted is that? All of this is the height of arrogance, because death is utterly contrary to God's Will for life. But we have it in our power to honor God's Will instead by releasing everyone from sin, guilt, and death.

5. You have <u>another</u> dedication that would keep the body incorruptible and perfect as long as it is useful for your holy purpose. The body no more dies than it can feel. <u>It does nothing</u>. Of itself it is neither corruptible nor incorruptible. It *is* nothing [Ur: *It is nothing*]. It is the result of a tiny, mad <u>idea</u> of corruption that can be corrected [Ur: *which can be corrected*]. For God has <u>answered</u> this insane idea with His Own; an Answer Which left Him not, and therefore brings the Creator to the awareness of every mind which heard His Answer and <u>accepted</u> It.

The body's condition depends solely on the purpose we give it. As we saw earlier, the body is merely a communication device like a telephone, which communicates whatever message we give it. It is nothing but an idea we made out of our insane purpose of sin, onto which we have projected our mad dedication to death. As long as we use it for these things, it is vulnerable to corruption, pain, and death. But in and of itself, it is not vulnerable to any of these things. We can change our purpose by accepting God's Answer to our insanity, and with this change comes a radically different body.

The "other dedication" referred to here is the goal that gave birth to our holy relationship: holiness, truth, peace. When we use the body *only* for this (a long-range goal for most of us), something amazing will happen: the body will become incorruptible and perfect. The Course means this quite literally, as we can see in the following passage:

> As [the purposes you gave the body] are laid aside, the strength the body has will always be enough to serve all truly useful purposes. The body's health is fully guaranteed, because it is not limited by time, by weather or fatigue, by food and drink, or any laws you made it serve before. You need do nothing now to make it well, for sickness has become impossible. (W-pI.136.18:2-4)

6. You who are dedicated to the incorruptible have been given through <u>your</u> acceptance, the power to <u>release</u> from corruption. What better way to teach the first and fundamental principle in a course on miracles than by showing you the one that <u>seems</u> to be the hardest [overcoming death] can be accomplished <u>first</u>? The body can but serve your purpose. As you look on [Ur: upon] it, so will it seem to be. Death, were it true, would be the final and complete disruption of communication, which <u>is</u> the ego's goal.

IV. The Obstacles to Peace

The ego's dedication to sin, guilt, and death serves its ultimate goal of severing communication with God forever. But by accepting the goal of our holy relationship, we dedicated ourselves to the incorruptible. This new dedication not only enables our own bodies to become incorruptible; it enables us to release *others* from corruption as well. Again, Jesus means this quite literally: He expects us to eventually become miracle workers who, just as he did, literally heal the sick and raise the dead (see T-1.I.24:1). *Raise the dead?* This seems impossible, but amazingly, we have the ability to overcome death *now.* And if we did overcome death, seemingly the most difficult thing of all, how could we doubt the truth of the Course's first and most fundamental principle: "There is no order of difficulty in miracles" (T-1.I.1:1)?

> 7. Those who fear death see not how often and how loudly they call to it, and bid it come to save them from communication. For death is seen as safety, the great dark savior from the light of truth, the answer to the Answer, the silencer of the Voice That speaks for God. Yet the retreat to death is not the end of conflict. Only God's Answer is its end. The obstacle of your seeming love for death that peace must flow across seems to be very great. For in it lie hidden all the ego's secrets, all its strange devices for deception, all its sick ideas and weird imaginings. Here is the final end of union, the triumph of the ego's making over creation, the victory of lifelessness on Life Itself.

When reading this material, we may protest: "But I'm not attracted to death—in fact, I'm terribly *afraid* of it!" Our fear of death, however, is actually a mask that keeps our underlying attraction buried in our unconscious. That's where it stays most of the time, though it does have its surface manifestations. For instance, the belief that death is "the end of conflict" is reflected in our belief that death ends the pain of this world; we can see it in expressions like "Goodbye, cruel world" and "Rest in peace."

However, the ego's ultimate purpose for death is something very few of us are in touch with: *to keep God out.* (This is a foretaste of the fourth obstacle to peace: the fear of God.) However buried this may be, it makes logical sense given all that we've read in this section. After all, the whole point of the obstacles to peace is to keep the peace of God at the heart of our holy relationship safely bottled up in order to keep our old goal of sin alive. Death is a great way to do this, because it is the ultimate proof of sin. It "saves" us from anything that would refute the reality of sin: communication, the light of truth, God's Voice. It represents the ego's ultimate victory in its war against God, "the victory of lifelessness on Life Itself." As long as we identify with the ego, we will see its victory as ours. But the only real end to the war is to hear God's Answer, the Voice of the side we are truly on.

> 8. Under the dusty edge of its distorted world the ego would lay the Son of God, slain by its orders, proof in his decay that God Himself is powerless before the ego's might, unable to protect the life that He created against the ego's savage wish to kill. My brother [Ur: brothers], child [Ur: children] of our Father, this is a *dream* of death. There is no funeral, no dark altars, no grim commandments nor twisted rituals of condemnation to which the <u>body</u> leads you. Ask not release of *it*. But <u>free</u> it from the merciless and unrelenting orders you laid upon it, and forgive it what you ordered it to do. In its exaltation you <u>commanded</u> it to die, for only death <u>could</u> conquer life. And what but insanity could look upon the defeat of God, and think it <u>real</u>?

Again, death represents the ego's ultimate victory over God, the ultimate proof that the ego's wish to kill is greater than God's Will for life. But as the Apostle Paul said, "O death, where is thy sting? O grave, where is thy victory?" (1 Corinthians 15:55). Its victory is nothing at all; "this is a dream of death." That entire grotesque scene from paragraphs 3 and 4 is nothing but a macabre fantasy from Edgar Allen Poe. It stems solely from our decision to use the body to serve the goal of sin—through the "exaltation" of the body, through our intense devotion to its comfort, protection, and enjoyment (see 18.VII.1:2). Freedom from death is no further away than our choice to use the body only for the goal of holiness.

Application. Say to your body:

> *I free you from the goal of sin.*
> *I free you from the merciless and unrelenting orders I laid upon*
> *you.*
> *I free you from my exaltation of you, in which I commanded you*
> *to die.*

IV. The Obstacles to Peace

I forgive you what I ordered you to do.
I dedicate you now to the goal of holiness.

9. The fear of death will go as its appeal is yielded to love's <u>real</u> attraction. The end of sin, which nestles quietly in the safety of your relationship, protected by your union with your brother [Ur: protected by your union], and ready to grow into a mighty force for God is very near. The infancy of salvation is carefully guarded by love, preserved from every thought that would attack it, and quietly made ready to fulfill the mighty task for which it was <u>given</u> you. Your newborn purpose is nursed by angels, cherished by the Holy Spirit and protected by God Himself. It <u>needs</u> not your protection; it is *yours*. For it is deathless, and within it lies the <u>end</u> of death.

You may have noticed that earlier (in the seventh paragraph), our attraction to death was called our "*seeming* love for death" (italics mine). Deep down at our core, we are truly attracted to love, and both our fear of death and the attraction it masks will fade away as love's real attraction reaches the surface. And the rebirth of love's real attraction in our minds came when we joined in our holy relationship. Now, our holy purpose rests within this relationship. It is in its infancy right now, nursed and protected by all the daycare providers Heaven has to offer: the angels, the Holy Spirit, and God Himself. But in time, this infant will grow up and become "a mighty force for God," a force that will overcome death entirely.

10. What danger can assail the wholly innocent? What can attack the guiltless? What fear can enter and disturb the peace of sinlessness? What has been given you, even in its infancy, is in full communication with God <u>and</u> you. In its tiny hands it holds, in perfect safety, every miracle you will perform, held out to <u>you</u>. The miracle of life is ageless, born in time but nourished in eternity. Behold this infant, to whom you gave a resting place by your forgiveness of your brother [Ur: *each other*], and see in it the Will of God. Here is the babe of Bethlehem reborn. And everyone who gives him shelter will follow him, <u>not</u> to the cross, but to the resurrection and the life.

What a great new spin on the Christmas story! Traditionally, of course, the "babe of Bethlehem" is Jesus himself, the pure and sinless

151

Son of God who will grow up to be the greatest of miracle workers and save us from our sins through his death on the cross. Here, the "babe of Bethlehem" is the holy purpose of our holy relationship, the infant "to whom you gave a resting place by your forgiveness of *each other*." Through this forgiveness, we see the sinless Son of God in each other. This infant, too, will grow up and hold out to us the miracles that *we* are to perform. And we who give Christ shelter in our holy relationship will follow him not to the crucifixion of our bodies (death), but to the resurrection and life that is the Will of God.

> 11. When anything seems to you to be a source of fear, when any situation strikes you with terror and makes your body tremble and the cold sweat of fear comes over it, remember it is <u>always</u> for *one* reason; the ego has perceived it as a symbol of fear, a sign of sin and death. Remember, then, that neither sign nor symbol should be <u>confused</u> with source, for they must <u>stand for</u> something <u>other</u> than themselves. Their meaning <u>cannot</u> lie in them, but must be sought in what they <u>represent</u>. And they may thus mean everything or nothing, according to the truth or falsity of the <u>idea</u> which they reflect. Confronted with such seeming uncertainty of meaning, judge it not. Remember the holy presence of the One <u>given</u> to you to be the Source of judgment. Give it to Him to judge <u>for</u> you, and say:
>
> *Take this from me and look upon it, judging it for me.*
> *Let me not see it as a sign of sin and death, nor use it for destruction.*
> *Teach me how **not** to make of it an <u>obstacle</u> to peace,*
> *but let You use it <u>for</u> me, to <u>facilitate</u> its coming.*

Application: Whenever we fear anything, this is a reflection of our fear of/attraction to death. So, we conclude with a practice aimed at undoing any form of fear we experience, a practice that will enable the thing we fear to become a *facilitator* of peace rather than an *obstacle* to it. Bring to mind something you are afraid of right now, and do the following:

Remember that the reason you are afraid is that the ego is seeing in this thing a symbol of fear, sin, and death.

Remember also that the thing you're afraid of has no meaning in itself. The meaning of a symbol lies in what it represents. It can thus mean everything or nothing. If the idea it represents is true, it means everything; if the idea it represents is false, it means nothing. Since fear, sin, and death are false ideas, the meaning the ego sees in this thing is nothing.

Remember also that because the thing you're afraid of has no meaning in itself, it doesn't *have* to be a symbol of fear, sin, and death. The only reason you fear it is because you see this meaning in it, but this is only a meaning the ego has attached to it. It could mean something else—something that doesn't frighten you at all.

You, then, do not really know what the thing you fear means. Confronted with this uncertainty of meaning, don't judge this thing and assume it *must* be a source of fear. Instead, remember the holy presence of the One given to you to be the Source of judgment: the Holy Spirit. Turn this thing over to Him by saying the words given to you as this subsection concludes:

> *Take this from me and look upon it, judging it for me.*
> *Let me not see it as a sign of sin and death, nor use it for destruction.*
> *Teach me how not to make of it an obstacle to peace, but let You use it for me, to facilitate its coming.*

D. The Fourth Obstacle: The Fear of God

Recap: You're familiar with the story by now. Two people have joined in a holy relationship, and the peace that is now the unconscious foundation of their relationship wants to rise to conscious awareness and extend to the world. But the remnant of their old goal of sin wants to re-establish itself, so it sets up obstacles to that peace.

Each obstacle is produced by the one after it, and serves to protect the one after it by convincing us to believe a lie. The desire to get rid of peace (first obstacle) is produced by the belief the body is valuable for what it offers (second obstacle), and protects that second obstacle by convincing us that our old goal will make us happier than the Holy Spirit's peace will. The belief that the body is valuable for what it offers is produced by the attraction of death (third obstacle), and protects that third obstacle by convincing us that giving up the body's "gifts" will sacrifice our happiness, even though what those "gifts" actually give us (and what we're really attracted to) is guilt, pain, and death.

Finally, as we'll see here, the attraction of death (third obstacle) is produced by the fear of God (the fourth obstacle), and protects that fourth obstacle by convincing us that the reason we fear God is that He is the Author of death. This is the lie that conceals the real content of the fourth obstacle: Identifying with the ego, we really fear God's *Life*—His infinite Love—because that would undo the ego. This is the secret all of the obstacles are designed to hide, because if we realized that this is what we're afraid of, we would immediately throw the ego out and joyously leap back into our Father's Arms.

> 1. What would you see <u>without</u> the fear of death? What would you feel and think if death held <u>no</u> attraction for you? Very simply, <u>you would remember your Father</u>. The Creator of life, the Source of everything that lives, the Father of the universe and of the universe of universes, and of everything that lies even <u>beyond</u> them would you remember. And as this memory rises in your mind, peace must still surmount a final obstacle, <u>after</u> which is salvation completed, and the Son of God <u>entirely</u> restored to sanity. For here your world *does* end.

When our fear of/attraction to death—the third obstacle—is removed, what we find behind it is *life*; the memory of God, the Source of everlasting and limitless life, will come streaming back into our awareness. At this point, the ego will be on the verge of extinction, but it has one more monkey wrench to throw into the works: the fourth obstacle, the fear of God. Only when this final obstacle is overcome is the rising of peace through the obstacles complete and salvation accomplished.

> 2. The fourth obstacle to be surmounted hangs like a heavy veil before the face of Christ. Yet as His face rises beyond it, shining with joy because He is in His Father's Love, peace will lightly brush the veil aside and run to meet Him, and to <u>join</u> with Him at last. For this dark veil, which seems to make the face of Christ Himself like to a leper's, and the bright Rays of His Father's Love that light His face with glory appear as streams of blood, fades in the blazing light <u>beyond</u> it when the fear of death is gone.

This paragraph introduces an image that is central to the rest of this section and to the entire Course: the veiled face of Christ. (This is the Course's first reference to "the face of Christ." The one earlier reference in 4.IV.1:5 was originally "the face of God," but was changed by the editors.) Let's unpack this image:

The face of Christ: This is a symbol for what we see with Christ's vision or true perception—the true Self of everyone, the holiness in all things. As a *face*, it is not reality itself, but the outer façade of reality, a perceptual reflection of it. This face is the last thing we'll see before God takes His final step.

The veil: The image here is of a facial veil. Broadly speaking, the veil is a symbol for anything that blocks our awareness of true perception. A veil *looks* dark and heavy, but it is actually thin and easily lifted once we have the desire to do so. A number of things are described as "veils" in the Course: time, guilt, fantasies, etc. All of the obstacles to peace are veils. The specific veil described in this paragraph, of course, is the fourth obstacle, the "darkest veil," the fear of God.

The distorting effect of the veil: The veil distorts the face of Christ so that His radiant glory looks like the face of a leper streaming with blood. This is a symbol for how we see our brothers when we look for sin in them (remember those hunting dogs?): the beautiful Christ in them is twisted into a bloody, horrifying monster doomed to sickness and death.

The lifting of the veil: This is a symbol for what happens when we forgive (as we'll see in the next subsection). The face of Christ will rise up, His light will shine away the darkness of the final veil, the peace the obstacles were designed to thwart will brush the veil aside, and Christ will be revealed in all His glory. We will run to meet Him and join with Him at last.

3. This is the darkest veil, upheld by the belief in death and protected by its attraction. The dedication to death and to its sovereignty is but the solemn vow, the promise made in secret to the ego never to lift this veil, not to approach it, nor even to <u>suspect</u> that it is there. This is the secret bargain made with the ego to keep what lies <u>beyond</u> the veil forever blotted out and unremembered. Here is your promise never to allow union to call you <u>out</u> of separation; the great amnesia in which the memory of God seems quite forgotten; the cleavage of your Self from you;—*the fear of God*, the final step in your dissociation.

As I mentioned, the fourth obstacle is the "darkest veil" of all. The third obstacle, the attraction of death, is both the tie that keeps the veil in place and the blindfold that keeps it from even being seen. Our dedication to death is our promise to the ego to keep this fourth obstacle—the fear of God—safely out of our awareness so that we'll never be able to undo it, and because we cannot undo it, to banish God from our memory forever. How this works will be explained in the next paragraph.

> 4. See how the belief in death would seem to "save" you. For if this were gone, what could [Ur: can] you fear but life? It is the attraction of death that makes life seem to be ugly, cruel and tyrannical. You are no more afraid of death than of the ego. These are your chosen <u>friends</u>. For in your secret alliance with them you have agreed never to let the fear of God be lifted, so you could look upon the face of Christ and join Him in His Father.

Here's how the attraction of death protects the fear of God. Our attraction to death "saves" us because it makes us think that God is the Author of death, and is thus "ugly, cruel and tyrannical." We now think we fear a punishing God bent on destroying us. We now have a great justification for being afraid of Him. But this "justification" is an ego ruse to keep us from recognizing that we really fear what the ego fears: God's *Life*, His Love (see also 19.IV(C).7). If we saw that we really feared God's Life, we would immediately see how insane that is and let it be undone so we could be with our Beloved again. But by fearing God's wrath, we don't suspect that option even exists.

> As in the previous paragraph, we see here our promise to our "friends" (the ego and death) to never let this final veil be lifted. We are steadfastly loyal to these "friends," yet they don't have our best interests at heart at all. It is as if we have invited con artists into our life, who promise us the moon even as they rob us blind behind our backs.5. Every obstacle that peace must flow across is surmounted in just the same way; the fear that <u>raised</u> it yields to the love beyond, and so the fear is gone. And so it is with this. The desire to get rid of peace and drive the Holy Spirit <u>from</u> you fades in the presence of the quiet recognition that you love Him. The exaltation of the body is given up in favor of the spirit, which you love as you could <u>never</u> love the body. And the appeal of death is lost forever as love's attraction stirs and calls to you. From <u>beyond</u> each of the <u>obstacles</u> to love, Love Itself has called. And each has been

surmounted by the power of the attraction of what lies <u>beyond</u>. Your <u>wanting</u> fear <u>seemed</u> to be holding them in place. Yet when you heard the Voice of Love <u>beyond</u> them, you answered and they disappeared.

Here is how we overcome the obstacles: by letting the fear that generated them give way to the love beyond. Another way of putting this is that the *attraction* of each obstacle—an attraction generated by fear—gives way to the love beyond. Here's how this works with the first three obstacles: Our attraction to the goal of sin, which makes us want to get rid of the Holy Spirit's peace, gives way to our love for the Holy Spirit. Our attraction to the "gifts" the body offers gives way to our love for the spirit. Our attraction to death gives way to love's real attraction. The final obstacle, the fear of God, will be overcome in the same way.

Application: Though this material is specifically about the process of the holy relationship, much of it could be applied on an individual basis as well. Right now, affirm your willingness to let peace flow past the first three obstacles, using these words:

> *I no longer desire to get rid of peace and drive the Holy Spirit from me, because I now recognize that I love Him.*

> *I no longer exalt my body, because I now recognize that I love the spirit as I could never love the body.*

> *I am no longer attracted to death, because love's real attraction has stirred in me and calls to me.*

> *I have heard the Voice of Love beyond these obstacles to peace, I have answered, and they will disappear.*

6. And now you stand in terror before what you swore never to look upon. Your eyes look down, remembering your promise to your "friends." The "loveliness" of sin, the delicate appeal of guilt, the "holy" waxen image of death, and the fear of vengeance of the ego you swore in blood not to desert, all rise and bid you <u>not</u> to raise your eyes. For you realize that if you look on <u>this</u> and <u>let</u> the veil be lifted, *they* <u>will be gone forever</u>. All of your "friends," your "protectors" and

your "home" will vanish. Nothing that you remember <u>now</u> will you remember.

7. It seems to you the world will utterly abandon you if you but raise your eyes. Yet all that <u>will</u> occur is <u>you</u> will leave the world forever. This is the re-establishment of *your* will. Look upon it, open-eyed, and you will nevermore believe that you are at the mercy of things <u>beyond</u> you, forces you can<u>not</u> control, and thoughts that come to you <u>against</u> your will. <u>It</u> *is* <u>your will to look on this</u>. No mad desire, no trivial impulse to forget again, no stab of fear nor the cold sweat of seeming death <u>can</u> stand against your will. For what attracts you from <u>beyond</u> the veil is also deep <u>within</u> you, unseparated from it and <u>completely</u> one.

Here is the image that is the theme of the entire rest of the section: the two holy relationship partners standing before the final obstacle, the final veil, the fear of God. (Later references will make it clear that there are two people standing before the veil.) Finally, at long last, we are ready to look upon the thing that we promised our "friends"—the ego and death, along with a few other familiar thugs: sin, guilt, and fear—that we would never bring to light. We are terrified of the vengeance our "friends" will visit upon us if we look. We are like a whistle-blower who works for a corrupt government, terrified of what the government will do to her for breaking her loyalty oath and exposing the Big Lie at the heart of the government, a revelation that will bring it toppling down. We realize that if we do this, there's no turning back.

It seems like we'll lose everything if we look, but in truth we'll *gain* everything. We will leave the world for our true home. We will re-establish our own will. We will no longer believe that fearful things can come to us against our will, for we will recognize that only our own decision to abandon our true will and listen to the propaganda of our false "friends" brought fearful things to us. We've had enough of that propaganda; we're determined not to be deceived again. We're ready now; the Love beyond the veil is calling to the Love within us. It's so close we can taste it.

Yet we are still in terror. Will we lift our eyes and look?

i. The Lifting of the Veil

We are now standing with our holy relationship partner before the final obstacle to peace: the fear of God, which seems to be the fear of

God's wrath but is really the ego's fear of God's Love. We are terrified at the prospect of looking up and lifting the veil that hides the face of Christ. What will undo this terror so we can lift our eyes and look?

The first three obstacles to peace were overcome when the fear that generated them yielded to the love beyond. So it is with the final obstacle: The fear of God yields to the attraction of the Love beyond the veil. This happens through forgiving and fully joining with our holy relationship partner. Each partner forgives the other and receives forgiveness from the other—each is savior to the other. Through this forgiveness, the old goal of sin that erected the obstacles is at last undone completely, and the holy relationship's goal of peace is at last accomplished. Through union with each other, we find union with God.

> 8. Forget not that you came this far <u>together</u>, you and your brother. And it was surely <u>not</u> the ego that led you here. No obstacle to peace can <u>be</u> surmounted through <u>its</u> help. <u>It</u> does not open up its secrets, and bid you look on them and go <u>beyond</u> them. <u>It</u> would not have you see its weakness, and learn it has <u>no</u> power to <u>keep</u> you from the truth. The Guide Who brought you here <u>remains</u> with you, and when you raise your eyes you <u>will</u> be ready to look on terror with no fear at all. But first, lift up your eyes and look on your brother [Ur: each other] in innocence born of <u>complete</u> forgiveness of his [Ur: each other's] illusions, and through the eyes of faith that sees [Ur: which see] them not.

As we stand in terror before the fear of God, we may be tempted to ask our old "friend," the ego, for help. But this is like asking Osama bin Laden for help with homeland security. The ego's obstacles to peace were set up precisely to keep us from getting to this place, because it doesn't want us to see how flimsy that final veil really is.

Only through joining in a holy relationship, which invited the Holy Spirit to give us His goal of peace, were we able to get this far at all. He has guided this entire journey, and He is still with us. Now, He gives us the key that will enable us to lift up our eyes and look on the fear of God *without* fear: lifting up our eyes and looking first upon *each other* with complete forgiveness. We must let go of all the "imagined slights, remembered pain, past disappointments, perceived injustices and deprivations" (16.VII.1:3) that still stand between us. Only our faith in each other and in the Holy Spirit Who took our relationship under His wing will lift us beyond the veil to God.

> 9. No one can look upon the fear of God unterrified, unless he has <u>accepted</u> the Atonement and learned illusions are not real. No one can stand before this obstacle alone, for he could not have <u>reached</u> this far unless his brother walked beside him. And no one would dare to <u>look</u> on it without <u>complete</u> forgiveness of his brother in his heart. Stand you here a while and tremble not. You will be ready. Let us join together in a holy instant, here in this place where the purpose, <u>given</u> in a holy instant, has led you. And let us join in faith that He Who brought us here together will <u>offer</u> you the innocence you need, and that you will <u>accept</u> it for my love and His.

A holy instant started this entire process: the one that gave birth to our holy relationship. In that holy instant, the Holy Spirit gave us the purpose of peace, and since then has led us through all of the obstacles to peace to the place we stand now. We never could have made it this far without Him or without each other. Now, as we stand in terror before the final obstacle, Jesus invites us to join him in *another* holy instant. In this holy instant, we join in faith in the Guide Who led us this far to give us what we need to make it the rest of the way: complete forgiveness of our partner in our heart. We won't dare look at the fear of God until we recognize that the terrifying illusions we see in our brother are not real.

> 10. Nor is it <u>possible</u> to look on this too soon. This is the place to which everyone must come when he is ready. Once he has found his brother he *is* ready. Yet merely to <u>reach</u> the [Ur: a] place is not enough. A journey without a purpose is still meaningless, and even when it is over it seems to make no sense. How can you <u>know</u> that it is over unless you realize its purpose <u>is</u> accomplished? Here, with the journey's end before you, you *see* its purpose. And it is here you choose whether to look upon it or wander on, only to return and make the choice again.

It's easy to imagine ourselves standing in terror before the fear of God and screaming, "I'm not ready!" Yet the very fact that we're here with our partner means we *are* ready. This by itself isn't enough, however; to reach our goal, we must actually *do* what we came to do. A person who is ready for a marathon still needs to actually run the race to accomplish her purpose of finishing it. In like manner, we who are ready to look fearlessly at the fear of God must actually *look* to accomplish our purpose of joining with the Love of God beyond the veil. In truth this has already been accomplished—"you but make a journey that is done" (W-pI.169.8:3)—but we won't *know* this consciously until we actually lift that final veil.

What happens if we don't do this? We "wander on, only to return and make the choice again." I wonder how many times we've been one step away from Heaven, only to chicken out at the last minute?

> 11. To look upon the fear of God <u>does</u> need some preparation. Only the sane can look on stark insanity and raving madness with pity and compassion, but <u>not</u> with fear. For only if they <u>share</u> in it does it seem fearful, and you <u>do</u> share in it until you look upon your brother [Ur: each other] with perfect faith and love and tenderness. Before complete forgiveness you still stand unforgiving. You are afraid of God *because* you fear your brother [Ur: each other]. Those you do not forgive <u>you fear</u>. And no one reaches love with <u>fear</u> beside him.

Why do we need to forgive our holy relationship partner before we can look upon the fear of God? Here is the logic:

- Those you do not forgive, you fear.
- Therefore, until you forgive your brother, you will fear him.
- Because you fear your brother, you fear God.
- As long as you fear God, you will not lift the veil and find God's Love.

Without forgiveness, each partner sees the other as a selfish, sinful attacker worthy of death—a leper whose face is streaming with blood, to bring back an image we saw earlier. With such a terrifying picture of each other, how can we look upon *God* without fear? We share the madness of fearing our loving Father. With forgiveness, though, each partner sees the face of Christ in the other. With this sane vision, we no longer share the madness of fearing our Father, and are thus able to look upon it with compassion rather than fear. It then becomes easy to set it aside and reach the Love beyond.

> 12. This brother who stands beside you still <u>seems</u> to be a stranger. You do <u>not</u> know him, and your <u>interpretation</u> of him is <u>very</u> fearful.

And you attack him still, to keep what seems to be <u>yourself</u> unharmed. Yet in his hands <u>is</u> your salvation. You see his madness, which you hate because you <u>share</u> [Ur: in] it. And all the pity and forgiveness that would <u>heal</u> it gives way to fear. Brother, [Ur: Brothers,] you <u>need</u> forgiveness of your brother [Ur: each other], for you will share in madness or in Heaven <u>together</u>. And you and he will raise your eyes in <u>faith</u> together, or not at all.

Even at this apparently advanced point in the journey, we still have a lot of forgiveness work to do. Our interpretation of our partner is still "very fearful." We still don't really know who the other is, and each of us is still playing the game of attacking the other in order to protect oursels. We're still sharing in the madness our holy relationship is meant to undo. That's why Jesus pleads with us: "Brothers, you need forgiveness of each other." When we joined in a holy relationship, our destinies became linked forever: Together we will either lose ourselves in madness or find ourselves in God.

It's crucial to remember that this material, with its vivid imagery, is talking about a real-life situation: Two people have joined in a holy goal and have worked together toward that goal, but their grievances against each other keep them from reaching the goal. Unforgiveness really does scuttle holy relationships; this certainly happened with Helen and Bill. Their relationship, which started out with such promise, deteriorated more and more into resentment, attack, and blame as the years went on. If they had indeed reached the final veil, it seems that their unforgiveness kept them from lifting it and they turned away. They *did* make progress, and they gave a priceless gift to the world (and they will return and get another chance to lift the final veil), but in the end, they shared in madness instead of Heaven. What will *our* choice be?

13. Beside [Ur: each of] you is one who offers you the chalice of Atonement, for the Holy Spirit is in him. Would you hold his sins <u>against</u> him, or accept his gift to <u>you</u>? Is this giver of salvation your friend or enemy? Choose which he is, remembering that you will <u>receive</u> of him according to your choice. He has <u>in him</u> the power to forgive <u>your</u> sin [Ur: sins], as you for <u>him</u>. Neither can give it to himself alone. And yet your savior stands beside each one. Let him be what he <u>is,</u> and seek not to make of love an enemy.

14. Behold your Friend, the Christ Who stands beside you. How holy and

how beautiful He is! You <u>thought</u> He sinned because you cast the veil of sin upon Him to <u>hide</u> His loveliness. Yet still He holds forgiveness out to you, to <u>share</u> His holiness. This "enemy," this "stranger" still offers you salvation as His Friend. The "enemies" of Christ, the worshippers of sin, know not Whom they attack.

The alternative to our fearful perception of our partner is seeing Christ in him. This is the process of salvation at the heart of the Course: We forgive our brother by seeing Christ in him, which sets him free to forgive us by seeing Christ in *us*. This process is absolutely essential, for "Neither can give [forgiveness] to himself alone."

Here's how it works: Forgiving our brother reveals Who *really* stands beside us. We saw a sinner before; now we see Christ. We saw a bloody leper before, because we threw a veil of sin over his head; now we see a holy and beautiful being. We saw an enemy before; now we see our Friend. We saw a fearful attacker before, whom we needed to attack to keep ourselves from harm; now we see one who can *free* us from all harm by forgiving our sins.

In short, we save our savior. We forgive our brother, which awakens the Christ in him, and then he returns the favor. In this context, this doesn't just mean that the Christ in our brother forgives us without our brother consciously doing so, though that does happen. This section is talking about two people actively forgiving *each other*; what's happening here is that when we give forgiveness to our partner, it heals him, and he will forgive us in gratitude for our gift of healing. And as we share holiness instead of madness, we will be able to look together upon the fear of God and awaken to the Love beyond the veil.

15. This is your brother, crucified by sin and waiting for release from pain. Would you not <u>offer</u> him forgiveness, when only he can offer it to you? For <u>his</u> redemption he will give you yours, as surely as God created every living thing and loves it. And he will give it truly, for it will be both offered and <u>received</u>. There is no grace of Heaven that you cannot <u>offer</u> to your brother [Ur: each other], and receive from your most holy Friend. Let him withhold it not, for by receiving it you offer it to <u>him</u>. And he <u>will</u> receive of you what <u>you</u> received of him. Redemption has been given you to give your brother [Ur: *each other*], and thus receive it. Whom you forgive <u>is</u> free, and what you give you <u>share</u>. Forgive the sins your brother <u>thinks</u> he has committed, and all the guilt you think you see in him [Ur: all the guilt *you* see in him].

Our partner is the Christ, but right now we see him as crucified—crucified by both the sins he thinks he has committed and those we think *we* see in him. In the rest of this paragraph, Jesus hammers home that theme of saving your savior in one sentence after another:

- Offer your partner forgiveness, and he will offer forgiveness to you (second sentence).
- Offer your partner redemption, and he will give you your redemption (third sentence).
- Offer your gift of redemption to your partner and he will give you redemption truly, for you who offered it will also receive it (fourth sentence).
- Offer redemption because redemption has been given you to give your partner, so you can receive it from him (eighth sentence).
- Offer forgiveness to your partner and set him free; you too will receive this freedom, because what you give you share (ninth sentence).
- A new twist: Offer forgiveness to your partner and you will receive it from him. By receiving it from him, you offer it to him again, for he will receive of you what you received of him (fifth through seventh sentences). (I assume this means that your receiving your partner's forgiveness will reinforce the forgiveness you gave to him.)

I think we can safely conclude that Jesus considers this process absolutely essential.

> 16. Here is the holy place of resurrection, to which we come again; to which we will <u>return</u> until redemption is accomplished <u>and received</u>. Think who your brother <u>is</u>, before you would condemn him. And offer thanks to God that he is holy, and has been given the gift of holiness for <u>you</u>. Join him in gladness, and remove all trace of guilt from his disturbed and tortured mind. Help him to lift the heavy burden of sin you laid upon him and he <u>accepted</u> as his own, and toss it lightly and with happy laughter <u>away</u> from him. Press it not like thorns against his brow, nor nail him to it, unredeemed and hopeless.

This place we have come to, standing before the fear of God, is meant to be the empty tomb—the place of resurrection. Right now, though, it looks like Golgotha. So many times we have wandered off and returned to this place; so many times we have been right on the verge of resurrection to everlasting life, only to nail each other to the cross yet again. Will we repeat this travesty yet again?

We can avert it by gratefully remembering that our partner is the Christ, and refusing to play the part of the Romans this time. We can help him remove the heavy cross of sin he has carried on his back for so long—sins we laid on him and he accepted as his own. We can refuse to nail him to that cross and mock him with a crown of thorns. (I imagine that crown is why the veiled face of Christ in paragraph 2 has streams of blood flowing down it.) We can help him toss the cross of sin away with happy laughter (reminiscent of the image in 19.IV(C).2 of tossing the black robes away and laughing at death). Instead of crucifying our brother the Christ yet again, we can offer him thanks that he is holy and join him in resurrection.

> 17. Give faith to your brother [Ur: Give each other faith], for faith and hope and mercy <u>are</u> yours to give. Into the hands that give, the gift is given. Look on your brother, and see in him the gift of God you would <u>receive</u>. It is almost Easter, the time of resurrection. Let us give redemption to each other and <u>share</u> in it, that we may rise as one in resurrection, [Ur: and] not <u>separate</u> in death. Behold the gift of freedom that I gave the Holy Spirit for [Ur: *both* of] you. And be you and your brother free together, as you offer <u>to</u> the Holy Spirit this <u>same</u> gift. And <u>giving</u> it, receive it <u>of</u> Him in <u>return</u> for what you gave. He leadeth you and me together, that we might meet here in this holy place, and make the <u>same</u> decision.

It was literally almost Easter when Helen took down this dictation. Here, Jesus calls upon Helen and Bill (and all of us) to celebrate the day that commemorates his resurrection in a far different way than the usual egg hunt and church services. Instead of just preaching and singing about how wonderful his resurrection was, Jesus wants us to give his gift of resurrection to *each other*. This is what we give when we forgive each other, when we have faith in each other to make it all the way home together. We offer our forgiveness of each other to the Holy Spirit so

He can return to us what we gave. By doing this, we meet with Jesus before the final veil and make our final decision to rise as one with him in resurrection.

> 18. Free your brother here, as I freed you. Give him the selfsame gift, nor look upon him with condemnation of <u>any</u> kind. See him as guiltless as I look on you, and <u>overlook</u> the sins he <u>thinks</u> he sees within himself. Offer your brother [Ur: each other] freedom and complete release from sin, here in the garden of seeming agony and death. So will we prepare <u>together</u> the way unto the resurrection of God's Son, and let him rise again to glad remembrance of his Father, Who knows no sin, no death, but <u>only</u> life eternal.

Because of our belief in sin, this place where we stand before the veil feels like the Garden of Gethsemane, the "garden of seeming agony and death." But again, it is really the place of resurrection. Both of us are burdened with the sins we think we see in ourselves. Jesus calls upon us to lift this burden by seeing each other as he sees us: pure, holy Sons of God, whom sin has never touched. In this way, we bring about the resurrection of God's Son to remembrance of his Father, Who knows *no* sin or death, but only everlasting life.

> 19. Together we will disappear into the Presence <u>beyond</u> the veil, not to be lost but <u>found</u>; not to be seen but [Ur: to be] <u>known</u>. And knowing, nothing in the plan God has established for salvation will be left undone. This is the journey's purpose, <u>without</u> which <u>is</u> the journey meaningless. Here is the peace of God, given to you eternally by Him. Here is the rest and quiet that you seek, the <u>reason</u> for the journey from its beginning. Heaven is the gift you <u>owe</u> your brother [Ur: each other], the debt of gratitude you offer to the Son of God in thanks for what he is, and what his Father created him to be.

Here we are at last: the end of the journey. The place we reach when we have overcome all of the obstacles to peace is the peace of God, the deep rest we have yearned for from time immemorial. We find this peace as we join together with each other and with Jesus and disappear into the Presence beyond the veil—not to be lost as the ego tells us, but to be truly found by our Beloved; not to be seen in a world of perception but to be known directly by our Creator. At last the goal of our holy relationship, the purpose of our journey from the very beginning, is accomplished. And all we need to do to reach this place is to forgive our partner, to give him the gift of Heaven in gratitude for the Holy Son of God he truly is.

> 20. Think carefully how you would look upon the giver of this gift, for as you look on <u>him</u> so will the gift <u>itself</u> appear to be. As <u>he</u> is seen as either the giver of guilt or of salvation, so will his <u>offering</u> be seen and so <u>received</u>. The crucified give pain because they <u>are</u> in pain. But the redeemed give joy because they have been <u>healed</u> of pain. Everyone gives as he receives, but <u>he</u> must choose what it will *be* that he receives. And he will <u>recognize</u> his choice by what he gives, and what is given <u>him</u>. Nor is it given anything in hell or Heaven to <u>interfere</u> with his decision.

Our partner gives *us* Heaven too, but will we recognize it? It all depends on how *we* choose to perceive him. If we crucify him by perceiving him as a sinner, he will give us pain in return for our "sin" of nailing him to the cross. If we redeem him by perceiving him as the resurrected Christ, he will give us joy in return for the healing we gave him. As I mentioned in my commentary on the fourteenth paragraph, our redeemed partner can give us joy in two ways: 1) the Christ in him gives us joy even without his conscious cooperation (since we will now be *interpreting* whatever he gives us differently), and 2) he consciously gives us joy in gratitude for the healing we gave him.

What we choose to give our partner is completely up to us, and what we give is what *we* want to receive. In fact, whatever we may *say* we want, the evidence for what we really want to receive lies in what we give and what we receive in return. Something to think about the next time a brother seems to give you pain.

> 21. You came this far because the journey <u>was</u> your choice. And no one undertakes to do what he believes is meaningless. What you had faith in still is faithful, and watches over you in faith so gentle yet so strong that it would lift you far beyond the veil, and place the Son of God safely within the sure protection of his Father. Here is the <u>only</u> purpose that gives this world, and the long journey <u>through</u> this world, whatever meaning lies in them. Beyond this, they <u>are</u> meaningless. You and your brother stand together [Ur: You stand together], still without conviction they <u>have</u> a purpose. Yet it is <u>given</u> you to <u>see</u> this purpose in your holy

Friend, and <u>recognize</u> it as your own.

As the section ends, we are back where we started: standing before the veil that covers the face of Christ, quaking in terror before the final obstacle to peace, the fear of God. To go beyond the veil and disappear into our Father's Love was the purpose of the journey of our holy relationship from the beginning. It is the only purpose that gives the *entire* journey through the world any meaning at all. We joined in this purpose, and placed our faith in it (even as we consciously resisted it). That purpose is still worthy of our faith, and even now is faithfully guiding us into our Father's loving Arms.

Yet as we stand here so close to the end, we still aren't sure this long journey has a purpose. The only way to recognize the purpose and go beyond the veil is to forgive our partner so we can *see* our shared purpose in the Christ that stands revealed before us. We have come to this place so many times before, only to turn away. What will we do this time?

Visualization: The Lifting of the Veil

This is a visualization created by Robert (I've altered it slightly). It is a fitting end to our journey through the obstacles to peace. Bring to mind your holy relationship partner if you have one. If you don't (and that is perfectly okay), choose a brother who makes the journey to God with you, one whom you have not entirely forgiven. Read the material below slowly and thoughtfully, applying everything you read to this person.

(See yourself standing before the veil across the face of Christ,
the veil being the fear of God.
You are terrified to look up.
Next to you stands this brother.)

The Guide Who brought you here remains with you, and when you raise your eyes you will be ready to look on terror [the veil, the fear of God] with no fear at all.

But first, lift up your eyes and look on your brother, [name], in innocence born of complete forgiveness of his illusions, and through the eyes of faith that sees them [his illusions] not.

168

No one can stand before this obstacle [the fear of God] alone,
for he could not have reached this far unless his brother walked
beside him.

And no one would dare to look on it without complete forgiveness
of his brother in his heart.

Stand you here a while and tremble not.

You will be ready.

Let us [you, Jesus and your brother] join together in a holy
instant, here in this place [before the veil] where the purpose,
given in a holy instant [the instant of joining that began this
journey], has led you.

And let us join in faith that He Who brought us here together will
offer you the innocence you need [to look on the fear of God],
and that you will accept it for my love and His.

To look upon the fear of God does need some preparation.

Only the sane can look on stark insanity and raving madness [the
madness of fearing the Love and perfect joy that lie in God]
with pity and compassion, but not with fear.

For only if they share in it [the madness] does it seem fearful,

and you do share in it until you look upon your brother, [name],
with perfect faith and love and tenderness.

Before complete forgiveness [the face of Christ] you still stand
unforgiving.

You are afraid of God because you fear your brother, [name].

Those you do not forgive you fear.

And no one reaches love with fear beside him.

[You will be afraid of love, afraid that it will take your fear—
which you cling to desperately—away.]

This brother, [name], who stands beside you still seems to be a
stranger.

[Reflect on this.]

You do not know him, and your interpretation of him is very
fearful.

And you attack him still, to keep what seems to be yourself
unharmed.

[But only what seems to be yourself.]

Yet in his hands, [fill in your own name and hear Jesus speaking this to you], is your salvation.
You see his madness, which you hate because you share it.
[If you didn't share his madness, it would only evoke compassion, not hate and fear.]
And all the pity and forgiveness that would heal it gives way to fear.
Brother, you need forgiveness of your brother, [name], for you will share in madness or in Heaven together.
And you and he will raise your eyes in faith together, or not at all.

Beside you is one who offers you the chalice of Atonement, for the Holy Spirit is in him.
Would you hold his sins against him, or accept his gift to you?
Is this giver of salvation your friend or enemy?
Choose which he is, remembering that you will receive of him according to your choice.

(Really visualize this. See this person approach you,
filled with the Holy Spirit, shining with holiness.
See his hands holding out the Holy Grail to you.
Take the cup from his hands,
lift it to your lips and drink in the Atonement.
Feel the wine of Atonement absolving you of all guilt,
liberating you from all fear and limitation.
Look into the eyes of the holy giver of this gift.
Imagine how thankful you would be for the hands that gave you this priceless gift.)

He has in him the power to forgive your sin, as you for him.
Neither can give it to himself alone.
And yet your Savior [the Christ, the true Self you share] stands beside each one.
Let Him be what He is [see your brother as the Christ he really is], and seek not to make of love an enemy.

Behold your Friend, the Christ Who stands beside you [how would you feel if you really believed this?].

How holy and how beautiful He is!
You thought He sinned because you cast the veil of sin upon Him
    to hide His loveliness.
[He only seems unholy because of what you projected onto him.]
Yet still He holds forgiveness out to you, to share His holiness.
This "enemy," this "stranger" still offers you salvation as His
    Friend....

(Picture your brother standing in front of you.
Right behind his body, picture a massive radiant face,
the face of love, the face of Christ, "shining with joy because He is in
His Father's Love" (19.IV(D).2:2).
Now visualize your current picture of your brother—as a body that
sins—
as an image on a cloth veil that is hanging in front of this glorious
face.
Realize that you cast this veil of sin upon this shining face of your
own free will,
in order to hide the intense loveliness of the face.
Without your projection, all you would see in this person is this face
of glory.
And so you walk up and lift the veil
and there behold who your brother really is.
There you see the face of love, the face of your true Self,
shining on you in perfect love.)

This [Friend, this Christ] is your brother, [name], crucified by
    sin and waiting for release from pain.
(Imagine your brother nailed to a cross, waiting for release from pain.)

Would you not offer him forgiveness, when only he can offer it to
    you [ask yourself this]?
For his redemption he will give you yours [is it worth it?],
as surely as God created every living thing and loves it....
There is no grace of Heaven that you cannot offer to your brother,
    [name], and receive from your most holy Friend....

Forgive the sins your brother, [name], thinks he has committed, and all the guilt you think you see in him.

Think who your brother [name] is, before you would condemn him [really think on this].

And offer thanks to God that he is holy [actually offer this thanks], and has been given the gift of holiness for you [could any gift be more desirable?].

Join him in gladness, and remove all trace of guilt from his disturbed and tortured mind.

Help him to lift the heavy burden of sin you laid upon him and he accepted as his own, and toss it lightly and with happy laughter away from him.

Press it not like thorns against his brow, nor nail him to it, unredeemed and hopeless.

(Picture your brother carrying his cross, struggling, bleeding, his face contorted in pain, with a crown of thorns on his brow.

Realize that you played the role of Pilate and gave him this cross, and that you played the role of the soldiers and pressed these thorns into his brow.

Now, though, see yourself walk up to him, happily, beaming with love.

You are here to undo what you've done. You are here to set him free.

You gently take the cross from him and toss it lightly and with happy laughter away from him, as if it were made of cardboard..

You do the same with the crown of thorns.

Now both of you are beaming at each other with love and happiness, tears of joy streaming down your faces.

You embrace and prepare together to look upon the veil and let it be lifted so that you can look on the face of Christ together.)

Give faith to your brother, [name], for faith and hope and mercy are yours to give.

Into the hands that give, the gift is given.

Look on your brother, and see in him the gift of God you would receive. [Really do this.]

Free your brother here, as I [Jesus] freed you.

Give him the selfsame gift, nor look upon him with condemnation of any kind.

See him as guiltless as I look on you, and overlook the sins he thinks he sees within himself.

Offer your brother, [name], freedom and complete release from sin, here in the garden of seeming agony and death [before the veil].

Together we [you, your brother, and Jesus] will disappear into the Presence beyond the veil, not to be lost but found; not to be seen but known.

(Really imagine this happening. Picture the veil being lifted and the three of you first gazing in rapture on the sublime face of Christ, and then being drawn by an irresistible force towards that face, past the veil, and into the Presence beyond the face, the Presence of God and Christ joined together.)

Commentaries on Chapter 20

THE VISION
OF HOLINESS

I. Holy Week
Commentary by Greg Mackie

This section and the next were dictated during Holy Week in 1967. They are an extension of the material I covered in the last section, "The Lifting of the Veil" (T-19.IV(D).i). As such, they are still discussing the same scenario: two holy relationship partners standing before the final obstacle to peace, the fear of God. Obviously, much of the material can be applied more generally as well, but this is the original context. This material presents a radically new interpretation of Holy Week.

> 1. This is Palm Sunday, the celebration of victory and the <u>acceptance</u> of the truth. Let us not spend this holy week brooding on the crucifixion of God's Son, but happily in the celebration of his <u>release</u>. For Easter is the sign of peace, not pain. A slain Christ has no meaning. But a <u>risen</u> Christ becomes the symbol of the Son of God's forgiveness on [Ur: upon] <u>himself</u>; the sign he looks upon himself as healed and whole.

Holy Week begins with Palm Sunday, which commemorates Jesus' triumphal entry into Jerusalem, where the multitudes spread palm fronds before him and shouted, "Blessed is he that cometh in the name of the Lord; Hosanna in the highest" (Matthew 21:9, KJV). It ends with Easter, which commemorates his resurrection. Here, Palm Sunday represents the "acceptance of the truth" that began our holy relationship—the holy instant in which we joined in the Holy Spirit's goal of truth—and Easter represents reaching that goal, the resurrection that comes when we forgive one another and go beyond the final veil.

What's de-emphasized here is the event that comes between Palm Sunday and Easter: the crucifixion. Jesus says that "a slain Christ has no meaning," a radical departure from traditional Christianity, in which Paul's statement that "we preach Christ crucified" (1 Corinthians 1:23) is virtually a summary of the faith. The traditional Holy Week liturgy spends much time "brooding on the crucifixion," and in traditional theology the crucifixion is *the* event which brought about the Atonement. But in the Course, it was the resurrection that brought about the Atonement (see

177

T-3.I.1:2), and it is this we should celebrate during Holy Week: both Jesus' resurrection and our own, the symbol that our own forgiveness has come to heal us and restore us to wholeness.

> 2. This week begins with palms and ends with lilies, the white and holy sign the Son of God is innocent. Let no dark sign [Ur: signs] of crucifixion intervene between the journey and its purpose; between the <u>acceptance</u> of the truth [Palm Sunday] and its <u>expression</u> [Easter]. This week we celebrate [Ur: eternal] life, <u>not</u> death. And we honor the perfect <u>purity</u> of the Son of God, and <u>not</u> his sins. Offer your brother [Ur: each other] the gift of lilies, <u>not</u> the crown of thorns; the gift of love and <u>not</u> the "gift" of fear. You stand beside your brother [Ur: each other], thorns in one hand and lilies in the other, uncertain which to give. Join now with me and throw away the thorns, offering the lilies to <u>replace</u> them. This Easter I would have the gift of your forgiveness offered by you to me, and <u>returned</u> by me to you. We <u>cannot</u> be united in crucifixion and in death. Nor can the resurrection be complete till <u>your</u> forgiveness rests on Christ, along with mine.

Holy Week is the celebration of life rather than death, of purity rather than sin. To celebrate it properly, then, we must not let the crucifixion and the sin it represents come between the *acceptance* of the truth (represented by Palm Sunday) and the *expression* of the truth (represented by Easter). The way we do this is described in beautiful imagery: We must offer each other the gift of lilies instead of the crown of thorns; love and forgiveness instead of fear and condemnation. In everyday terms, we must be kind to our partner when he leaves the toilet seat up instead of giving him "the look." By joining with Jesus in forgiving each other, we offer *him* forgiveness and receive it back from him. Only in this way will the resurrection that began with Jesus' resurrection two thousand years ago be complete.

> 3. A week is short, and yet this holy week is the symbol of the whole journey the Son of God has undertaken. He started with the sign of victory, the promise of the resurrection, <u>already</u> given him [Palm Sunday]. Let him not wander into the temptation of crucifixion, and <u>delay</u> him there. Help him to go in peace <u>beyond</u> it, with the light of his own innocence lighting his way to his redemption and release. Hold him not back with thorns and nails when his redemption is so near. But

178

let the whiteness of your shining gift of lilies speed him on his way to resurrection [Easter].

Holy Week is a microcosm of the entire spiritual journey. That journey began as soon as we separated, but it began in a more substantial way in that "Palm Sunday" holy instant when we joined in a holy relationship—like the instant Helen and Bill joined in search of a better way. All through the journey, though, we are tempted to crucify each other with our many grievances, a temptation we give in to all too often. This temptation is still in force as we stand together before the final veil. But here, we have the opportunity to end the journey by helping each other go in peace beyond crucifixion. We accomplish this through offering each other forgiveness, the gift of lilies, which speeds us both (and everyone) to the "Easter" resurrection than brings the journey to a close.

> 4. Easter is not the celebration of the *cost* of sin, but of its *end*. If you see glimpses of the face of Christ behind the veil, looking between the snow white petals of the lilies you have received and <u>given</u> as your gift, you will behold your brother's [Ur: each other's] face and <u>recognize</u> it. I was a stranger and you took me in, not knowing who I was. Yet for your gift of lilies you <u>will</u> know. In your <u>forgiveness</u> of this stranger, alien to you and yet your ancient Friend, lies <u>his</u> release and <u>your</u> redemption <u>with</u> him. The time of Easter is a time of <u>joy</u>, and not of mourning. Look on your risen Friend, and celebrate his holiness along with me. For Easter is the time of <u>your</u> salvation, along with mine.

Traditionally, Holy Week *is* the celebration of the cost of sin, for it celebrates Jesus dying to pay for our sins. But Jesus taking on our punishment doesn't really end our sins, for "what must be punished, must be true" (T-19.III.2:5). Jesus calls us now to a new way of celebrating Holy Week that truly *ends* sin.

That way, as we've seen, is through forgiveness, through giving the gift of lilies instead of the crown of thorns. Our partner was a stranger when we took him in and joined him in a holy relationship; little did we know that in doing so we took in Jesus, and the Christ Whom Jesus symbolizes (a reference to Matthew 25:34-40; see also T-19.IV(D).12-14). Yet our gift of lilies will reveal the face of Christ peering between their petals, and we will learn that this "stranger" is in fact our ancient

Friend. As we join Jesus in beholding our risen Friend in our brother, we are resurrected with him. This is how Jesus wants us to celebrate Easter.

Visualization: Holy Week

This is another of Robert's visualizations. Think of someone who makes the journey to God with you, perhaps the same one you used in the previous section's visualization:

Now picture this person in a white robe, sitting astride a donkey, riding through the gates of Jerusalem.
It is Palm Sunday.
The crowds are lining the street to see the Son of God triumphantly enter the Holy City.
They are cheering and laying palm fronds down before her.
Realize that this entry into Jerusalem symbolizes this person's acceptance of the truth, her point of entry onto the spiritual path.
She entered the path as the Son of God, with the promise of total victory given her.
The cheering crowds, the entire victorious scene, are proclaiming that spiritual victory is already hers.
Their cheers are saying, "You are going to make it. We *know* you will."

She gets off of the donkey and begins to walk, full of optimism.
You go up to her and begin to walk beside her.
She pauses before a fork in the road, wondering which way to take, the left or the right.
As she does, you realize that you have a gift for her in each hand.
In one hand, you hold a crown of thorns, its points poking at your palm.
In the other hand, you hold beautiful lilies, with snow white petals.

You look at the crown of thorns.
It symbolizes all of the sins you see in her, and all the ones she sees in herself.
It is what all of your resentments and irritations about her affirm that

she deserves.

Each thorn represents payment for some unkind word, some inconsiderate deed, some ugly trait of hers.

Your eyes narrow, remembering every one of these sins, and you drop the lilies in the dust, using both hands to lift the crown of thorns onto her head and press it down.

She meekly accepts this gift, for she knows she is guilty.

And she walks on, taking the left hand path. As she does, soldiers immediately come up, lay a cross on her shoulder for her to carry, begin to whip her and jeer at her.

Crowds form around her to witness the gruesome spectacle.

You see that the road she is on leads straight to Golgotha, the place of crucifixion.

You deeply regret what you have done and wish you could roll back the hands of time.

Then you find that they *have* been rolled back.

She is back standing at the fork in the road, and you are standing beside her.

Jesus is standing there with you, also. He speaks to you:

"You stand beside your sister, thorns in one hand and lilies in the other, uncertain which one to give.

Join now with me and throw away the thorns, offering the lilies to replace them."

With Jesus' hand on your shoulder, you toss the thorns aside,

And hold out the lilies to your white-robed sister.

These lilies represent her shining innocence.

Their whiteness represents her perfect holiness as a Son of God.

More specifically, they represent the manifestation of her holiness: her resurrection.

They represent her Easter morning, her ultimate spiritual victory, the very thing she has entered the Holy City to achieve.

By giving them to her you are saying:

"You will make it. You are so holy that the only destiny that fits you is resurrection.

This gift is the expression of my certainty that you will get there."

She accepts this gift from you.

The lilies begin to literally shine and so does she.

A light seems to come out from them, pointing out the right-hand path to her.

She takes it, with renewed confidence and a brisker step.

As she walks up the gently sloping road, you see her behaving more and more like the Christ.

She touches people and they are healed. She speaks to them, and they are comforted.

Days pass and Sunday comes around again.

You find yourself outside the city, standing before your friend's tomb, just before sunrise.

This tomb does not imply that she has been crucified for her sins, for you helped her escape that road.

This is the tomb of her ego, which has walled her off from true life for so long.

The edge of the sun appears above the horizon and, very quietly, the stone rolls away from the entrance.

A light shines from inside the tomb and she emerges, bathed in light. She has left the prison of her ego.

The light is so bright that you can barely make out a form inside it.

But you can see her face, and from the wisdom and love and peace on it, you can see that she has overcome everything in her but God.

You can make out one more form in the light: In her hand she holds a single white lily; your gift to her.

Jesus once again is beside you. He has come to celebrate this great event.

Hear him speak to you:

"Look on your risen Friend, and celebrate her holiness along with me. For Easter is the time of your salvation, along with mine."

II. The Gift of Lilies
Commentary by Robert Perry

1. Look upon all the trinkets made to hang upon the body, or to cover it or for its use. See all the useless things made for its eyes to see. Think on the many offerings made for its pleasure, and remember all these were made to make seem lovely what you hate. Would you employ this hated thing to draw your brother to you, and to attract <u>his</u> body's eyes? Learn you but offer him a crown of thorns, not recognizing it for what it is, and trying to justify your <u>own</u> interpretation of its value by <u>his</u> acceptance. Yet still the gift proclaims his worthlessness to <u>you</u>, as his acceptance and delight acknowledges the lack of value <u>he</u> places on himself.

Application. You can do this either mentally, or by flicking through a magazine or photo album:

> Look upon all the trinkets made to hang upon the body.
> Look on the clothing made to cover it.
> Look on all the things we put on it to make other eyes enjoy it.
> Now realize that all these things were made to make seem lovely what you hate.
> Realize that by offering this hated thing to others, you are offering them a crown of thorns.

Why do we hate the body? Because, in some deep place in us, we hold the body responsible for dragging us down from Heaven, making us separate, base, and aggressive—making us *animal*. To get the sense of this, imagine that you had a mind transplant into a body that was hideous and misshapen and full of overpowering antisocial urges. Would you then doll it up to attract other people to you? Especially realizing the real nature of the bait you were offering? And if you did, wouldn't you just be trying to convince yourself this body wasn't so bad by getting someone else to like it? And if someone did get excited about it, what would that say about the value he put on *himself*?

> 2. Gifts are not made through bodies, if they be truly given and received. For bodies can neither offer nor accept; hold out nor take. Only the mind can value, and only the mind decides on what it would receive and give. And every gift it offers depends on what it <u>wants</u>. It will adorn its chosen home most carefully, making it ready to <u>receive</u> the gifts it wants by offering them to those who come unto its chosen home, or those it would <u>attract</u> to it. And there they will exchange their gifts, offering and receiving what their minds judge to be worthy of them.

All that bodies can do is exchange mindless, meaningless forms. That is not real giving and receiving. Only minds can truly give and receive, for only they can *value*. Yet this doesn't mean they cannot value wrongly. If the mind sees the body as its home, it will adorn that home in order to advertise the gifts it has to offer, which are offered in exchange for the gifts it wants to receive.

Application: What are the gifts that you use your body to advertise? What gifts are you hoping to receive from others in return? What does this say about what you consider to be worthy of you?

> 3. Each gift is an <u>evaluation</u> of the receiver <u>and the</u> *giver*. No one but sees his chosen home as an altar to <u>himself</u>. No one but seeks to <u>draw</u> to it the worshippers of what he placed <u>upon</u> it, making it <u>worthy</u> of their devotion. And each has set a light upon his altar, that they may see what he has placed upon it and take it for their own. Here is the value that you lay upon your brother and on <u>yourself</u>. Here is your gift to <u>both</u>; your judgment on the Son of God for what he is. Forget not that it is <u>your</u> savior to whom the gift is offered. Offer him thorns and *you* are crucified. Offer him lilies and it is <u>yourself</u> you free.

Think of your body as an altar to yourself. Upon this altar you place sacred objects in order to make the altar worthy of the devotion of your desired worshippers. Finally, you set a light on it, so that people cannot fail to see those sacred objects and be drawn to worship there. Yet if what you offer is of the body, then your sacred objects are really just cheap plastic. Worse, they are just crowns of thorns disguised as jeweled crowns. And if you think your brother is worthy only of a crown of thorns, then you will think you too are worthy only of that.

Yet you can do this differently. You can place lilies of forgiveness on your altar. Imagine that being what you advertised. What if your whole way of being was a kind of billboard that constantly gave the message, "When you come here, you receive the gift of forgiveness"?

> 4. I have great need for lilies, for the Son of God has not forgiven me. And can I offer <u>him</u> forgiveness when he offers thorns to me? For he who offers thorns to anyone is against me still, and who is whole <u>without</u> him? Be you his friend for me, that I may be forgiven and you may look upon the Son of God as whole. But look you first upon the altar in your chosen home, and see what you have laid upon it to offer me. If it be thorns whose points gleam sharply in a blood-red light, the body is your chosen home and it is separation that you offer me. And yet the thorns are gone. Look you still closer at them now, and you will see your altar is no longer what it was.

The logic in the first sentences seems to go like this: If a person offers thorns to anyone, he offer thorns to Jesus. Offering thorns to Jesus blocks Jesus from giving lilies to this person. Being without lilies makes this person incapable of realizing he is truly part of the Sonship. While he sees himself as separate from the Sonship, the Sonship cannot perceive itself as whole. Therefore, *you* need to give this person lilies, for by doing so, you can undo the entire cycle.

The question, then, is: Does anyone come to mind who is constantly offering thorns? And then: How can you offer this person lilies instead?

But first, says Jesus, look upon your altar and see whether you are offering thorns or lilies to others and thereby to Jesus. He says that if you look deeply enough, you will realize that the thorns have been replaced by lilies. The belief in sin has been uprooted and replaced by the Holy Spirit's peace.

> 5. You look still with the body's eyes, and they <u>can</u> see but thorns. Yet you have asked for <u>and received</u> another sight. Those who accept the Holy Spirit's purpose as their own share also His vision. And what enables Him to <u>see</u> His purpose shine forth from every altar now is yours as well as His. He sees <u>no</u> strangers; only dearly loved and loving

friends. He sees no thorns but only lilies, gleaming in the gentle glow of peace that shines on everything He looks upon and loves.

This is yet another reference to the deep-level transformation that took place when the holy relationship began. At that point, we were given a new kind of sight, which looks past the body. Rather than seeing a collection of bodies hawking their wares and strutting their stuff, this vision sees a holy purpose shine forth from every person's altar. It sees only dearly loved and loving friends, whose altars are piled with gleaming lilies, bathed in the gentle glow of peace. Would we like to see the world this way?

> 6. This Easter, look with <u>different</u> eyes upon your brother [Ur: each other]. You *have* forgiven me. And yet I cannot <u>use</u> your gift of lilies while you see them not. Nor can <u>you</u> use what I have given unless you <u>share</u> it. The Holy Spirit's vision is no idle gift, no plaything to be tossed about a while and laid aside.

You have been given the gift of vision, within which is contained the forgiveness of everyone, including Jesus. But until you give this gift to your brother, until you actually use it, it can't do you any good. Isn't it strange how we treat the spiritual gifts we are given? We do treat them as playthings, as Jesus implies here, to be picked up, tossed about a while and laid aside, forgotten.

Application: Are there any spiritual gifts that you've been given that you've treated as playthings, to be played with a bit and then laid aside?

> Listen and hear this carefully, nor think it but a dream, a careless thought to play with, or a toy you would pick up from time to time and then put by. For if you do, so will it be to you.

I believe these lines refer to the following paragraph. He is readying us to take that paragraph much more seriously than we normally would. So let's do that. Let's listen to this paragraph and hear it carefully, and not see it is only a dream, a toy to play with and then set aside. Let's read it very slowly and insert our name at the asterisks.

> 7. You have the vision now * to look past <u>all</u> illusions. It has been given

186

you * to see no thorns, no strangers and <u>no</u> obstacles to peace. *The fear of God is <u>nothing</u> to you now. Who is afraid to look upon illusions, <u>knowing</u> his savior stands beside him? <u>With</u> him, * your vision has become the greatest power for the <u>undoing</u> of illusion that God Himself could give. For what God gave the Holy Spirit, * <u>you</u> have received. The Son of God looks unto <u>you</u> * for his release. For * you have asked for <u>and been given</u> the strength to look upon this final obstacle, and see no thorns nor nails to crucify the Son of God, and crown him king of death.

How do you feel having read it that way? How do you feel about this power you've been given? Do you really want to treat it like a three-year-old treats a new toy, to be idly played with for a day and then discarded?

8. Your chosen home is on the other side, <u>beyond</u> the veil [the veil before the face of Christ]. It has been carefully prepared for you, and it is ready to receive you now. You will not see it with the body's eyes. Yet all you need you have. Your home has called to you since time began, nor have you ever failed entirely to hear. You heard, but knew not <u>how</u> to look, nor <u>where</u>. And now you <u>know</u>. In you the knowledge lies, ready to be unveiled and freed from all the terror [the fear of God] that kept it hidden. There *is* no fear in love. The song of Easter is the glad refrain the Son of God was <u>never</u> crucified. Let us lift up our eyes together, not in fear but <u>faith</u>. And there <u>will</u> be no fear in us, for in our vision will be <u>no</u> illusions; only a pathway to the open door of Heaven, the home we share in quietness and where we live in gentleness and peace, as one together.

Our real home is not the body; it is Heaven. Which one would you prefer as a home? Our real home is not a house we deck out with gaudy lights to draw gawking onlookers. This home has been prepared *for* us. It has called to us since time began and we have heard, we just didn't know how or where to look. But now we have this *vision*, the vision to see past the body, past the veil, past the fear of God. If now we will only raise our eyes with our holy relationship partner and with Jesus, we will see what we have longed for eons to see: "a pathway to the open door of Heaven," a pathway *home*.

9. Would you not have your holy brother lead you there? His innocence will light your way, offering you its guiding light and sure protection, and shining from the holy altar within him where you laid the lilies of forgiveness. Let him be to you the savior from illusions, and look on him with the new vision that looks upon the lilies and brings <u>you</u> joy. We go beyond the veil of fear, lighting each other's way. The holiness that leads us is <u>within</u> us, as is our home. So will we find what we were <u>meant</u> to find by Him Who leads us.

What we see before us is a *pathway* to the open door of Heaven, which means we still have to walk along that pathway to get to the door. Yet we are walking through the dark, and it is easy to lose our way. How often do we have that nagging suspicion that we have walked slightly off the path? How do we make sure that we stay on? The surprising answer here is that our brother lights the way for us. The lilies of forgiveness that we have given him lie on his inner altar, and shine out from there, lighting our way.

Application: Picture yourself on the path in the dark, afraid that you'll wander off the path and get lost. Now imagine someone beside you, to whom you have given lilies of forgiveness. Envision those lilies lying on his or her inner altar, and radiating the gentle glow of peace. That glow shines onto the path in front of you, lighting your way. Feel the relief of knowing that you need never lose your way again.

10. This is the way to Heaven and to the peace of Easter, in which we join in glad awareness that the Son of God is risen from the past, and has awakened to the present. Now is he free, unlimited in his communion with all that is within him. Now are the lilies of his innocence untouched by guilt, and perfectly protected from the cold chill of fear and withering blight of sin alike. Your gift has saved him from the thorns and nails, and his strong arm is free to guide you safely through them and <u>beyond</u>. Walk with him now rejoicing, for the savior from illusions has come to greet you, and lead you home with <u>him</u>.

By giving lilies to this brother, you have saved him. Because of your gift, the lovely white lilies of his innocence are protected from both the freezing chill of fear and the fungal rot of sin, as well as from the thorns and nails of crucifixion. And now he will return the favor. He will now become your savior from illusions. His strong arm is free to guide you safely through the perils of crucifixion and beyond. Is there someone in your life who fits this description—someone who has been saved by your love and forgiveness, and whose inner light is now bright enough to turn around and save you?

> 11. Here is your savior and your friend, <u>released</u> from crucifixion through <u>your</u> vision, and free to lead you now where <u>he</u> would be. He will not leave you, nor forsake the savior in [Ur: the savior from] <u>his</u> pain. And gladly will you and your brother [Ur: will you] walk the way of innocence together, singing as you behold the open door of Heaven and <u>recognize</u> the home that called to you. Give joyously to your brother [Ur: one another] the freedom and the strength to lead you there. And come before his [Ur: each other's] holy altar where the strength and freedom wait, to offer and receive the bright awareness that leads you home. The lamp is lit in you for your brother [Ur: The lamp is lit in both of you, for one another]. And by the hands that <u>gave</u> it to him [Ur: each other] shall you be led past fear to love.

What a beautiful vision of mutuality. The two of you need each other. Neither of you can make it back alone. Yet each of you carries within you a holy altar, on which sits a lamp, and this lamp lights the way *for the other*. And so each of you shines this light upon the other, giving him the strength to lead *you* home. And then each of you comes before the other's altar, to draw strength and freedom from it, almost as if you are standing before a warm fire on a cold night. In this way, you lead each other home. And as you finally come near the open door of Heaven, you break into song together, singing that glad refrain, "The Son of God was never crucified."

Are we prepared to accept this kind of mutuality on the journey home? Are we ready to accept that we can't do it alone? That we need each other? Each of us needs to light the way home for someone else, and each of us needs to let someone else light the way home for *us*.

III. Sin as an Adjustment
Commentary by Robert Perry

1. The belief in sin is an <u>adjustment</u>. And an adjustment is a <u>change</u>; a shift in perception, or a belief that what was so before has been made <u>different</u>. Every adjustment is therefore a <u>distortion,</u> and calls upon defenses to uphold it <u>against</u> reality. Knowledge requires <u>no</u> adjustments and, in fact, is lost if any shift or change is undertaken. For this reduces it at once to mere perception; a way of <u>looking</u> in which <u>certainty</u> is lost and <u>doubt</u> has entered. To this <u>impaired</u> condition *are* adjustments necessary, because it is not true [Ur: *Because they are not true*]. Who need adjust to truth, which calls on only what he <u>is,</u> to understand?

We rely on adjustment every day. We speak of being "well adjusted," a positive goal that takes many years of growing up to achieve. A child's fantasies of what he wants the world to be simply do not fit the actual world, and so he needs to adjust those fantasies, or there will be constant friction between him and everyone else.

But this paragraph speaks of adjustment as a negative thing. Why? Because to adjust is to make something different, and if reality is changeless, then adjustment is simply a distortion, a twisting of what is. It is reality seen in a funhouse mirror. In our natural state, we need no adjustment. We are in complete harmony with reality. Adjustments are only needed when there is lack of fit, yet the fit between us and reality is perfect. Therefore, for us to know the truth requires no adjustment. It requires us only to be what we are.

2. Adjustments of <u>any</u> kind are of the ego. For it is the ego's fixed belief that all relationships <u>depend</u> upon adjustments, to make of them what it would have them be. <u>Direct</u> relationships, in which there are <u>no</u> interferences, are <u>always</u> seen as dangerous. The ego is the self-appointed mediator of <u>all</u> relationships, making whatever adjustments it deems necessary and <u>interposing</u> them <u>between</u> those who would meet, to keep them separate and <u>prevent</u> their union. It is this studied interference that makes it difficult for you to recognize your holy relationship for what it <u>is</u>.

III. Sin as an Adjustment

In every relationship, the ego is eager to tell us how to make it work. It says, "Look, the two of you can make a great couple, even though you are starting off so far apart. All you need to do is listen to me. You, dear, will need to make a lot of compromises for him. That's your job as the woman, you know. And you, honey, will need lots of training from her. By the time it's over, you might even be civilized."

The problem with this, though, is that just as we have an inherently perfect fit with reality, so we have an inherently perfect fit with each other. Joining with another, then, doesn't require an endless series of adjustments. Rather, it requires both parties to "un-adjust," to return to the original nature they possessed before all the adjustments were introduced. Yet the unity that would result from this is exactly what the ego is afraid of. So it steps in as a mediator—the mediator from hell. For this mediator is *self*-appointed and steps in between *harmonious* parties in order to keep them *apart*. And every adjustment he recommends makes it harder for the two people to recognize their pre-existent unity.

Unfortunately, most of what we say and do in relationships comes from following the advice that this mediator whispered in our ear.

> 3. The holy do not interfere with truth. They are <u>not</u> afraid of it, for it is <u>within</u> the truth they recognize [Ur: *recognized*] their holiness, and rejoice [Ur: rejoiced] at what they see [Ur: saw]. They look [Ur: looked] on it directly, <u>without</u> attempting to <u>adjust</u> themselves to it, or it to them. And so they see [Ur: saw] that it was <u>in</u> them, <u>not</u> deciding first where they would have it be. Their looking merely asks [Ur: asked] a question, and it is what they see [Ur: *what they saw*] that answers them [Ur: that answered]. <u>You</u> make the world and <u>then</u> adjust to it, <u>and it to you</u>. Nor is there any difference between yourself and it in your perception, <u>which made them both</u>.

Perception is a constant game of adjusting. We adjust what we see to fit our desires and expectations. And we adjust our desires and expectations to fit what we see. We constantly play with both sides of the equation to bring about a fit between self and world. We call this maturity. In all of our adjusting, though, we don't realize that we are adjusting a false self to a false world, and that we made both of them.

But that is not how the holy work. They merely observe, without bias, without distortion, and without fear. While they look, they merely ask,

"What is the truth that lies before me now?" Through this process, they discover a radiant reality, one that not only fits them, but is one with them, even *within* them. This radiant reality is holy, and therefore reveals that *they* are holy.

> 4. A simple question yet remains, and needs an answer. Do you like what you have made?—a world of murder and attack, through which you thread your timid way through constant dangers, alone and frightened, hoping at most that death will wait a little longer before it overtakes you and you disappear. *You made this up.* It is a picture of what you think you are; of how you see yourself. A murderer *is* frightened, and those who kill fear death. All these are but the fearful thoughts of those who would adjust themselves to a world made fearful by their adjustments. And they look out in sorrow from what is sad within, and see the sadness there.

Application: While busy playing the adjustment game, we should all pause for a moment and ask ourselves: Do we like this game? So think about all the adjusting that you have had to do, adjusting of your desires, of your behavior, of your life, to fit into this world. Then think about all the adjusting you have tried to impose on the world, and how successful (or not) you've been, along with how you feel about being so pushy (or not). Then ask yourself who, on the whole, has won this game—you or the world. Finally, return to the beginning question: "Do I like this adjustment game?"

If you really think deeply about these questions, you will come up with a picture like Jesus gives here: "a world of murder and attack, through which you thread your timid way through constant dangers, alone and frightened, hoping at most that death will wait a little longer before it overtakes you and you disappear." He says we made this world, but why would we make a world like this? Because deep down, we believe that we have made *murderous adjustments* to ultimate reality, and as a result we believe that this is the world we deserve.

> 5. Have you not [Ur: Have you] wondered what the world is really like; how it would look through happy eyes? The world you see is but a judgment on yourself. It is not there at all. Yet judgment lays a

sentence on it, <u>justifies</u> it and <u>makes it real</u>. Such is the world you see; a judgment on yourself, and made by <u>you</u>. This sickly picture of yourself is carefully preserved by the ego, whose image it <u>is</u> and which it loves, and placed <u>outside</u> you in the world. And <u>to</u> this world must <u>you</u> adjust as long as you believe this picture <u>is</u> outside, and has you at its mercy. This world *is* merciless, and were it outside you, you <u>should</u> indeed be fearful. Yet it was <u>you</u> who made it merciless, and now if mercilessness <u>seems</u> to look back at you, <u>it can be corrected</u>.

Imagine a dictator who loudly claims that he has only tried to serve his people. But when he goes to sleep, his defenses drop and his guilt takes over his dreams. He dreams of a courtroom in which he is on trial for his crimes. The judge, the jury, the prosecuting attorney, the onlookers, and the media are all condemning him. This dream is his own judgment on himself. It is a picture of what, underneath all the conscious bravado, he thinks he really is.

We are that dictator, and this world is our dream. Our lives takes place inside this imaginary courtroom, and it is this courtroom which we spend our lives adjusting to. When you look about you now, you are looking at your courtroom. No wonder the adjustment game is so hard. It's not like we're adjusting to paradise.

This is the bad news, and the good. Don't you see the good side of this? *It's only a dream.* It's being dreamt from guilt in your mind, guilt which can be healed. If you looked at the same world through happy eyes, rather than guilty eyes, it would look completely different. That is the good news.

6. Who in a holy relationship can long remain unholy? The world the holy see is one with them, just as the world the ego looks upon is like itself. The world the holy see is beautiful because they see their innocence in it. They did not <u>tell</u> it what it was; they did not make adjustments to fit their orders. They gently questioned it and whispered, "What are you?" And He Who watches over all perception answered. Take not the judgment of the world as answer to the question, "What am I?" The world <u>believes</u> in sin, but the belief that made it as you see it is <u>not</u> outside you.

We have a choice. We can look upon a world made by our adjustments, a world whose essential nature is to frown on us for our sins, and ask of it, "What am I?" We all know what its answer is. It is the answer we have been both fighting off and reluctantly internalizing our whole lives.

Or we can look on the world in complete innocence, not attempting to make a single adjustment. Rather than asking "What am I?" we can ask "What are you?" In other words, we can see the world as it really is. We will then discover that it is one with us, and that it proclaims our innocence, not our guilt.

Imagine two people in the second mode being in relationship with each other. That would be a truly realized holy relationship.

> 7. Seek not to make the Son of God <u>adjust</u> to his insanity. There <u>is</u> a stranger in him, who wandered carelessly into the home of truth and who will wander off. He came <u>without</u> a purpose, but he will not remain before the shining light the Holy Spirit offered, and you accepted. For there the <u>stranger</u> is made homeless and *you* are welcome. Ask not this transient stranger, "What [Ur: who] am I?" He is the only thing in all the universe that does not know. Yet it is he you ask, and it is to <u>his</u> answer that you would adjust. This one wild thought, fierce in its arrogance, and yet so tiny and so meaningless it slips unnoticed through the universe of truth, becomes your guide. To it you turn to ask the <u>meaning</u> of the universe. And of the one blind thing in all the seeing universe of truth you ask, "How shall I look upon the Son of God?"

When you adjust yourself to the world, you are really adjusting yourself to your own ego. When you ask the world "What am I?" you are really asking that of your ego. For it made the world. The ego is just a homeless stranger that wandered into the home of your mind and kicked you out. Now, you spend your days standing outside, poking your head in the window, and having friendly chats with this stranger. You regard him as the master of the house and something of a wise man, despite his unsavory combination of fierce arrogance and total ignorance. Worst of all, you humbly ask him who you are, and when in response he spins elaborate theories, which are obviously total lies, you believe every word.

We need to apply this comical image to ourselves. We draw conclusions about who we are based on watching ourselves thread our timid way through a dangerous world. Isn't that how we form our self-images? Yet in doing so, we are living out that comical image. We are believing the lies of the homeless stranger.

The key here is to refuse to adjust our concept of ourselves to what the world tells us we are. The world will always tell us that we are lowly *homo sapiens*, yet we are the Sons of God. Let us resolve to not bend an inch for the world's judgment of our holy nature.

> 8. Does one ask judgment of what is totally <u>bereft</u> of judgment? And if you <u>have</u>, would you <u>believe</u> the answer, and <u>adjust</u> to it as if it were the truth? The world you look on <u>is</u> the answer that it gave you, and <u>you</u> have given it power to <u>adjust</u> the world to <u>make</u> its answer true. You asked this puff of madness for the meaning of your unholy relationship, and adjusted it according to its insane answer. How happy did it make you? Did you meet your brother [Ur: Did you meet] with joy to bless the Son of God, and give him thanks for all the happiness that he held out to you? Did you <u>recognize</u> your brother [Ur: each other] as the eternal gift of God to you? Did you see the holiness that shone in both you and your brother [Ur: in both of you], to bless the other? That is the purpose of your <u>holy</u> relationship. Ask not the means of its attainment of the one thing that still would have it be unholy. Give it <u>no</u> power to <u>adjust</u> the means and end.

Notice how the homeless stranger that barged into your house is also the self-appointed mediator that barged into your relationship. Very telling images of the ego, aren't they?

Application: Think of a relationship that you would consider unholy (special). Realize that you adjusted the relationship according to the advice of the self-appointed mediator, the homeless stranger. Now ask yourself these questions:

> *How happy did it make me?*
> *Did I meet with joy to bless the Son of God—[name]—and give him thanks for all the happiness that he held out to me?*
> *Did we recognize each other as the eternal gift of God to us?*
> *Did we see the holiness that shone in both of us, to bless the other?*

It is because the answers are "no" that we seek the holy relationship. Its purpose is to enable us to sincerely answer "yes" to each of these questions. When it is formed, that meddling mediator gets kicked out. Now, we are back in the house, but he's still knocking. Do we really want to invite him back in and say, "Now that I'm in a holy relationship, can you guide us in how to reach our goal?"

> 9. Prisoners bound with heavy chains for years, starved and emaciated, weak and exhausted, and with eyes so long cast down in darkness they remember not the light, do not leap up in joy the instant they are made free. It takes a while for them to understand what freedom is. You groped but feebly in the dust and found your brother's [Ur: each other's] hand, uncertain whether to let it go or to take hold on life so long forgotten. Strengthen your hold and raise your eyes unto your strong companion, in whom the meaning of your freedom lies. He seemed to be crucified beside you. And yet his holiness remained untouched and perfect, and with him beside you, you shall this day enter with him to Paradise, and know the peace of God.

Helen and Bill are still in the old mold. They don't realize the profound change that has taken place. Even though they have formed a holy relationship, they are still taking their advice from the mediator from hell. Even though the concentration camp has been liberated, they still huddle in their dark cell, as if nothing has happened. Even though they finally found a brother's hand in the dust, they still act is if they are lost in the desert, all alone.

They have it all wrong. They are each seeing the other as a footnote, when they need to see that person as the *Christ*. In a moving passage, Jesus references the famous image of the thief on the cross, which I'll quote here:

> One of the criminals who were hanged there was hurling abuse at Him....But the other...was saying, "Jesus, remember me when You come in Your kingdom!" And He said to him, "Truly I say to you, today you shall be with Me in Paradise." (Luke 23)

Jesus has applied this image to our holy relationship. Now *we* are the thief, and we need to look over at our brother, the one who seems to be crucified next to us, all too human and wounded, and acknowledge that *he* is the Christ. If we do, he has the power to take us to Paradise.

10. Such [Paradise] is my will for you and your brother [Ur: for *both* of you], and for each of you for one another and for <u>himself</u>. Here there is only holiness and joining without limit. For what is Heaven but union, direct and perfect, and <u>without</u> the veil of fear upon it? Here are we one, looking with perfect gentleness upon each other and on ourselves. Here all thoughts of <u>any</u> separation between us become impossible. You who were a prisoner [Ur: prisoners] in separation are now made free in Paradise. And here would I unite with you, my friend, my brother and my Self [Ur: my friends, my brothers and my Self].

This brother beside us may look beaten up and bedraggled, but if we see him for who he is, he can take us to Paradise, to Heaven. There, there are no adjustments and no need for them. Can we even imagine such a state? Adjustments only make sense when there is a lack of fit, and everything in Heaven fits perfectly, allowing for direct, unmediated, unlimited union. This is Jesus' will for us, to go from being prisoners in separation to being free in Paradise. And there, the fit with him is perfect, too, and so there he would unite with us. For he regards us his friends, as his brothers, and even as his own Self.

11. Your gift unto your brother [Ur: each other] has given me the certainty our union will be soon. Share, then, this faith [that this union will be soon] with me, and know [Ur: who *know*] that it [the faith] is justified. There is no fear in perfect love *because* it knows no sin, and it <u>must</u> look on others as on itself. Looking with charity within, what can it fear <u>without</u>? The innocent see safety, and the pure in heart see God within His Son, and look unto the Son to lead them to the Father. And where else would they go but where they will to be? You and your brother [Ur: Each of you] now will lead the other to the Father as surely as God created His Son holy, and kept him so. In your brother is the light of God's eternal promise of <u>your</u> immortality. See <u>him</u> as sinless, and there can *be* no fear in you.

Jesus is certain that our union with him in Heaven, and with each other, will be soon. We need to share his faith. And we would if we could only look with the eyes of innocence, rather than the eyes of adjustment. Innocent eyes look within and see innocence there, and then look without and see purity in our brother. They see such purity that they look to him to lead us home. Are we willing to see that much purity in him? To see him as not just tolerable, but as containing something so holy that we look to that holiness to light our pathway to Heaven? If we are, all our fears will melt away. And we will know that Heaven is right around the corner.

IV. Entering the Ark
Commentary by Robert Perry

1. Nothing can hurt you unless you give it the power to do so. Yet *you* give power as the laws of this world <u>interpret</u> giving; as you give you <u>lose</u>. It is not up to you to give power at all. Power is of God, <u>given</u> by Him and <u>reawakened</u> by the Holy Spirit, Who knows that as you give you <u>gain</u>. He gives <u>no</u> power to sin, and therefore it <u>has</u> none; nor to its results as this world sees them,—sickness and death and misery and pain. These things have not occurred because the Holy Spirit sees them not, and gives no power to their seeming source [sin]. Thus would He keep you free of them. Being without illusion of what you are, the Holy Spirit merely gives <u>everything</u> to God, Who has already given <u>and</u> <u>received</u> all that is true. The <u>un</u>true He has neither received <u>nor</u> given.

As we all know, we readily give our power away, but we aren't really giving it to other people. If we genuinely gave them power, our own power would be increased. Rather, we give our power away to sin and its results—sickness, death, misery, and pain. This is what gives sin the power to hurt us. What we are doing, then, is not giving power to our brother, but to our perception of sin in our brother. That's what is hurting us. We need to realize that we are giving power to the powerless. When the Holy Spirit looks on that sin in our brother, He doesn't see anything. He merely sees a cry for help coming out of a sense of weakness. If we will only see as He does, then, we will be free of all that hurts us now.

Application: Think of several things you see as having power over you, and say,

> *Nothing can hurt me unless I give it the power to do so.*
> *The Holy Spirit doesn't give any power to this, and so I don't either.*

2. Sin has no place in Heaven, where its results are alien and can no more enter than can their source [sin itself]. And therein lies your need

to see your brother sinless. In him *is* Heaven. See sin in him <u>instead</u>, and Heaven is lost to <u>you</u>. But see him as he <u>is</u>, and what is yours shines from him to you. Your savior gives you <u>only</u> love, but what you would <u>receive</u> of him is up to you. It lies in him to overlook <u>all</u> your mistakes, and therein lies his <u>own</u> salvation. And so it is with <u>yours</u>. Salvation is a lesson in giving [giving forgiveness to your brother], as the Holy Spirit interprets it. It is the reawakening of the laws of God [the law that giving and receiving are the same] in minds that have established <u>other</u> laws, and given them power to enforce what God created not.

There is no sin in Heaven. So if you see sin in your brother, you will not see Heaven. If you see him as he really is, however, you will see Heaven shining its love and blessing on you, awakening you, saving you. This is the gift you are supposed to give him. You are supposed to overlook all his mistakes, giving no power to the apparent sin in him, and acknowledging only his innate holiness. If this is the way that you give power, you will receive what you give. Rather than giving away your power to the merciless tyrant of sin, you will be exercising the law of God—that giving and receiving are the same.

Notice the mutuality here. You are called to overlook your brother's mistakes and reawaken the holiness in him, and he is called to do the same for you.

> 3. Your insane laws were made to <u>guarantee</u> that you would make mistakes, and give them power over you by <u>accepting</u> their results as your just due. What <u>could</u> this be but madness? And is it <u>this</u> that you would see within your savior <u>from</u> insanity? He is as free from this as you are, and in the freedom that you see in <u>him</u> you see your own. For this you <u>share</u>. What God has given follows <u>His</u> laws, and His alone. Nor is it possible for those who follow them to suffer the results of any other source.

Our laws make sure that we will make mistakes, see them as sins, and then see their results as our just punishment. Our laws, in other words, guarantee that we will see our lives held in the bony claw of sin. Jesus says that this, however, is madness. It flies in the face of reality. Is this madness what we want to see in our brother, the one who is meant to *save* us from madness? His reality is utterly free of the myth of sin's power, and if we see him as free of it, we will see ourselves as free, too.

4. Those who choose freedom will experience only <u>its</u> results. Their power is of God, and they will give it only to what <u>God</u> has given, [and He gave it] to <u>share</u> with them. Nothing but this can touch them, for they see <u>only</u> this, sharing their power according to the Will of God. And thus their freedom is established <u>and maintained</u>. It is upheld through <u>all</u> temptation [Ur: temptations] to imprison and to <u>be</u> imprisoned. It is of <u>them</u> who learned of freedom that you should ask what freedom <u>is</u>. Ask not the sparrow how the eagle soars, for those with little wings have not accepted for <u>themselves</u> the power to share with you.

If we want to know what freedom is, we need to look to those who have found it. We need to look to those spiritual giants who have been liberated. While the world we see is held in sin's bony claw, they seem remarkably at peace. They seem immune to this supposed power. Those who have not yet been liberated will tell us that freedom is all sorts of things, mostly the body's ability to do what it wants and get what it wants. But they are sparrows. Instead, we need to ask what freedom is from those who fly on eagles' wings, not sparrows' wings. They will tell you that freedom is seeing power only in what is of God, that freedom is looking on sin and giving it no power whatsoever.

Application: Think of the life of one of your spiritual heroes. Can you see in that life the idea that all power is of God, that anything which is not of God has no power at all?

5. The sinless give as they received. See, then, the power of sinlessness within your brother, and share with him the power of the <u>release</u> from sin you offered <u>him</u>. To each who walks this earth in seeming solitude is a savior given, whose special function here is to release him, and so to free himself. In the world of separation each is appointed separately, though they are all the same. Yet those who <u>know</u> that they are all the same need not salvation. And each one <u>finds</u> his savior when he is ready to look upon the face of Christ, and see Him sinless.

If you see the power of sinlessness within your brother, that power will shine forth onto your face. If you give your brother release from sin, you will share in that release. Notice that here again we are called on to save our savior. We cannot save ourselves. Instead, we save our savior, setting him free to save us. It's a different notion of salvation, isn't it?

Every single person alive, however alone he may seem, has been assigned a savior. This savior's whole purpose in life is to save this person, and thereby free himself. Yet this person will only find his savior when he is truly ready to receive the gift.

Application: Ask the Holy Spirit within, "Who is waiting to be given salvation (release from the perception of being sinful) by me?"

> 6. The plan is not of you, nor need you be concerned with anything except the part that has been given you to learn. For He Who knows the rest will see to it without your help. But think not that He does not need your part to help Him with the rest. For in your part lies all of it, without which is no part complete, nor is the whole completed without your part.

These lines are priceless. Our tendency is to worry about global issues that are really beyond our sphere, and while we worry, to neglect that small function that we *have* been called to. The irony is that the Holy Spirit doesn't need our help with the whole picture, but He does need us to do our little part. Indeed, He needs that little part for the *sake* of the whole picture, for it somehow contains the whole picture in miniature. It's as if He's baking a loaf of bread, and while we look over His shoulder, telling Him what He should do differently, we are neglecting to hand Him the yeast, which is the only element we are supposed to supply. How will the loaf turn out without that yeast?

> The ark of peace is entered two by two, yet the beginning of another world goes with them. Each holy relationship must enter here, to learn its special function in the Holy Spirit's plan, now that it shares His purpose. And as this purpose is fulfilled, a new world rises in which sin can enter not, and where the Son of God can enter without fear and where he rests a while, to forget imprisonment and to remember freedom. How can he enter, to rest and to remember, without you? Except you be there, he is not complete. And it is his completion that he remembers there.
> 7. This is the purpose given you. Think not that your forgiveness of your brother [Ur: each other] serves but you two alone. For the whole

new world rests in the hands of every two who enter here [into the ark] to rest. And as they rest, the face of Christ shines on them and they remember the laws of God, forgetting all the rest and yearning only to have His laws perfectly fulfilled in them and all their brothers. Think you when this [the laws being perfectly fulfilled in everyone] has been achieved that you will rest <u>without</u> them? You could no more leave one of them outside than I could leave you, and forget part of myself.

When I first got into the Course, that first line—"the ark of peace is entered two by two"—was quoted all the time. It's a beautiful line, yet to appreciate its full meaning, we have to think carefully about how the image of Noah's ark relates to this discussion. In the biblical image, the world is in the process of being destroyed for its sins. Everything is drowning and dying. Yet there is one place of safety in this universal deluge: the ark. This ark safely carries two members of every species, so that when the waters subside, they can be the seeds of a new earth, an earth ruled by God's covenant with the survivors and by God's promise never to destroy it again.

Now let's apply that to what is said in this section. The earth seems to be ruled by the power of sin and so is pervaded by its results—sickness, pain, death—all of which are supposed punishment for sin. Yet amidst all the chaos and destruction, there is one safe place: the holy instant. It is not a wooden boat; it is the temple within. What enters here are not pairs of animals, but pairs of people joined in a common purpose. "Each holy relationship must enter here." As these two enter this holy place to rest together, they forget the power of sin that rages outside its walls, and remember the power of God's law—that giving and receiving are the same. In this place of rest, they yearn "only to have His laws perfectly fulfilled in them and all their brothers." And they learn their unique contribution to this goal. They learn their joint special function, their little part in the Holy Spirit's larger plan. His plan, of course, is for a new world to arise "in which sin can enter not." They are one of the seeds of this world. And when that world has come, they will rest in its peace just as much as everyone else. They will not be like Moses, guiding people to the Promised Land but unable to enter himself.

How would you live your life differently if you really believed that you were one of the seeds of a new world, a world set free from the power of sin?

8. You may wonder how you can <u>be</u> at peace when, while you are in time, there is so much that must be done <u>before</u> the way to peace is open. Perhaps this seems impossible to <u>you</u>. But ask yourself if it is possible that <u>God</u> would have a plan for your salvation that does <u>not</u> work. Once you accept <u>His</u> plan as the <u>one</u> function that you would fulfill, there <u>will</u> be nothing else the Holy Spirit will not <u>arrange</u> for you <u>without</u> your effort. He will go before you making straight your path, and leaving in your way no stones to trip on, and no obstacles to bar your way. <u>Nothing</u> you need will be denied you. Not one seeming difficulty but will melt away <u>before</u> you reach it. You need take thought for nothing, careless of everything except the only purpose that you would fulfill. As <u>that</u> was given you, so will its fulfillment be. God's guarantee will hold against <u>all</u> obstacles, for it rests on certainty and <u>not</u> contingency. <u>It rests on</u> *you.* And what can be more certain than a Son of God?

This, too, is a beloved passage, yet we need to understand it in context. You've been given your special function as a savior of the world, a function in which you are supposed to draw everyone into peace. And yet, how can you yourself be at peace when your function keeps you so busy (you may recall those busy doings on which you are sent from "I Need Do Nothing")? There is just so much to be done between now and the dawning of that sinless world. Once they get off the ark, those zebras have a lot of work to do in populating the new world. If you have ever had a full-time spiritual or healing ministry, you know exactly how busy it can keep you.

How can we be at peace in the midst of all that the Holy Spirit asks us to do? The answer is: If we accept our special function as our *only* function, the Holy Spirit will take care of the minutiae involved in that function. In every such function, there is a core and a periphery. There is the laying on of hands and there is the paying of the bills. The promise here is that if we devote ourselves completely to the former, He will take care of the latter. That is why "You need take thought for nothing, careless of everything except the only purpose that you would fulfill."

The classic example of this is Jesus finding Helen a fur coat. He wanted to save her time for this, because, as he said, he had a better use for her time. Here are his comments as recorded in Ken Wapnick's *Absence from Felicity* (p. 235):

The reason I direct everything that is unimportant is because it is no way to waste *your* free will. If you insist on doing the trivial your way, you waste too much time and will on it. Will cannot be free if it is tied up in trivia. It never gets out.

I will tell you *exactly* what to do in connection with everything that does not matter. That is not an area where choice should be invested. There is better use of time. [He wanted her to take notes, something he explicitly mentioned during a long discourse on wasted time.]

You have to remember to ask Me to take charge of all minutiae, and they will be taken care of so well and so quickly that you cannot bog down in it.

V. Heralds of Eternity
Commentary by Robert Perry

1. In this world, God's Son comes closest to himself in a holy relationship. There he begins to find the certainty his Father has in him. And there he finds his function of restoring his Father's laws to what was held <u>outside</u> them, and finding what was lost. Only in time can anything <u>be</u> lost, and [Ur: but] never lost forever. So do the parts of God's Son gradually join in time, and with each joining is the end of time brought nearer. Each miracle of joining is a mighty herald of eternity. No one who has a single purpose, unified and sure, can <u>be</u> afraid. No one who <u>shares</u> his purpose with him can *not* be one with him.

That first line should rock our whole view of spirituality. If someone asked you how we come closest to our divine nature in this world, what would you say? Would you say, "We come closest to our true nature in a relationship in which we are joined in a common purpose"? Not very likely. Yet that is what this paragraph says. It says that in a holy relationship we find the certainty that God has in us; we find a Self that is worthy of God's infinite confidence.

But then it goes even further. It says that in a holy relationship we also find our function, which is to undo all that has been lost in time. And what has been lost? Oneness. With the advent of time, the parts of God's Son seemed to shatter into countless separate fragments. The job of each holy relationship is to put those fragments back together. "So do the parts of God's Son gradually join in time." One holy relationship, then, is like a reverse virus introduced into the whole system, causing *all* the parts to gradually come back together.

2. Each herald of eternity sings of the end of sin and fear. Each speaks in time of what is far <u>beyond</u> it. Two voices raised together call to the hearts of everyone, to let them beat as one. And in that single heartbeat is the unity of love proclaimed and given welcome. Peace to your holy relationship, which has the power to hold the unity of the Son of God together. You give to your brother [Ur: one another] for <u>everyone,</u> and in your gift is everyone made glad. Forget not Who has given <u>you</u> the

gifts you give, and through your <u>not</u> forgetting this, will you remember Who gave the gifts to Him to give to you.

What a beautiful image. Each holy relationship is a herald, announcing the imminent arrival of eternity. To perform this heralding function, both partners lift their voices together in song. Their song announces the end of separation and the dawn of unity. It calls to the hearts of everyone, and as the Sonship listens, all hearts respond, and begin to beat as one. Just imagine every single heart beating in unison. This one heartbeat signifies the Sonship realizing its unity. This, then, is the function of the holy relationship. Yes, each partner is engaged in saving the other, but this exchange of salvation is for a purpose that goes far beyond the two of them. It's for the sake of everyone.

If you feel you are in such a relationship, try to apply this image to it. See your relationship as a song that calls to everyone, to announce the end of separation, and to draw them into unity.

3. It is impossible to overestimate your brother's value. Only the ego does this ["This person's special love will be my total salvation"], but all it means is that it <u>wants</u> the other for <u>itself</u>, and therefore values him too little [he becomes a pawn, a toy]. What is inestimable clearly cannot <u>be</u> evaluated. Do you recognize the fear that rises from the meaningless attempt to judge what lies so far <u>beyond</u> your judgment you cannot even <u>see</u> it? Judge not what is invisible to you or you will <u>never</u> see it, but wait in patience for its coming. It will be <u>given</u> you to see your brother's worth when all you <u>want</u> for him is peace. And what you want for <u>him</u> you will receive.

4. How can you estimate the worth of him who offers peace to you? What would you want <u>except</u> his offering [peace]? His worth has been established by his Father, and you will <u>recognize</u> it as you receive his Father's gift through him. What is in him will shine so brightly in your grateful vision that you will merely love him and be glad. You will not think to judge him, for who ["who" begins a new sentence in the Urtext] would <u>see</u> the face of Christ and yet insist that judgment still has meaning? For this insistence is of those who do <u>not</u> see. Vision <u>or</u> judgment is your choice, but never <u>both</u> of these.

It seems so natural to evaluate the worth of others, doesn't it? Yet Jesus tells us that their worth is inestimable. Their worth is infinite, literally.

Think about that for a moment.

Imagine someone saying to you, "Please give us the equation for the unified field theory that will solve all the problems in physics—you know, that one that no one has discovered yet." You would probably feel fear, simply because it's so far over your head. What you don't realize is that this is what you feel every time you try to assess your brother's worth, which is even more over your head. Further, just as thinking you know that equation would blind you to the real answer, so thinking you know your brother's worth makes his real worth invisible to you.

Application: Choose someone in your life and apply the following to this person:

Think of how you have been constantly evaluating this person's worth. You have been constantly measuring it against standards that you carry.

Yet do you really know this person's worth?

Do you really see directly into her soul?

Admit to yourself that you have no clue about her true worth.

Let your mind be clear of all thoughts, to reflect this admission of unknowing.

In this blank, open state, wait patiently for the truth of who she is to dawn on your mind, wanting only to know her reality, and wanting only peace for her.

Now imagine that, after patient waiting, her reality dawns on your mind, like a great orb of light rising over your mental horizon.

Its rays shine their warmth on you. It is the warmth of golden peace.

As she gives you this priceless gift, which you have sought for so long, you finally realize her true, inestimable worth.

Feel your heart brimming with inexpressible gratitude.

"What is in [her] will shine so brightly in your grateful vision that you will merely love [her] and be glad.

You will not think to judge [her].

Who would *see* the face of Christ and yet insist that judgment still has meaning?"

5. Your brother's body is as little use to you as it is to him. When it is used <u>only</u> as the Holy Spirit teaches, it has no function. For minds <u>need</u> not the body to communicate. The sight that <u>sees</u> the body has no use which serves the purpose of a holy relationship. And while you look upon your brother thus, the means and end [of the holy relationship] have <u>not</u> been brought in line. Why should it take so many holy instants to let this be accomplished, when one would do? There *is* but one. The little breath of eternity that runs through time like golden light is all the same; nothing before it, nothing afterwards.

Hold on—I thought the holy relationship was where the sex got really great, where we went to those Tantra workshops and learned how to have six-hour orgasms. But now Jesus is saying that the body, and even the sight of the body, is useless to a holy relationship, and that focusing on our brother's body is in conflict with the goal of the holy relationship. I think, though, that he's talking about an exceedingly high state here. We do begin by focusing on bodies. Then, slowly, we realize that the body is just a communication device between minds, just a plastic telephone. Yet finally, when we use the body only for communication, it falls away (which is what happened to Jesus' body). Since minds are already one, why would they need a body to communicate?

It seems to take a lengthy process punctuated by countless holy instants to reach this state, yet something is amiss here. For each holy instant is the exact same one, simply experienced at different times. It's as if you had a time machine and, at different points scattered over years, you used it to repeatedly travel to the exact same moment in time.

6. You look upon each holy instant as a <u>different</u> point in time. <u>It never changes</u>. All that it ever held or will ever hold is here right now. The past takes nothing <u>from</u> it, and the future will <u>add</u> no more. Here, then, is <u>everything</u>. Here is the loveliness of your relationship, with means and end in perfect harmony <u>already</u>. Here is the perfect faith that you will one day offer to your brother <u>already</u> offered you; and here the limitless forgiveness you will give him <u>already</u> given, the face of Christ you yet will look upon <u>already</u> seen.

That moment you travel to in the holy instant is the very end of time. There, your holy relationship is fully realized. It's reached the end of the road. All the unconditional love and innocent faith that you want to give your brother now is already there, full-blown. This is why it is so supremely important to visit the holy instant now, so you can carry the grace of that future state back into the present.

Helen experienced an example of this, and it is one of the most meaningful visions she ever had (see *Absence from Felicity*, p. 106). In this vision, she and Bill were in a church and Bill was playing the "Hallelujah Chorus" on an organ, his face lit with joy. "We had finally reached our goal," she wrote. I love that line. The vision culminated in her and Bill and Jesus all kneeling before an altar, on which the symbol of the ego had been obliterated, leaving only the symbol of God. Then Jesus said to her, "That altar is within you." At this, Helen burst into tears and was unable to regain her composure for some time.

It's hard to imagine that this experience, in which she visited the point at which they had reached their goal, didn't give Helen something to bring back into the current relationship.

> 7. Can you <u>evaluate</u> the giver of a gift like this? Would you <u>exchange</u> this gift for <u>any</u> other? This gift returns the laws of God to your remembrance. And merely <u>by</u> remembering them, the laws that held you prisoner to pain and death <u>must</u> be forgotten. This is no gift your brother's <u>body</u> offers you. The veil [the body] that hides the gift hides him as well. He *is* the gift, and yet he knows it not. No more do you. And yet, have faith that He Who sees the gift in you and your brother [Ur: in *both* of you] will offer and receive it for you <u>both</u>. And through His vision will <u>you</u> see it, and through His understanding <u>recognize</u> it and love it as your own.

We are looking at our holy relationship partner's body (or any brother's body) and thinking, "Given how I see this body behaving, this person doesn't have that much to offer me." And when the Course asks us to forgive this person, part of us responds, "But that just doesn't fit the facts in front of me." Yet there is an answer. We need to have faith that the Holy Spirit sees in this person, beyond his misbehaving body, an unparalleled gift for us. When we look upon who he really is, something shines from him to us that is more precious than anything this world can offer. In this light, we can well ponder Jesus' question: "Can you *evaluate* the giver of a gift like this?"

8. Be comforted, and feel the Holy Spirit watching over you in love and perfect confidence in what He sees. He knows the Son of God, and shares his Father's certainty the universe rests in his gentle hands in safety and in peace. Let us consider now what he must learn, to <u>share</u> his Father's confidence in him. What <u>is</u> he, that the Creator of the universe should offer it [the universe, i.e., the Sonship] to him and <u>know</u> it rests in safety? He looks upon himself not as his Father knows him. And yet it is impossible the confidence of God should be misplaced.

Along this path, we screw up a lot. Yet we can be comforted, knowing that the Holy Spirit watches over us with love and with *confidence*. For He shares God's certainty in us, certainty that we will make it, and certainty that we will bring the entire universe with us. That's a tall order. Why are God and the Holy Spirit so confident that we are up to this task? What do we have to learn to share Their confidence? That is what Jesus promises to reveal to us in the next section.

VI. The Temple of the Holy Spirit
Commentary by Robert Perry

1. The meaning of the Son of God lies solely in his relationship with his Creator. If it were elsewhere it <u>would</u> rest on contingency, but there *is* nothing else. And this is wholly loving and forever. Yet has the Son of God invented an unholy relationship between him and his Father. His <u>real</u> relationship is one of perfect union and unbroken continuity. The one he made is partial, self-centered, broken into fragments and full of fear. The one created by his Father is wholly self-encompassing and self-<u>extending</u>. The one he made is wholly self-<u>destructive</u> and self-<u>limiting</u>.

The previous section promised to explain to us why God is so confident that we can save the world, and what we need to learn to share that confidence. This paragraph is the beginning of the answer. God is confident in us because our whole meaning lies in our relationship with Him. Our meaning, therefore, rests on the most real and immovable thing there is, for ultimately it rests on God Himself. That is why He is so confident in us and in the task He's given us.

We, however, took the beautiful, perfectly loving relationship we have with Him in truth and screwed it all up. Rather than a single, collective, all-inclusive relationship with God, we broke it into billions of separate relationships with Him, each one consumed with the fearful thought, "What is that heartless Guy going to do to me next?" No wonder we lost confidence in ourselves.

2. Nothing can show the contrast better than the experience of both a holy and an unholy relationship. The first is based on love, and rests on it serene and undisturbed. <u>The body does not intrude upon it.</u> Any relationship in which the body enters is based <u>not</u> on love, but on idolatry. Love wishes to be known, <u>completely</u> understood and shared. <u>It has no secrets</u>; nothing that it would keep apart and hide. It walks in sunlight, open-eyed and calm, in smiling welcome and in sincerity so simple and so obvious it cannot <u>be</u> misunderstood.

212

The contrast between our two relationships with God is perfectly exemplified in the contrast between a holy and an unholy relationship on earth. The holy relationship rests serenely and securely on the solid rock of love. Being based on love, it is all about sharing, not hiding. It conceals nothing, but instead exudes a sincerity that is "so simple and so obvious it cannot be misunderstood." This is an earthly reflection of the perfect, undefended openness of our true relationship with God, in which there is nothing hidden and nothing held back.

Application: Do you have a relationship in your life that "walks in sunlight, open-eyed and calm, in smiling welcome and in sincerity so simple and so obvious it cannot be misunderstood." Do you want such a relationship?

3. But idols do not share. Idols <u>accept</u>, but never make return. They can <u>be</u> loved, but cannot love. They do not understand what they are offered, and any relationship in which they enter has <u>lost</u> its meaning. The love of <u>them</u> has <u>made</u> love meaningless. They live in secrecy, hating the sunlight and happy in the body's darkness, where they can hide and keep their secrets hidden along with them. And they have <u>no</u> relationships, for no one else is welcome there. They smile on no one, and those who smile on them they do not see.
4. Love has no darkened temples where mysteries are kept obscure and hidden from the sun. <u>It does not seek for power</u>, but for <u>relationships</u>. The body is the ego's chosen weapon for seeking power *through* relationships. And its relationships <u>must</u> be unholy, for what they <u>are</u> it does not even <u>see</u>. It wants them solely for the offerings on which its idols thrive. The rest it merely throws away, for all that <u>it</u> could offer is seen as valueless. Homeless, the ego seeks as many bodies as it can collect to place its idols in, and so establish them as temples to itself.

The meaning of "idols"—a very flexible word in the Course—is hard to discern here. I am taking it to mean those *ideas* that prop up our ego, such as "I am separate," "I'm the best," "I own my spouse," etc. These idols are part of a larger image, in which your body is a temple to your ego. On the altar in this darkened temple your ego places its idols— again, those ideas that prop it up.

Now we can understand the unholy relationship game as this section describes it. It consists of beckoning people to come to your temple and lay their offerings before your idols. This is supposed to make those idols stronger, so that now they have the power to answer your prayers.

In practical terms, this means that if you get someone to laugh at your jokes, it's as if they have come to your temple to lay their offerings before the idol labeled, "I'm especially entertaining." If you get someone to give you sex, it's as if they have laid their offerings before the idol labeled, "I'm attractive and lovable." If you get someone to pay attention to you, they are giving offerings to your idol labeled, "I'm worth attention." If these people worship at your temple often enough, you get to actually place one of your idols in *their* body. Their body, in other words, becomes shelter for your idol, proof of the idol's strength and validity. To put this more literally, their body becomes walking proof that you, in fact, are attractive and lovable (to use one of the examples above).

This is what the unholy relationship is all about—getting other people to feed our idols. These idols are the epitome of self-absorption. Think about a relatively harmless one: "I'm especially entertaining." That idol is not really in relationship with anyone. It does not even see them. It only sees the offerings they give to it. If they give it something else, something it isn't fed by, it just chucks the offering in the trash. To this idol, a person is nothing but a pair of hands bringing it food. Period.

Can you admit that you do engage in relationships in this way, at least to some degree? How do you feel about admitting this?

> 5. The Holy Spirit's temple is <u>not</u> a body, but a <u>relationship</u>. The body is an isolated speck of darkness; a hidden secret room, a tiny spot of senseless mystery, a meaningless enclosure carefully protected, yet hiding nothing. Here the unholy relationship escapes reality, and seeks for crumbs to keep itself alive. Here it would drag its brothers, holding them here in its idolatry. Here it is "safe," for here love <u>cannot</u> enter. The Holy Spirit does not build His temples where love can never be. Would He Who <u>sees</u> the face of Christ choose as His home the only place in all the universe where it can <u>not</u> be seen?

That first line is quite a shocker. In contrast to centuries of spiritual wisdom (see 1 Cor 6:19), Jesus says that the Holy Spirit's temple is *not* a body. The body was made to house, protect, support, and conceal those idols. And idols by definition are God's replacement.

Application: Make a brief list of the idols—those ideas that support your particular ego (such as "I'm of superior intelligence")—that you see your body containing, protecting, supporting, and concealing.

Can you see that you drag other people to your body to give their "crumbs" to these idols? Now can you understand why the Holy Spirit's temple is not a body, but a relationship?

> 6. You <u>cannot</u> make the body the Holy Spirit's temple, and it will <u>never</u> be the seat of love. It is the home of the idolater, and of love's <u>condemnation</u>. For here is love made fearful and hope abandoned. Even the idols that are worshipped here are shrouded in mystery, and kept <u>apart</u> from those who worship them. This is the temple dedicated to no relationships and no return. Here is the "mystery" of separation perceived in awe and held in reverence. What God would have *not* be is here kept "safe" from Him. But what you do <u>not</u> realize is what you fear within your brother, and would not <u>see</u> in <u>him,</u> is what makes God seem fearful to you, and kept unknown.

The problem with the body is that it's pure separation. When someone strokes your skin, who feels it besides you? When someone strokes the idols housed in your body, who feels that besides you? Chances are that they don't even know which idol they are stroking, right? You just smile; the rest is private. The body, then, is the enshrinement of the idea of separation. It is a temple to the religion of separation. Being all about separation, it symbolizes the fear of oneness with God. But what we don't realize is that we fear God *because* we fear our brother.

> 7. Idolaters will <u>always</u> be afraid of love, for nothing so severely threatens them as love's approach. Let love draw near them and <u>overlook</u> the body, as it will surely do, and they retreat in fear, feeling the seeming firm foundation of their temple begin to shake and loosen. Brother, you tremble with them. Yet what you fear is but the herald of escape. This place of darkness is <u>not</u> your home. Your temple is <u>not</u> threatened. You are an idolater no longer. The Holy Spirit's purpose lies safe in your <u>relationship,</u> and <u>not</u> your body. You have <u>escaped</u> the body. Where you are the <u>body</u> cannot enter, for the Holy Spirit has set <u>His</u> temple there.

From our point of view, nothing says love better than someone approaching our body with food for our idols. In fact, nothing else says love at all. So what do we do when someone approaches us, full of love, "open-eyed and calm, in smiling welcome" and in unmistakable sincerity, yet *overlooking the body*? We feel the firm foundation of our temple begin to shake, and we tremble with it. Yet this kind of love is the herald of our escape from the ego's lonely temple. And this is the very love that entered our relationship when we invited the Holy Spirit into it. Now we must choose between the ego's temple—the body—and *His* temple—our holy relationship.

> 8. There is no order in relationships. They either <u>are</u> or not. An unholy relationship is <u>no</u> relationship. It is a state of isolation, which <u>seems</u> to be what it is <u>not</u>. No more than that. The instant that the mad idea of making your relationship with God unholy seemed to be possible, <u>all</u> your relationships were made meaningless. In that unholy instant time was born [unholy relationships were born in the unholy instant], and bodies made to house the mad idea [of making your relationship with God unholy] and give it the <u>illusion</u> of reality. And so it <u>seemed</u> to have a home that held together for a little while in time, and vanished. For what could house this mad idea <u>against</u> reality but for an instant?

The first four lines of this paragraph have always struck me as extremely important. They follow perfectly from the preceding paragraphs. A relationship in which our partner exists simply to feed our idols is not a relationship at all. It is pure aloneness dressed up as relationship.

This state of affairs traces back to the dawn of time, when we made that unholy caricature of our relationship with God, which we saw in paragraph 1. This new relationship with God was based on separateness. The idea of separateness became the heart of our whole religion, and this made all of our relationships into dances of isolation. We built the temple of the body to house this mad idea, and thus make it seem real and mysterious and sacred. This idea is the mother of all our idols; it is the idol labeled "I am separate." Oddly enough, this idol is why bodies pass away so quickly. "For what could house this mad idea against reality but for an instant?"

> 9. Idols <u>must</u> disappear, and leave no trace behind their going. The unholy instant of their seeming power is frail as is a snowflake, but without its

loveliness. Is this the substitute you <u>want</u> for the eternal blessing of the holy instant and its unlimited beneficence? Is the malevolence of the unholy relationship, so seeming powerful and so bitterly misunderstood and so invested in a <u>false</u> attraction your preference to the holy instant, which offers you peace and understanding? [He expects your answer to be no.] Then lay aside the body and quietly <u>transcend</u> it, rising to welcome what you <u>really</u> want. And from His holy temple, look you not back [like Lot's wife] on what you have awakened <u>from</u>. For no illusions <u>can</u> attract the mind that has <u>transcended</u> them, and left them far behind.

Application: Jesus is clearly employing his usual "gross out" method. He is trying to make us feel ill about how we currently conduct relationships. So let's try to make this method work for us. Say the following:

Do I really want to continually live out the unholy instant, in which I drag my brothers to my body, to offer their crumbs to my idols, before I dispense with them (my brothers)?
Do I really want to remain attracted to this essentially malevolent style of relationship?
Wouldn't I rather live in the holy instant, instead of the unholy one?
Then let me lay aside my love affair with this body and how it gets treated.
Let my mind rise free of it, to welcome in the peace and understanding of the holy instant.

(Pause.)

And from this holy temple, I will not look back on my former temple, which was really just a prison cell.
No illusions can attract me now.
Why would I want to go back to sleep when I've had a taste of the waking state?

10. The holy relationship reflects the <u>true</u> relationship the Son of God has with his Father in reality. The Holy Spirit rests within it in the certainty it will endure forever. Its firm foundation is eternally upheld by truth, and love shines on it with the gentle smile and tender blessing it offers to its own. Here the unholy instant is exchanged in gladness for the holy one of safe return. Here is the way to true relationships held gently open, through which you and your brother walk together, leaving the body thankfully behind and resting in the Everlasting Arms. Love's arms are open to receive you, and give you peace forever.

Notice the contrast Jesus is drawing with the unholy relationship, which is such a private, dark affair, where we just use others to drop their money into our offering basket. Imagine instead being in a relationship that is the home of the Holy Spirit. This relationship's foundation is so firm that it can never dissolve, ever. Therefore, the Holy Spirit rests within it, secure in the stability of His home. Imagine being in a relationship that love shines on, as constant as the sun, and so the two of you continually bask in love's "gentle smile and tender blessing." Imagine being in a relationship that frequently falls into holy instants. In these instants, both of you see before you an open door, through which lies "the way to true relationships." Through this door, you walk together, leaving the separateness of the body gladly behind. There, just down the road, you see God's Everlasting Arms, which are open to receive you, and give you peace and protection forever.

Now which would you prefer: the holy relationship or the unholy relationship?

11. The body is the ego's idol; the belief in sin made flesh and then projected outward. This produces what <u>seems</u> to be a wall of flesh <u>around</u> the mind, keeping it [the mind] prisoner in a tiny spot of space and time, beholden unto death, and given but an instant in which to sigh and grieve and die in honor of its master [the ego]. And this unholy instant <u>seems</u> to be life; an instant of despair, a tiny island of dry sand, bereft of water and set uncertainly upon oblivion. Here does the Son of God stop briefly by, to offer his devotion to death's idols and then pass on. And here he is more dead than living. Yet it is also here he makes his choice again between idolatry and love. Here it is given him to choose to spend this instant paying tribute to the body, or <u>let</u> himself be given freedom from it. Here he can <u>accept</u> the holy instant, offered

him to <u>replace</u> the unholy one he chose before. And here can he learn relationships are his <u>salvation,</u> and <u>not</u> his doom.

The first five sentences are a devastating description of what we call life. There are really two images here. In the first, the idea of sin becomes flesh. It turns into a wall of meat that then wraps around the mind, imprisoning it in "a tiny spot of space and time." In this prison cell, the mind has only a brief instant to enjoy, "an instant in which to sigh and grieve and die" in honor of the judge that put it there—the ego.

In the second image, this life is like being marooned on a tiny desert island (the body), that has no fresh water and is surrounded not by the sea, but by "oblivion"—nonexistence. We swim to the shore of this island in order to pray at death's altar, and then we return from whence we came—oblivion. And even during our brief furlough from oblivion, we are "more dead than living." A short-lived living-death in the prison cell of meat or on the desert island on the sea of oblivion—these are Jesus' images of what we call life. It kind of takes all the adrenaline out of "Seize the day," doesn't it? What's there to seize?

But there is good news. While in this cell, while on this island, we can make another choice. We can choose the holy instant over the unholy instant of three score and ten. We can transcend our quarantine and choose *relationship*.

> 12. You who <u>are</u> learning this may still be fearful, but you are <u>not</u> immobilized. The holy instant <u>is</u> of greater value now to you than its unholy seeming counterpart, and you <u>have</u> learned you <u>really</u> want but one. This is no time for sadness. Perhaps confusion, but hardly discouragement. <u>You have a</u> *real* <u>relationship,</u> and it <u>has</u> meaning. It is as like your real relationship with God as equal things are like unto each other. Idolatry is past and meaningless. Perhaps you fear your brother [Ur: each other] a little yet; perhaps a shadow of the fear of God [the final obstacle to peace] remains with you. Yet what is that to those who have been given one <u>true</u> relationship <u>beyond</u> the body? Can they be long held back from [lifting the veil and] looking on the face of Christ? And can they long withhold the memory of their relationship with their Father <u>from</u> themselves, and keep remembrance of His Love <u>apart</u> from their awareness?

After that incredibly depressing view of life on earth, Jesus sounds a note of hope, which is clearly addressed directly to Helen and Bill: "I know you are confused and I know you are afraid. The picture I have painted *is* bleak, but you have your ticket out of here. You have your holy relationship. You have 'been given one true relationship beyond the body.' You have no idea what a blessing this is. It contains your whole way out. At its heart, idolatry has been banished. So pick your head up and keep walking forward. 'This is no time for sadness.' It is all right if you still stand trembling before the final obstacle to peace. That won't last long. It's only a matter of time before you lift the veil together and look on the face of Christ, and then pass together beyond the veil into the full memory of His Father."

And now we have the answer to what Jesus brought up at the end of the last section—why our Father has such confidence in us, and how we can learn of that confidence. He has the confidence because our whole being rests on our relationship with Him. And we learn of that confidence through the earthly reflection of our relationship with Him—our holy relationship with our brother.

VII. The Consistency of Means and End
Commentary by Robert Perry

1. We have said much about discrepancies of means and end, and how these must be brought in line before your holy relationship can bring you <u>only</u> joy. But we have also said the means to meet the Holy Spirit's goal will come from the same Source as does His purpose. Being so simple and direct, this course has <u>nothing</u> in it that is not consistent. The <u>seeming</u> inconsistencies, or parts you find more difficult than others, are merely indications of areas where means and end are still discrepant. And this produces great discomfort. This <u>need</u> not be. This course requires almost <u>nothing</u> of you. It is impossible to imagine one that asks so little, or could offer more.

The first line is right: Jesus has repeatedly mentioned the need for a holy relationship's means to be in line with its goal. Just as the goal is holy, the means need to be holy as well. Our first reaction to this may be, "Yeah, but those holy means are just too difficult. In fact, this whole Course is just too difficult, especially certain parts of it." Jesus' response is, no, everything in the Course is the same. The means are all consistent with the goal and the means are all equally easy, for they are simply given to us by the Holy Spirit. For this reason, "This course requires almost nothing of you."

Is this our experience of the Course? I don't think so. So what's the story? Why do we experience the teaching, say, about the special relationship or about the body as being so much harder to accept and implement than other teachings in the Course? The reason is that "means and end are still discrepant" in us. In other words, we want to reach the Course's *end* through *means* of our choosing, means that don't really fit that end. This ends up making the real means seem unattractive and therefore very difficult.

2. The period of discomfort that follows the sudden change in a relationship from sin to holiness may [Ur: should] now be almost over. To the extent you still experience it, you are <u>refusing</u> to leave the means to Him Who changed the purpose. You recognize you <u>want</u> the goal.

> Are you not also willing to <u>accept</u> the means? If you are not, let us admit that *you* are inconsistent. A purpose is <u>attained</u> by means, and if you <u>want</u> a purpose [Ur: goal,] you <u>must</u> be willing to want the means as well. How can one be sincere and say, "I want this above all else, and yet I do not want to learn the means to get it?"

"The period of discomfort" is the Course's understated term for the painful stage a new holy relationship goes through since its new goal is completely discordant with its old structure (see T-17.V). Unfortunately, many holy relationships never get out of this period, Helen and Bill's being one of those. What is the way out? To stop insisting on pursuing the goal with *your* means and accept instead the *Holy Spirit's* means.

The final sentence captures the attitude that so many of us have toward the Course: "I want its goal above all else, but I don't really want to learn nor apply the means to get there." Can you see yourself in this sentence? If so, the problem is not the *Course's* inconsistency, but yours.

> 3. To obtain the <u>goal</u> the Holy Spirit indeed asks little. He asks no more to give the means as well. The means are second to the goal. And when you hesitate, it is because the <u>purpose</u> [the goal] frightens you, and <u>not</u> the means. Remember this, for otherwise you will make the error of believing the <u>means</u> are difficult. Yet how <u>can</u> they be difficult if they are merely <u>given</u> you? They <u>guarantee</u> the goal, and they are <u>perfectly</u> in line with it. Before we look at them a little closer, remember that if you think <u>they</u> are impossible, your wanting of the <u>purpose</u> has been shaken. For if a <u>goal</u> is possible to reach, the means to do so <u>must</u> be possible as well.

Here's the real problem. We are not really sure we want the goal. It actually frightens us a little. That's why we prefer means that don't really get us there. And that's why we experience the *real* means as difficult. Things that are objectively easy can seem incredibly difficult when you don't want to do them. This is the case with the means the Course instructs us to use. On an objective level, these means are extremely easy, for the Holy Spirit will simply give them to us. He will infuse us with them.

Yet still we find them difficult because we don't like the goal they lead us to. As an analogy, imagine that two beautifully wrapped packages land on your doorstep. How difficult is it to open a package? Both of them, therefore, are a snap to open. However, you happen to know that one holds a million dollars in crisp new bills, whereas the other holds literally thousands of huge, feisty cockroaches, which will immediately scurry all over your home and your feet. Objectively, both would be equally easy to open, yet I suspect that you would experience one of them as easier and the other as much harder.

We see the Course's means—which are as easy as opening the gift-wrapped package—as hard only because we see its goal as analogous to a seething mass of cockroaches.

> 4. It *is* impossible to see your brother as sinless and yet to look upon him as a body. Is this not perfectly consistent with the goal of holiness? For holiness is merely the result of letting the effects of sin be lifted, so what was <u>always</u> true is <u>recognized</u>. To see a <u>sinless</u> [i.e., holy] body is impossible, for holiness is <u>positive</u> and the body is merely neutral. It is <u>not</u> sinful, but neither is it sinless [holy]. As nothing, which it <u>is</u>, the body cannot meaningfully be invested with attributes of Christ <u>or</u> of the ego. <u>Either</u> must be an error, for both would place the attributes where they cannot <u>be</u>. And <u>both</u> must be undone for purposes of truth.

Now we have an insight into what the goal and means are. The *goal* is holiness, the full realization of our "always true" holiness. This is also called salvation. The *means* is seeing your brother as holy (seeing with vision). In other words, if you want to reach the realization of your own holiness (goal), then see your brother as holy (means).

And here also is the problem. We have been trying to reach the goal of holiness by seeing our brother as a body. This is our chosen means, which is incompatible with the real means. We can't see our brother as holy *and* see him as a body, because bodies aren't holy. They are merely neutral.

> 5. The body *is* the means by which the ego tries to make the unholy relationship seem real. The unholy instant *is* the time of bodies. But the *purpose* here is sin. It cannot <u>be</u> attained but in illusion, and so the illusion of a brother as a body is quite in keeping with the purpose of unholiness. <u>Because</u> of this consistency, the means remain unquestioned while the end is cherished. Seeing [Ur: Vision] adapts to wish, for sight is <u>always</u> secondary to desire. And if you see the body, you have chosen judgment and <u>not</u> vision. For vision, like relationships, <u>has</u> no order. You either <u>see</u> or not.

Even though the body is neutral, when we see a brother as a body, we aren't emphasizing its neutrality, nor his. We are actually pursuing a whole other set of means and end. Our end is sin—we secretly aim to believe that we ourselves are sinful. As a means to this, we want to see our brother as sinful. We want to see him through the eyes of judgment. For this reason, we see him as a body. If he is defined by his body, which is always doing things wrong, then he has to be a sinner.

This teaching turns upside down our experience of things. We are thinking, "I want the goal of holiness and I do want to see my brother as holy, but look at what he's showing me. How can I see him as holy given what he's doing?" The answer is: Seeing him as defined by what his body does is a *choice*, and you only make this choice when you want to see him through judgment, when you want to collect evidence to hang him. And you want this so you can turn around and condemn yourself.

> 6. Who sees a brother's body has laid a <u>judgment</u> on him, and sees him not. He does not <u>really</u> see him as sinful; he does not see him at all. In the darkness of sin he is <u>invisible</u>. He can but be <u>imagined</u> in the darkness, and it is here that the illusions you hold about him are <u>not</u> held up to his reality. Here [in the darkness] are illusions and reality kept <u>separated</u>. Here are illusions <u>never</u> brought to truth, and <u>always</u> hidden from it. And here, in darkness, is your brother's reality <u>imagined</u> as a body, in unholy relationships with other bodies, serving the cause of sin an instant before he dies.

Reflect on that first line. If you see another person as a body, if you see him defined by how his body looks and what it does, you have "laid a judgment on him." Even before any specific judgments are made, just seeing him as a body is a judgment, a condemnation. Has this occurred to you? Yet there's more in that first line. Seeing him as a body also means that you don't see him. Think about it. When you look on someone's body, are you seeing directly into his mind, his soul, his spirit? He could be a robot, without any of these things, for all you know. Or he could be the Son of God dreaming he's human. You don't know, because all you see is his exterior.

We need to realize that right now we are blind when it comes to seeing our brother. Like a blind person, we can only imagine what he really looks like, what his spirit looks like. And that is what we are doing—imagining.

Application: Think of someone you know. Notice that you picture this person as a body. Notice how your assessment of this person's inner identity is based mainly on your memories of what his or her body has done and said. Now say to yourself:

> *When I see my brother (or sister) as a body, I am seeing him (or*
>   *her) not.*
> *His reality is invisible to me.*
> *And in the darkness of my blindness, I merely imagine how he*
>   *really looks.*
> *All that I see of him is just my imagination, not his reality.*

7. There is indeed a difference between this vain imagining and vision. The difference lies not in <u>them</u>, but in their purpose. Both are but <u>means</u>, each one appropriate to the end for which it is employed. Neither can serve the purpose of the other, for each one is a *choice* of purpose, employed on its behalf. Either is meaningless <u>without</u> the end for which it was intended, nor is it valued as a <u>separate</u> thing apart from the intention. The means seem real because the <u>goal</u> is valued. And judgment <u>has</u> no value unless the <u>goal</u> is sin.

Seeing your brother as your eyes show him to you—as a sinning body—is totally different than seeing him through the eyes of Christ, as a sinless spirit. Yet the real difference between these two "lies not in them, but in their purpose." When you choose one, you are really choosing the goal it leads to. That's why you choose it. If you choose to see your brother as a body, then, that is really a choice to achieve the goal of sinfulness for yourself.

8. The body can<u>not</u> be looked upon <u>except</u> through judgment. To see the body [as real—to see it with your mind, not just your eyes] is the sign that you <u>lack</u> vision [true perception, which looks directly on the light of your brother's holiness], and have <u>denied</u> the means the Holy Spirit offers you to serve <u>His</u> purpose. How can a holy relationship achieve its purpose through the means of sin? Judgment you taught <u>yourself</u>; vision is learned from Him Who would <u>undo</u> your teaching. <u>His</u> vision cannot <u>see</u> the body <u>because it cannot look on sin</u>. And thus it leads you to reality. Your holy brother, sight of whom is <u>your</u> release,

225

is no illusion. Attempt to see him not in darkness, for your imaginings about him <u>will</u> seem real there. You <u>closed</u> your eyes [your true eyes, the eyes of Christ] to shut him out. Such was your <u>purpose</u>, and while this purpose seems to have a [Ur: *any*] meaning, the means for its attainment will be evaluated as <u>worth</u> the seeing, and so you will <u>not</u> see.

Seeing our brother as a body seems to be a given. Seeing him any *other* way seems unnatural, or supernatural. Yet seeing him as a body is what is unnatural. It represents a refusal to see him as he really is, a choice to close our eyes to shut him out. It represents a rejection of true vision. Yet—and here's the unfortunate part—vision is the Holy Spirit's means for achieving the goal of the holy relationship. How can we achieve that goal if we refuse to touch the means?

Now what Jesus said earlier should be much clearer. To summarize, we say, "I yearn for the goal of salvation, but the means—seeing my brother as holy, seeing him through vision—is just way too hard." But what we really mean is, "Seeing with vision *would* be easy, but I really don't want to do it. I prefer to see my brother as a sinful body, because that serves the goal I want more than salvation, the goal of sin."

> 9. Your question should not be, "How can I see my brother without the body?" Ask only, "Do I <u>really</u> wish to see him sinless?" And as you ask, forget not that <u>his</u> sinlessness is *your* escape from fear. Salvation [or holiness] is the Holy Spirit's goal. The means is vision. For what the seeing look upon *is* sinless [holy]. No one who loves can judge, and what he sees is <u>free</u> of condemnation. And what he sees he did <u>not</u> make [through his imagination], for it was <u>given</u> him to see, as was the vision that made his seeing possible.

To see a brother as sinless, we need to completely de-link his identity from his body and what his body does. His identity and his body need to be two entirely separate things in our mind. In fact, we already sense this. We innately sense that in order to see him sinless, we have to mentally separate *him* from his *body*. Because of this, if we sincerely desire to see him sinless, we will automatically drop his body from our picture of who he is.

VII. The Consistency of Means and End

Application:

> *Do I **really** wish to see my brother sinless?*
> *If so, I will automatically drop his body from my picture of who*
>   *he is.*
> *While his body does its crazy dance,*
> *I will see his identity as an unwavering light, ever changeless and*
>   *radiantly holy.*
> *I want to see him this way, for his sinlessness is **my** salvation.*

VIII. The Vision of Sinlessness
Commentary by Robert Perry

1. Vision will come to you at first in glimpses, but they will be enough to show you what is given you who see your brother sinless. Truth is restored to you through your desire, as it was lost to you through your desire for something else. Open the holy place that you closed off by valuing the "something else," and what was never lost will quietly return. It has been saved for you. Vision would not be necessary had judgment not been made. Desire now its whole undoing, and it is done for you.

When we decided to judge instead of know, we closed the door on the abode of truth within us, and it seemed to disappear. We doubted that we could ever get it back. Yet it has been saved for us, and all we need do to get it back is desire it, really want it. Yet how do we want something with all our heart that has been outside of our awareness for so long?

This is where vision comes in. Vision is not knowledge, yet it is as close as we can come to knowledge here. At first, we just get glimpses of vision, yet those glimpses can be the most precious experiences we have. Suddenly that familiar, damaged person seems like our dearest friend, shining with a purity that is so humbling it makes our knees buckle. These glimpses are what kindle our desire for the truth that we lost.

2. Do you not want to know your own Identity? Would you not happily exchange your doubts for certainty? Would you not willingly be free of misery, and learn again of joy? Your holy relationship offers all this to you. As it [your holy relationship] was given you, so will be its effects. And as its holy purpose [goal] was not made by you, the means by which its happy end is yours is also not of you. Rejoice in what is yours but for the asking, and think not that you need make either means or end. All this is given you who would but see your brother sinless. All this is given, waiting on your desire but to receive it. Vision is freely given to those who ask to see.

Application. Ask yourself:

> *Do I not **want** to know my own Identity?*
> *Would I not happily exchange my doubts for ultimate certainty?*
> *Would I not willingly be **free** of misery, and learn again of joy?*

Now pick someone in your life who is important to you, and say,

> *All this is given me if I simply desire to see [name] sinless.*

The logic in this particular paragraph goes like this: If I want to see my brother sinless, I will be given vision, in which I really do see him as sinless. Since vision is the means to the goal of the holy relationship, I will achieve that goal, which is salvation. And through salvation I will regain the knowledge of the truth, which includes knowledge of my Identity, perfect certainty, and complete joy.

3. Your brother's sinlessness is given you [by the Holy Spirit] in shining light, to look on with the Holy Spirit's vision and to rejoice in along with Him. For peace will come to all who ask for it with real desire and sincerity of purpose, <u>shared</u> with the Holy Spirit and at one with Him on what salvation <u>is</u>. Be willing, then, to see your brother sinless, that Christ may rise before your vision and give you joy. And place <u>no</u> value on your brother's body, which holds him to illusions of what he is. It is <u>his</u> desire to see his sinlessness, as it is <u>yours</u>. And bless the Son of God in your relationship, nor see in him what you have <u>made</u> of him.

Vision is not talked about much among Course students, but it's what the whole Course is trying to lead us to. It is literally a different kind of sight than physical sight, in which spiritual eyes within us "see" the holiness in others just as clearly as our physical eyes see their body now. The more you understand what the Course means by vision, the more unattainable it seems. How do we acquire this entirely new ability, one that doesn't seem part of normal human equipment? This makes acquiring something like psychic abilities seem like peanuts.

Jesus' answer, over and over again, is "just want it." Really, sincerely desire it, and the Holy Spirit will simply give it to you. All we need do is transfer our motivation away from gloating over the sin we see in others to *yearning* to see the purity in them.

> 4. The Holy Spirit <u>guarantees</u> that what God willed and gave you shall be yours. This is <u>your</u> purpose [goal] now, and the vision that makes it [the goal] yours is ready to be given. You have the vision that enables you to see the body not. And as you look upon your brother, you will see an altar to your Father, holy as Heaven, glowing with radiant purity and sparkling with the shining lilies you laid upon it. What can you value more than this? Why do you think the body is a better home, a safer shelter for God's Son? Why would you rather look on <u>it</u> than on the truth? How can the engine of destruction be <u>preferred</u>, and chosen to <u>replace</u> the holy home the Holy Spirit offers, where <u>He</u> will dwell <u>with</u> you?

Application:

Think of someone in your life and look at this person in your mind.
Picture the person's face and its familiar expressions.
Picture his or her hands and their familiar gestures.
Picture this person's body and its familiar clothing.
Notice how that body is tainted in your eyes by the inconsiderate and destructive things it has done.
Now imagine that Jesus walks up and says, "I have a pair of miracle glasses for you to try on.
They will allow you to see this person as he or she really is.
Would you like to put them on?"
You of course say yes.
You put the glasses on and open your eyes.
You are surprised, because the person's body is nowhere to be seen.
Instead, all you see is an altar to God.
It is as holy as Heaven.
It is glowing with an unearthly light—the radiance of purity.
There on this altar, in between lovely candles, is a beautiful collection of sparkling lilies.
You realize that these are the gifts of love and forgiveness you have given this person.

Those gifts were not lost or forgotten, but instead have become the centerpiece of his or her altar.

You are astonished.

Could this be how this person really looks through eyes of truth?

Now Jesus speaks to you.

"What can you value more than this?" he asks.

"Why do you think the body is a better home for this person? Why would you rather look on it than on the truth?"

You realize he is asking you if you want to continue wearing the glasses, or go back to your old way of seeing.

What is your answer?

5. The body is the sign of weakness, vulnerability and <u>loss</u> of power. Can such a savior <u>help</u> you? Would you turn in your distress and need for help unto the <u>helpless</u>? Is the pitifully <u>little</u> the perfect choice to call upon for strength? Judgment <u>will</u> seem to make your savior weak. Yet it is *you* who need his strength. There is no problem, no event or situation, no perplexity that vision will not solve. All is redeemed when looked upon with vision. For this is not *your* sight, and brings with it the laws beloved of Him Whose sight it <u>is</u>.

If your brother is that holy altar, then the light can shine forth from him and illuminate you. If he is that altar, then he can awaken you. He can save you. But if he is the body that you see, how can he do that? Can this weak and vulnerable mound of flesh actually wake you up? If he is his body, you have no one to save you. This is why it is so crucial to choose which eyes you will see him through. If you see him through the eyes of judgment, you will see a body, powerless to save you. If you see him through vision, you will see the altar, shining illumination into your very being.

6. Everything looked upon with vision falls gently into place, according to the laws brought <u>to</u> it by His calm and certain sight. The end [Ur: ,] for everything <u>He</u> looks upon [Ur: ,] is <u>always</u> sure. For it will meet His purpose [His end], seen in <u>unadjusted</u> form and suited perfectly to meet it [His purpose]. Destructiveness becomes benign, and sin is turned to blessing under His gentle gaze. What can the body's eyes perceive, with power to <u>correct</u>? Its eyes <u>adjust</u> to sin, unable to overlook it in

231

any form and seeing it everywhere, in everything. Look through its eyes, and everything will stand condemned before you. All that could save you, you will never see. Your holy relationship, the source of your salvation, will be deprived of meaning, and its most holy purpose bereft of means for its accomplishment.

When you look through the eyes of vision, all the chaos and destructiveness before you looks entirely different. You see everything fall into its proper place. Even vicious attacks look like beautiful opportunities for blessing. The reason it all looks so different is that vision sees everything as a means to the Holy Spirit's goal. Everything shines with the pure potential of serving His goal, as well as the certainty that, in the end, it *will*.

When we see through the body's eyes, the contrast couldn't be greater. We see the power of sin running roughshod over the world. I just read comments by Father Gabriele Amorth, the Pope's "caster out of demons." He said, "Of course the Devil exists and he can not only possess a single person but also groups and entire populations. I am convinced that the Nazis were all possessed." When we see the world with the body's eyes, it's as if not just the entire population of Nazis, but the entire population of the *world* is possessed. This is why Jesus says, "Look through its eyes, and everything will stand condemned before you." Who of us can't identify with that line?

> 7. Judgment is but a toy, a whim, the senseless means to play the idle game of death in your imagination. But vision sets all things right, bringing them gently within the kindly sway of Heaven's laws. What if you recognized this world is an hallucination? What if you really understood you made it up? What if you realized that those who seem to walk about in it, to sin and die, attack and murder and destroy themselves, are wholly unreal? Could you have faith in what you see, if you accepted this? And would you see it?

Your physical eyes are dream eyes, and what they see before them are dream figures. All those bodies that appear to be possessed by the power of sin are not there. They are open-eyed dreams—what we call hallucinations.

Application: Look around the place you are in and let your gaze rest on one object after another, randomly. With each one say,

That [blank] is just a dream figure [or dream object].
It is no more real than the dreams I see at night.

Then try to get a sense that the entire scene you see is just a dream, viewed through the eyes of a dream body. How does that feel?

Of course, behind each dream body is a dreaming Son of God, but that Son of God is precisely what your eyes *don't* see.

8. Hallucinations disappear when they are <u>recognized</u> for what they are. This <u>is</u> the healing and the remedy. Believe them not and they <u>are</u> gone. And all <u>you</u> need to do is recognize that <u>you did this</u>. Once you <u>accept</u> this simple fact and take unto <u>yourself</u> the power you <u>gave</u> them, <u>you</u> are released from them. One thing is sure; hallucinations serve a purpose, and when that <u>purpose</u> is no longer held <u>they</u> disappear. Therefore, the question never is whether you want <u>them</u>, but <u>always</u>, do you want the purpose that they serve? This world <u>seems</u> to hold out many purposes, each different and with different values. Yet they are all the same. Again there is no order; only a <u>seeming</u> hierarchy of values.

9. Only two purposes are possible. And one is sin, the other holiness. Nothing is in between, and which you choose determines what you see. For what you see is merely <u>how</u> you elect to meet your goal. Hallucinations serve to meet the goal of madness. They are the means by which the <u>outside</u> world, projected from within, <u>adjusts</u> to sin and <u>seems</u> to witness to its reality. It still is true that nothing <u>is</u> without. Yet upon nothing are <u>all</u> projections made. For it is the <u>projection</u> that gives the "nothing" <u>all</u> the meaning that it holds.

Let's try to follow the chain of ideas here:

Everything I am seeing before me now is an hallucination; it's not really there.

I projected it all from my mind. I made it up.

I only see it because I believe it is real.

I believe it is real because it serves a purpose that I want.

The purpose these hallucinations serve is sin.
They witness to the reality of sin.
The sinning, dying, attacking, murdering bodies are constant "proof" that sin is real.
When I stop wanting to prove that sin is real, I will stop seeing the physical world.

> 10. What has <u>no</u> meaning cannot <u>be</u> perceived. And meaning <u>always</u> looks within to find itself, and *then* looks out. <u>All</u> meaning that you give the world outside must thus reflect the sight you saw <u>within</u>; or better, <u>if</u> you saw at all or merely judged <u>against</u>. Vision is the means by which the Holy Spirit translates your nightmares into happy dreams; your wild hallucinations that show you all the fearful outcomes of imagined sin into the calm and reassuring sights with which He would replace them. These gentle sights and sounds are looked on happily, and heard with joy. They are <u>His</u> substitutes for all the terrifying sights and screaming sounds the ego's purpose brought to your horrified awareness. They step <u>away</u> from sin, reminding you that it is <u>not</u> reality which frightens you, and that the errors which you made <u>can</u> be corrected.

We can look out at the world and see totally different meanings, for the meaning we see in the world comes from within, not without. If we look within and see sin, we will look out upon a world of "terrifying sights and screaming sounds." If we look within and see holiness, we will look on a world of "gentle sights and sounds" that "are looked on happily, and heard with joy."

The world does seem frightening, yet could what we have heard so often actually be true—that we are frightened not by the reality of what's out there, but by our own projections? Are we on a secret campaign to prove to ourselves that sin is the ultimate power? Is that the real story behind our negative view of people and events?

> 11. When you have looked on what seemed terrifying, and <u>seen</u> it change to sights of loveliness and peace; when you have looked on scenes of violence and death, and <u>watched</u> them change to quiet views of gardens under open skies, with clear, life-giving water running happily beside them in dancing brooks that never waste away; who need <u>persuade</u> you to accept the gift of vision? And <u>after</u> vision, who is there who <u>could</u> refuse what <u>must</u> come after? Think but an instant just on this; <u>you</u> can

behold the holiness God gave His Son. And <u>never</u> need you think that there <u>is</u> something else for you to see.

Accepting vision is all about desire, motivation. And we get that motivation from experiencing the sudden shift from seeing through eyes of judgment to seeing through eyes of love. If you experience this often enough and powerfully enough, no one needs to convince you to accept the gift of vision. And once vision comes, you will need no arm-twisting to accept the gift that transcends even vision, the eternal gift of knowledge.

Application: Imagine a scene from your life that was particularly dark and upsetting. Now try to imagine seeing that same scene, only in such a way that the feeling would best be captured as a quiet view of a garden under an open sky, with clear, life-giving water running happily beside it in a dancing brook that never runs dry. Is this something you would want?

Commentaries on Chapter 21

REASON AND
PERCEPTION

Introduction
Commentary by Robert Perry

1. Projection makes perception. The world you see is what you <u>gave</u> it, nothing more than that. But though it is no <u>more</u> than that, it is <u>not</u> less. Therefore, to <u>you</u> it <u>is</u> important. It is the witness to your state of mind, the <u>outside</u> picture of an <u>inward</u> condition. As a man thinketh, so does he perceive. Therefore, seek not to change the <u>world</u>, but choose to change your mind <u>about</u> the world. Perception is a <u>result</u> and <u>not</u> a cause. And that is <u>why</u> order of difficulty in miracles is meaningless. <u>Everything</u> looked upon with vision is healed and holy. <u>Nothing</u> perceived without it means anything. And where there is no meaning, there is chaos.

The importance of that first line, "Projection makes perception," has grown and grown in my mind over the years. To put it in ordinary parlance: We see what we want to see. We do not see what is real; we see simply an "outside picture of an inward condition." This has many implications. First, it means that if we want to know our actual state of mind, we need to look at the meanings we see in the world. Second, it means that if we want to feel happier, we need to rearrange our thoughts, not rearrange the furniture of the world. Third, it means that there is no order of difficulty in miracles, because both cancer and colds are just projections of the mind.

By the way, "seek not to change the world" doesn't mean that we should not help others. That line is speaking to our belief that our happiness comes from rearranging external events. Remember, the Course tells us many times that our function is to save the world.

2. Damnation is your judgment on <u>yourself</u>, and this you <u>will</u> project upon the world. See <u>it</u> as damned, and all you see is what <u>you</u> did to hurt the Son of God. If you behold disaster and catastrophe, you tried to crucify him. If you see holiness and hope, you joined the Will of God to set him free. There is no choice that lies between these two decisions. And you will see the <u>witness</u> to the choice you made, and learn from this to <u>recognize</u> which one you chose. The world you see but shows you how much joy <u>you</u> have allowed yourself to see in you, and to

accept as <u>yours</u>. And, if this *is* its meaning, then the power to <u>give</u> it joy <u>must</u> lie <u>within</u> you.

This paragraph gives us more specific guidance on how to use the outer picture we see to assess our inward condition. If we see a world full of disaster and catastrophe, a world pressing upon us and haranguing us, we are seeing an outward picture of our condemnation of ourselves. If we see "holiness and hope," we are seeing a reflection of our decision to accept our innocence and rise in joyous resurrection.

Application: Think about your perception of the world. How much do you see it as a cruel and unfair place, full of dangers and senseless disasters? When it turns its gaze on you, how much do you see it as misunderstanding you, shunning and neglecting you, using you, not giving you your due, treating you unfairly? Try to quantify the world's attack level as you see it on a scale of 1 to 10. Now consider this: The attack level you see is the projection of your verdict on yourself. That is the world you secretly feel you deserve. Try to let that in. Without that verdict, you would look out on the same forms and see nothing but "holiness and hope."

I. The Forgotten Song
Commentary by Robert Perry

1. Never forget the world the sightless "see" <u>must</u> be imagined, for what it <u>really</u> looks like <u>is</u> unknown to them. They must infer what <u>could</u> be seen from evidence forever indirect; and <u>reconstruct</u> their inferences as they stumble and fall because of what they did <u>not</u> recognize, or walk unharmed through open doorways that they <u>thought</u> were closed. And so it is with you. You do <u>not</u> see. Your cues for inference are wrong, and so you stumble and fall down upon the stones you did not recognize, but fail to be aware you <u>can</u> go through the doors you <u>thought</u> were closed, but which stand open before unseeing eyes, waiting to <u>welcome</u> you.

Here we see Jesus' skill at crafting a great metaphor. The first sentences are talking literally about the blind. They point out the obvious, that the blind have to infer their world from indirect evidence, and then revise those inferences as they encounter things they did not expect. But we all knew that. Why is he telling us this?

Then he says, "And so it is with you. You do not see." Oh, this is about *us*. We are the blind. How can that be? We see the objects in front of us. Ah, but do we see *meaning*? No. This leaves us forever trying to infer what things mean based on indirect cues. But these cues are wrong, and so just when we think we can sail smoothly ahead, we stumble over unforeseen obstacles. And just when we think we are trapped, with no way out, we fail to see the open doorway standing right in front of us.

Seeing meaning is far more important than seeing form. Appearances can so easily deceive; what we want is the truth behind them. And that is precisely what we do not see. We can move through a room just fine, but we are terrible at moving through *life*. When it comes to the important stuff, we really are the blind.

Application: Have you ever felt like you were sailing along down a smooth path only to find yourself stumbling over stones you didn't know were there? Can you think of a specific example?

2. How foolish is it to attempt to judge what could be seen instead. It is not necessary to <u>imagine</u> what the world must look like. It must be <u>seen</u> before you recognize it for what it is. You can be <u>shown</u> which doors are open, and you can <u>see</u> where safety lies; and which way leads to darkness, which to light. Judgment will <u>always</u> give you false directions, but vision <u>shows</u> you where to go. Why should you guess?

The process of inferring based on indirect cues is the same process that Jesus has already been talking about, the process of *imagining* based on *judgment*. In both cases, you are assembling an inaccurate mental picture that rests not on direct perception, but on shaky guesswork. Now he is saying, "Why do that? You don't need to guess. You can just take the blindfold off." Taking the blindfold off means seeing through vision. Vision shows us where the obstacles are and where the open doors are. With it, we glide effortlessly through life. Now when it comes to the important stuff, *we can see*.

3. There is no <u>need</u> to learn through pain. And gentle lessons are acquired joyously, and are remembered gladly. What gives you happiness you <u>want</u> to learn and <u>not</u> forget. It is not this you would deny. <u>Your</u> question is whether the means by which this course is learned <u>will</u> bring to you the joy it promises. If you <u>believed</u> it would, the <u>learning</u> of it would be <u>no</u> problem. You are not a happy learner yet because you still remain uncertain that vision gives you <u>more</u> than judgment does, and you <u>have</u> learned that both you <u>cannot</u> have.

No one likes to learn through pain. However, we are undecided about which brings us less pain—judgment or vision. Sure, the Course promises that vision will make us glowingly happy, but will the Course keep this promise? "If you believed it would, the learning of it would be no problem."

What, then, do we believe? Are we truly convinced that seeing people as a sinless, changeless light will really bring us joy—more joy than the way we see now? I hate to say this, but the answer is no. If the answer were yes, we would find the Course itself, and everything in it, a total cinch. We would be seeing with vision right now, and would be so filled with celestial love that we could hardly restrain ourselves from kneeling at everyone's feet.

4. The blind become <u>accustomed</u> to their world by their adjustments to it. They think they know their way about in it. They learned it, not through joyous lessons, but through the stern necessity of limits they believed they could not overcome. And <u>still</u> believing this, they hold those lessons dear, and cling to them <u>because</u> they cannot see. They do not understand the lessons *keep* them blind. This they do <u>not</u> believe. And so they keep the world they learned to "see" in their imagination, believing that their choice is that or nothing. They hate the world they learned through pain. And everything they think is in it serves to remind them that <u>they</u> are incomplete and bitterly deprived.

5. Thus they <u>define</u> their life and where they live, <u>adjusting</u> to it as they think they must, afraid to lose the little that they have. And so it is with all who see the body as all they have and all their brothers have. They try to reach each other, and they fail, and fail again. And they <u>adjust</u> to loneliness, believing that to <u>keep</u> the body is to <u>save</u> the little that they have.

Jesus now returns to the subject of the blind. It is a poignant picture of the private side of blindness. Yet again, of course, he is really talking about us. As the blind, we live in a world full of limits. In particular, they are limitations on *joining*. We want to join, but when we try to, we end up running into or tripping over obstacles—all of which amount to the obstacle of the body. Hitting up against this obstacle thousands of times gradually teaches us that joining is just not possible here. We hate all the bruises we have received from our attempts at joining, but we also gradually adjust to their message: Joining is a nice dream, a dream that cannot come true. And though we hate the bruising lessons we have been taught, we also cling to them, for we figure that if we don't remember them well, we will get bruised even more.

What we don't realize is that this process of reluctantly adjusting to a world of limits actually keeps us blind. If we refused to adjust, the scales would fall off our eyes. With eyes open, we would see how easy it is to walk right past those bodies and join with our brothers.

Listen, and try to think if you remember what we will speak of now.

6. Listen,—perhaps you catch a hint of an ancient state not quite forgotten; dim, perhaps, and yet not altogether unfamiliar, like a song whose name is long forgotten, and the circumstances in which you heard completely unremembered. Not the whole song has stayed with

you, but just a little wisp of melody, attached not to a person or a place or anything particular. But you remember, from just this little part, how lovely was the song, how wonderful the setting where you heard it, and how you loved those who were there and listened with you.

7. The notes are nothing. Yet you have kept them with you, not for themselves, but as a soft reminder of what would make you weep if you remembered how dear it was to you. You <u>could</u> remember, yet you are afraid, believing you would lose the world you learned since then. And yet you know that nothing in the world you learned is half so dear as this. Listen, and see if you remember an ancient song you knew so long ago and held more dear than any melody you taught yourself to cherish since.

This is one of the most beloved passages in the Course, and for good reason. In this, Jesus takes the common experience in which remembering just a few notes of an old song can bring on a wave of nostalgia, evoking an entire time in our life and the people with whom we shared that time.

But, of course, that is not what Jesus is really talking about. He is talking about remembering a song not from the fifties, but from eternity. He is talking about those moments where something causes a wave of vague nostalgia for a lost and nameless paradise to wash over us. We have this undefined sense that there was a time and place where everything was perfect, and the joy of this thought and the longing to be there are almost too much to bear. In those moments, we are remembering a wisp of melody from the song of Heaven, and this wisp brings back for us that entire "time" in our existence.

Why is it just a wisp? Because we are afraid that if we remembered the whole song—which we could—we would lose everything we have painstakingly built since those carefree days. And we would.

Application: Do you have a sense at times of some better place or state, some distant paradise, some higher realm, some nobler estate, some sort of pristine perfection you wished you were living in?

What sorts of things give you this sense?

Is it possible that this haunting sense you have is not some fantasy, but an actual memory, a fragment of a memory of a real realm you really did live in? How does that make you feel?

8. Beyond the body, beyond the sun and stars, past <u>everything</u> you see and yet somehow familiar, is an arc of golden light that stretches as you look into a great and shining circle. And all the circle fills with light before your eyes. The edges of the circle disappear, and what is in it is no longer contained at all. The light expands and covers everything, extending to infinity forever shining and with no break or limit anywhere. Within it <u>everything</u> is joined in perfect continuity. Nor is it possible to imagine that anything <u>could</u> be outside, for there <u>is</u> nowhere that this light is not.

Now he sets aside the song metaphor and instead builds a visual image, step by step. First it's an arc of light. Then it's a circle of light. Then the circle fills with light. Then its edges disappear, so that the light covers everything, "extending to infinity forever shining and with no break or limit anywhere." What is this limitless light?

9. This is the vision of the Son of God, whom you know well. Here is the sight of him who knows his Father. Here is the memory of what you <u>are</u>; a <u>part</u> of this, with <u>all</u> of it within, and <u>joined</u> to all as surely as all is joined in you. <u>Accept</u> the vision that can show you this, and <u>not</u> the body.

Above I asked what is this limitless light. Here is the answer: "This is the vision of the Son of God." This is what we see when we take the blindfold off and look on our brother with vision. We see who our brother really is, and who we really are, and who everyone really is—all part of this endless light. Which do you think would give you more joy, seeing this or seeing the body? Think of those visionaries who see Mary. They become completely transfixed on the holy vision before them, and totally unaware of everything else, including doctors testing them. If we saw this light, we would be like them, "unheeding of the body's witnesses before the rapture of Christ's holy face" (W-pI.151.8:4).

You <u>know</u> the ancient song, and know it well. Nothing will ever be as dear to you as is this ancient hymn of love the Son of God sings to his Father still.
10. And now the blind can see, for that same song they sing in honor of their Creator gives praise to them as well. The blindness that they made will not withstand the memory of this song. And they will look

upon the vision of the Son of God, remembering who he is they sing of. What is a miracle but this remembering? And who is there in whom this memory lies not? The light in one awakens it in all. And when you see it in your brother, you *are* remembering for everyone.

Clearly, the song and the light are intimately related. We who make up that limitless light—the Sonship—are the ones singing the song. We sing it in praise of our Creator and in praise of ourselves and each other. If we will just let ourselves remember the song, we will also remember "who he is [we] sing of." We will remember the Son of God. And then we will see him. Our eyes will open and we will be caught up in the rapturous vision of that infinite light. Our blindness "will not withstand the memory of this song."

Application. Close your eyes and visualize the following, step by step:

"Beyond the body, beyond the sun and stars, past everything you see and yet somehow familiar, is an arc of golden light that stretches as you look into a great and shining circle.
And all the circle fills with light before your eyes.
The edges of the circle disappear, and what is in it is no longer contained at all.
The light expands and covers everything, extending to infinity forever shining and with no break or limit anywhere.
Within it everything is joined in perfect continuity.
Nor is it possible to imagine that anything could be outside, for there is nowhere that this light is not.
This is the vision of the Son of God, whom you know well.
Here is the sight of him who knows his Father.
Here is the memory of what you are:[you are] a part of this, [imagine that] with all of it within [you], and [you are] joined to all [of it] as surely as all [of it] is joined in you." (T-21.I.8:1-9:3)

And while you look on this endless light, imagine that you hear a heavenly song coming from it, an achingly beautiful, celestial song.
It is the most beautiful thing you have ever heard.

As you listen to this song, you realize that it is a hymn of love, being sung by the Son—the endless light—to his Father.

It sings of an ancient love, so beautiful and sweet and deep that you think it will make your heart burst to keep listening to it.

And now you realize that when you have felt that sense of a better place, a higher state, a perfect realm, you were actually remembering a little wisp of this ancient hymn.

And now you remember that the setting where you heard it was no music hall; it was Heaven.

And that those you loved who listened with you were all your fellow Sons of God, infinite in number.

And that you not only listened to the song, but that you joined your voice to it as well.

There is one final step: remembering this song allows you to see the person next to you (choose someone) for who he really is.

He is not his body. He is not his personality. He is not what his behavior shows to your body's eyes.

That is the condition of blindness, where you guess what he is based on indirect evidence.

Now you realize that he was one of those you loved who listened with you.

He was one of those who sang this beautiful song with you.

He is part of that endless light; *part* of it and *all* of it.

So as you look on him in your mind, see past the body, past the identity your judgment has built up from the evidence of his behavior.

Let your mind see that arc of golden light, that stretches into a circle, that then fills with light, whose edges then disappear, whose light expands to cover everything.

Then realize that *this* is your brother.

"This is the vision of the Son of God, whom you know well."

"What is a miracle but this remembering?

And who is there in whom this memory lies not?

The light in one awakens it in all.

And when you see [this light] in your brother, you *are* remembering for everyone."

247

II. The Responsibility for Sight
Commentary by Robert Perry

1. We have repeated how little is asked of you to learn this course. It is the same small willingness you need to have your whole relationship transformed to joy; the <u>little</u> gift you offer to the Holy Spirit for which He gives you <u>everything</u>; the very little on which salvation rests; the tiny change of mind by which the crucifixion is changed to resurrection. And being true, it is so simple that it cannot fail to be <u>completely</u> understood. Rejected yes, but <u>not</u> ambiguous. And if you choose <u>against</u> it now it will <u>not</u> be because it is obscure, but rather that this <u>little</u> cost seemed, in <u>your</u> judgment, to be <u>too much</u> to pay for peace.

Jesus has indeed repeatedly told us that his course asks almost nothing of us. All it asks, as he said a few sections ago, is that we desire to see our brother through vision, rather than through judgment. That's it. That is the hinge on which literally everything turns. It is simple and completely unambiguous. We can't complain that we don't understand it. Therefore, if we choose against it, the only possible reason is "that this little cost seemed, in your judgment, to be too much to pay for peace." You wish he would give us more wiggle room, don't you?

2. This is the <u>only</u> thing that you need do for vision, happiness, release from pain and the <u>complete</u> escape from sin, <u>all</u> to be given you. Say <u>only</u> this, but <u>mean</u> it with <u>no</u> reservations, for here the power of salvation lies:

> *I **am** responsible for what I see.*
> *I choose [Ur: **chose**] the feelings I experience, and I decide upon [Ur: **decided on**] the goal I would achieve.*
> *And everything that <u>seems</u> to happen <u>to</u> me I ask for [Ur: **asked for**], and receive as I have [Ur: **had**] asked.*

Deceive yourself no longer that you are helpless in the face of what is done <u>to</u> you. Acknowledge but that <u>you</u> have been mistaken, and <u>all</u> effects of your mistakes will disappear.

II. The Responsibility for Sight

This is a beloved paragraph among Course students, yet a very in-your-face one as well. It follows directly from the first paragraph. That one said, "All you need do is offer the Holy Spirit this one little gift." Now this one says, "Okay, here it is. Why not offer that little gift right now?"

So let's do it. All we need do for all the Course's promises to come, for all the happiness we've ever wanted to be ours, is to say these lines. But it's not enough to say them. We have to mean them, with no reservations. And we can do that, if we just remember that they are the gateway to all the longings of our heart, to everything we have ever truly wanted. Let's do it now:

> *I **am** responsible for what I see.*
> *I **chose** the feelings I experience,*
> *and I **decided on** the goal I would achieve.*
> *And everything that **seems** to happen to me*
> *I **asked for**, and receive as I had asked.*

3. It is impossible the Son of God be merely driven by events <u>outside</u> of him. It is impossible that happenings that come to him were <u>not</u> his choice. His power of decision is the <u>determiner</u> of every situation in which he seems to <u>find</u> himself by chance or accident. No accident nor chance is <u>possible</u> within the universe as God created it, <u>outside</u> of which is nothing. Suffer, and <u>you</u> decided sin was your goal. Be happy, and you <u>gave</u> the power of decision to Him Who <u>must</u> decide for God for you. This is the little gift you offer to the Holy Spirit, and even this He gives to you to give yourself. For <u>by</u> this gift is given you the power to release your savior, that <u>he</u> may give salvation unto <u>you</u>.

We are the Son of God. How can we be overpowered by things outside our will? This is our dream. None of it is random. Our mind is pulling the strings on all of it, just as in our nighttime dreams. If the dream is frightening and punitive, we chose it in order to prove to us what sinners we are. But we can make another choice. We can lay claim to our power to see differently, and then give this power to the Holy Spirit. He will then give it back to us as the power to see our brother sinless. This will release that brother, who is really our sleeping savior, allowing him to open his eyes and fulfill the function for which he was born: to give salvation to us.

4. Begrudge not then this little offering. <u>Withhold</u> it, and you keep the world as now you see it. <u>Give it away</u>, and everything <u>you</u> see goes with it. Never was so much given for so little. In the holy instant is this exchange effected and <u>maintained</u>. Here is the world you do <u>not</u> want brought to the one you <u>do</u>. And here the one you do is <u>given</u> you <u>because</u> you want it. Yet for this, the <u>power</u> of your wanting must first be <u>recognized</u>. You must accept its <u>strength</u>, and <u>not</u> its weakness. You must perceive that what is strong enough to <u>make</u> a world can let it go, and <u>can</u> accept correction if it is willing to see that it was wrong.

Notice how he keeps telling us just how much is contained in this one decision. It is the decision to claim the power of our desire, the power to see what we want to see, and then give this power to the Holy Spirit.

Application: Look around you and say,

I accept that my desire was strong enough to make this world.
I accept that my desire is strong enough to let it go.
And my desire is big enough to accept correction, and admit that
*   it was wrong.*

If we can repeat these lines with sincerity, we will enter a holy instant, in which the old world passes away, and the new one is laid before us in all its glory.

5. The world you see is but the idle witness that you were <u>right</u>. This witness is insane. You trained it in its testimony, and as it gave it <u>back</u> to you, you listened and convinced yourself that what it saw was true. <u>You did this to yourself</u>. See only this, and you will also see how circular the reasoning on which your "seeing" rests. This was <u>not</u> given you. This was your <u>gift</u> to you <u>and to your brother</u>. Be willing, then, to have it taken <u>from</u> him and be replaced with truth. And as you look upon the change in <u>him</u>, it will be given you to see it in <u>yourself</u>.

Hear the story of the mad lawyer. This lawyer was completely innocent, but, being mentally ill, he dearly wanted to believe in his guilt. So he managed to get himself put on trial for a crime he did not commit. And he managed to be the prosecuting attorney in this trial as well. He had no proof of his guilt, of course, so he hired a witness, and trained this witness carefully over weeks to repeat a foolproof story that established the lawyer's guilt beyond doubt. This witness was the lynchpin in his case. The training worked. When the witness got up on the stand, he played his part perfectly, repeating all the lies with the appearance of complete honesty. Of course, the lawyer had taught him these lies, so he knew they weren't true. And yet, as he listened to this witness, he thought, "Oh my God, this is horrifying. I was right. I really did commit this crime!"

Unfortunately, this lawyer also managed to get his brother put on trial with him, as partners in this crime. Therefore, the testimony of this witness was sure to convict the brother as well.

We, of course, are this lawyer. The world is the witness. And the brother is our brother. What does this story do to the myth of our powerlessness in the face of the world?

> 6. Perhaps you do not see the need for you to give this little offering. Look closer, then, at what it <u>is</u>. And, very simply, see in it the whole exchange of separation for salvation. All that the ego is, is an idea that it is possible that things could <u>happen</u> to the Son of God <u>without</u> his will; and thus without the Will of his Creator, Whose Will cannot <u>be</u> separate from his own. This is the Son of God's <u>replacement</u> for his will, a mad revolt against what must forever be. This is the statement that he <u>has</u> the power to make God power<u>less</u> and so to take it [power] for himself [Ur: from *himself*], and leave himself <u>without</u> what God has willed <u>for</u> him [power]. This is the mad idea [that power can be taken from God and us] you have enshrined upon your altars, <u>and which you worship</u>. And anything that threatens this seems to <u>attack</u> your faith, for here is it invested. Think not that you are faithless, for your belief and trust in <u>this</u> is strong indeed.

This little offering—admitting that I have the power to see what I want to see—contains "the whole exchange of separation for salvation." This is because the separation was an attempt to wrench ourselves away from God, to take power away from Him and invest it in ourselves. Yet if our will and God's Will are one, then taking power away from Him means taking it from us as well. As the Father goes, so goes the Son. Therefore, the proof that we had really disempowered the Father would be that we found ourselves disempowered. The proof that something had happened outside of God's Will (the separation) was that things now happened outside of our own will.

This is the idea—the idol—that we have put on our altar and that we worship. (Remember this image from "The Temple of the Holy Spirit"?) We say we are faithless, but our faith in this idea—that things happen to us outside our will—is rock solid. Just let someone challenge this, and the gloves come off.

> 7. The Holy Spirit can <u>give</u> you faith in holiness and vision to see it easily enough. But you have not left open and unoccupied the altar where the gifts <u>belong</u>. Where <u>they</u> should be, <u>you</u> have set up your idols to something <u>else</u>. This <u>other</u> "will," which seems to <u>tell</u> you what must happen, you give [Ur: *gave*] reality. And what would <u>show</u> you otherwise must therefore seem unreal. All that is asked of you is to <u>make room</u> for truth. You are <u>not</u> asked to make or do what lies <u>beyond</u> your understanding. All you are asked to do is *let it in*; only to stop your <u>interference</u> with what will happen <u>of itself</u>; simply to recognize again the presence of what you <u>thought</u> you gave away.

The Holy Spirit could give us faith in our brother's holiness and vision to look on that holiness, so that it would be plain as day to us. He could do this with absolute ease. Then why hasn't it happened? Because there is no room on our inner altar to lay His gifts. Instead, something else is on that altar. That something is an alien presence that is seemingly outside our control. Our altar is its control room, from which it pulls all the strings in our life, causing the chaotic hurricane that blows around us. This other will that seems so beyond our control is nothing but the will of our ego.

Our job is simple: take a broom and sweep that alien off the altar. Once this is done, the Holy Spirit will lay His gifts on it without any further input from us.

> 8. Be willing, for an instant, to leave your altars free of what <u>you</u> placed upon them, and what is <u>really</u> there you <u>cannot</u> fail to see. The holy instant is <u>not</u> an instant of creation, but of <u>recognition</u>. For recognition comes of vision and <u>suspended</u> judgment. Then only it is possible to look within and see what <u>must</u> be there, plainly in sight, and wholly <u>independent</u> of inference and judgment. Undoing is not <u>your</u> task, but

it *is* up to you to welcome it or not. Faith and desire go hand in hand, for everyone believes in what he wants.

Now we learn that that hideous alien is not really on the altar at all. We only think he is there. We only infer that he must be there. It's a guess, an assumption. When we no longer want him there, we will look within with clearer eyes and instantly recognize that the Holy Spirit's gifts (faith in holiness and vision to see it) have been there all along. The hovering hologram of the alien presence had blocked our view of what was really there on the altar.

This is all we have to do: want the alien gone. If we do, the Holy Spirit will unplug the hologram. "Undoing is not your task, but it is up to you to welcome it or not."

> 9. We have already said that wishful thinking is how the ego deals with what it wants, to make it so. There is no better demonstration of the power of wanting, and therefore of <u>faith</u>, to make its goals seem real and possible. Faith in the <u>unreal</u> leads to <u>adjustments</u> of reality to make it fit the goal of madness. The goal of sin induces the perception of a fearful world to <u>justify</u> its purpose. What you desire, you <u>will</u> see. And if its reality is false, you will <u>uphold</u> it by <u>not</u> realizing all the adjustments <u>you</u> have introduced to <u>make</u> it so.

The mad lawyer is an ideal illustration of what this paragraph is talking about. The story there was all about his wishful thinking. He wanted to believe in his sinfulness, but it wasn't so. Yet that didn't stop him. He did two things. First, he set about adjusting reality, adjusting the real story to fit what he wanted to be true. He did this by training the witness to lie. Second, once he listened to the witness, he forgot that he had trained this witness, so now the story seemed like objective truth.

Our ego wanted to see a reality that witnessed to our sinfulness. Never mind that no such reality exists. It set about adjusting reality, until it had molded a world that did nothing but climb on the stand and swear that we did it. Then the ego says, "This is devastating testimony. I have not tampered with this witness. He must be telling us the truth."

> 10. When vision is <u>denied</u>, confusion of cause and effect becomes inevitable. The <u>purpose</u> now becomes to <u>keep obscure</u> the cause of the effect, and make effect appear to <u>be</u> a cause. This seeming independence

of effect enables it to be regarded as <u>standing by itself</u>, and capable of serving as a <u>cause</u> of the events and feelings its maker thinks <u>it</u> [the effect] causes. Earlier, we spoke of your desire to create your own creator, and be father and not son to him. This is the same desire. The Son is the effect, whose Cause he would deny. And so he seems to *be* the cause, producing real <u>effects</u>. Nothing can have effects <u>without</u> a cause, and to confuse the two is merely to fail to understand them both. 11. It is as needful that you recognize you <u>made</u> the world you see, as that you recognize that you did <u>not</u> create yourself. *They are the same mistake*. Nothing created <u>not</u> by your Creator has <u>any</u> influence over you. And if you think what <u>you</u> have made can <u>tell</u> you what you see and feel, and place your faith in its ability to do so, you <u>are</u> denying your Creator and <u>believing</u> that you made yourself. For if you think the world you made has power to make you what <u>it</u> wills, you <u>are</u> confusing Son and Father; effect and Source.

The ego's whole system is an attempt to confuse cause and effect, and actually reverse them. This system started with the idea that we, God's effect, could actually detach ourselves from His causation. We could become self-created and self-sufficient. Then we could take things one step further and turn around and actually cause Him. Now we would be First Cause.

But now this power that we have supposedly laid hold of must be denied. For the power we used to produce the separation could be used to undo it. Now the world that we caused must be seen as independent of us, as self-caused. Then it must turn around and seem to cause us, to cause our feelings, our perceptions, our life events, to even cause us to come into existence and go out of existence.

The first reversal of cause and effect (we become God's cause) is the height of grandiosity. The second reversal of cause and effect (the world becomes our cause) is the ultimate in disempowerment. They seem so different, yet they are the exact same error, the reversal of cause and effect. Indeed, they both deny God's causation. They both say that what God created not has power over us.

Application: We can undo both errors by seeing external events differently. Think of some event that seems to have you in its grip, to be exerting a terrible causation over you. Now say,

This does not cause me.
I caused it.
*But my Creator did **not** cause it.*
Therefore, it has no power over me.

12. The Son's creations <u>are</u> like his Father's. Yet in creating <u>them</u> the Son does not delude himself that he is <u>independent</u> of his Source. His union with It is the <u>Source</u> of his creating. <u>Apart</u> from this he <u>has</u> no power to create, and what he makes is meaningless. It changes <u>nothing</u> in creation, depends <u>entirely</u> upon the madness of its maker, and can<u>not</u> serve to justify the madness. Your brother thinks he made the world with you. Thus he denies creation. With you, he thinks the world he made, made <u>him</u>. Thus he denies he <u>made</u> it.

When we create in Heaven, our creative power flows from God through us. We are fully aware that the Source of our creative power is the Source of our being. What we create as a result is eternally real. That changes, however, when we try to create apart from God. When we make this world, this making does not flow from God. And so what we make is meaningless, powerless. "It changes nothing in creation, depends entirely upon the madness of its maker, and cannot serve to justify the madness."

This, I believe, is the missing piece in the New Age idea that "you created that." Yes, we made that illness, that poverty, that divorce—we made all of it. But God didn't create it. And therefore it has no power over us.

13. Yet the truth is you and your brother were both created by a loving Father, Who created you together and as one. <u>See</u> what "proves" otherwise [see the world], and you <u>deny</u> your whole reality. But grant that <u>everything</u> that seems to stand <u>between</u> you and your brother, keeping you from each other and separate from your Father, <u>you made in secret</u>, and the instant of release has come to you. <u>All</u> its effects are gone, because its source has been uncovered. It is its seeming <u>independence</u> of its source that keeps you prisoner. This <u>is</u> the same mistake as thinking <u>you</u> are independent of the Source by Which <u>you</u> were created, and have never left.

We cannot reflect too often on the image of the world as witness.

That is its whole purpose—to get up on the stand and testify to a certain view of reality, a certain view of our brothers, and a certain view of ourselves. In this view, we were not created by God. We were created by the relentless reproductive march of DNA. In this view, we are not one with our brother. We all stand alone inside different bodies, with different histories and life experiences. In this view, we are not one with God. We live here in this world, and where is God in this godforsaken place?

It is therefore not enough to say, "I caused this heart attack." We have to realize that we engineered the whole thing, down to the very structure of time and space, and that none of it is true. Unless we go all the way with this, we will believe this witness. We will accept its testimony. And then we are sunk.

Instead, we have to realize that this world is purely our effect, our dream. Thinking that it is independent of our causation is the same mistake as thinking that we are independent of God's causation.

Application: First think of someone close to you. Then look around you at all the things that seem to have power over you, noting the power each one seems to possess. Then say,

> *My brother [name] and I caused this.*
> *But God did not.*
> *Therefore, it has nothing to say about who we are.*
> *And it certainly has nothing to say about whether or not we can join.*

III. Faith, Belief and Vision
Commentary by Robert Perry

1. All special relationships have sin as their goal. For they are <u>bargains</u> with reality, toward which the seeming union is adjusted. Forget not this; to bargain is to set a limit, and any brother with whom you have a limited relationship, <u>you hate</u>. You may attempt to <u>keep</u> the bargain in the name of "fairness," sometimes demanding payment of yourself, perhaps more often of the other. Thus in the "fairness" you attempt to ease the guilt that comes from the accepted <u>purpose</u> of the relationship. And that is why the Holy Spirit must change its purpose to make it useful to <u>Him</u> and harmless to <u>you</u>.

At the base of each special relationship is an unspoken bargain: "I will love you and join with you only to the extent that you _____." Think about different relationships you have, and see if, with each one, that sentence doesn't readily complete itself in your mind.

Jesus makes several points about this. First, he says the bargain means you have a limited relationship. Think of those words "only to the extent that." They imply that the extent to which we will love and join with that person is not unlimited. It has a cap. It is "only to the extent that." Second, Jesus says that this means we really hate that person. The whole idea of the bargain is that they have to pay us before we love and join with them. When you have to pay someone to join with you, do they really love you? Third, he says that the hate-based nature of bargains makes the relationship a source of guilt. We try to ease this guilt by saying, "But the bargain is a fair one. I have nothing to feel guilty about." But we don't really say this to erase the guilt. We say it to keep the bargain, so that it can *continue* making us feel guilty, only at acceptable levels. For our whole goal in the relationship is sin—to convince ourselves we are sinners.

2. If you <u>accept</u> this change, you have accepted the <u>idea</u> of making room for truth. The *source* of sin is gone. You may <u>imagine</u> that you still experience its effects, but it is <u>not</u> your purpose and you no longer <u>want</u> it. No one allows a purpose to be <u>replaced</u> while he <u>desires</u> it, for

nothing is so cherished and protected as is a goal the mind accepts. This it will follow, grimly or happily, but <u>always</u> with faith and with the persistence that faith <u>inevitably</u> brings. The power of faith is <u>never</u> recognized if it is placed in sin. But it is <u>always</u> recognized if it is placed in love.

The only way out is to let the Holy Spirit change the goal of the relationship, from sin to holiness. This change is what makes a relationship holy. Even after this (as we have seen in "The Obstacles to Peace"), the old goal of sin will still hang around and seem to produce effects. Yet that doesn't matter. By setting a different goal, we have changed everything. When an alcoholic sets the goal of staying sober, it means that, even though he may have lapses, he doesn't really want the life of drinking he had before. When we set the goal of holiness, it means we don't really want sin anymore.

Everything is determined by the goal we set. Whatever it is, we will put our mind behind it, giving it our faith and our persistence. The problem, however, is that when our goal is sin, we are blind to this power. We don't realize that all the power lies in our devotion to sin; we think it lies in sin itself.

> 3. Why is it strange to you that faith can move mountains? This is indeed a little feat for such a power. For faith can keep the Son of God in chains as long as he believes he <u>is</u> in chains. And when he is <u>released</u> from them it will be simply because he no longer <u>believes</u> in them, <u>withdrawing</u> faith that they can hold him, and placing it in his freedom <u>instead</u>. It is impossible to place equal faith in opposite directions. What faith you give to sin you <u>take away</u> from holiness. And what you offer holiness has been <u>removed</u> from sin.

We have heard all our lives that "faith can move mountains." Yet that is nothing compared to an even greater feat that faith can perform: it can hold the Son of God in chains. Imagine what it would take to bind the omnipotent Son of God. Yet faith can do it. Of course, in this case, it is the Son of God's *own* faith. When he places faith in attaining the goal of sin, he loses sight of his power (as we just saw). He puts himself in chains. When he transfers that faith to reaching the goal of holiness, he withdraws faith from the chains, and they vanish.

The power of your faith, then, is everything. Nothing in this world can stand in its way, not mountains and not self-imposed chains.

> 4. Faith and belief and vision are the means by which the goal of holiness is reached. Through them the Holy Spirit leads you to the real world, and <u>away</u> from all illusions where your faith was laid. This is <u>His</u> direction; the only one He ever sees. And when you wander, He <u>reminds</u> you there <u>is</u> but one. <u>His</u> faith and <u>His</u> belief and vision are all for you. And when you have accepted them completely <u>instead</u> of yours, you will have need of them no longer. For faith and vision and belief are meaningful only <u>before</u> the state of certainty is reached. In Heaven they are unknown. Yet Heaven is <u>reached</u> through them.

Once we have set the goal of holiness, how do we reach it? We give holiness our *faith*, we give holiness our *belief*, and we see holiness with *vision*. That is the whole path, the act of giving these three things to holiness. We lose sight of this so easily, both as we focus on the things of the world, and as we focus on more peripheral elements of the spiritual path. We may lose sight of it for long periods of time. Yet the Holy Spirit will always call us back. He will keep doing that until we never forget again, until every ounce of our power is given to faith, belief, and vision. And then we will pass beyond them altogether, as faith in holiness, belief in holiness, and the vision of holiness are replaced with the *certainty* of holiness, which is what happens in Heaven.

> 5. It is impossible that the Son of God <u>lack</u> faith, but he <u>can</u> choose where he would have it <u>be</u>. Faithlessness is not a lack of <u>faith</u>, but faith in <u>nothing</u>. Faith given to illusions does <u>not</u> lack power, for <u>by</u> it does the Son of God believe that he is powerless. Thus is he faithless to <u>himself</u>, but <u>strong</u> in faith in his illusions <u>about</u> himself. For faith, perception and belief <u>you</u> made, as means for <u>losing</u> certainty and finding sin. This mad direction was your <u>choice</u>, and by your <u>faith</u> in what you chose, you made what you desired.

We are all trying to work up more faith, yet Jesus says that we already have abundant faith. Right now, we have rock-like faith in the essential sinfulness and nothingness of our being. This faith is incredibly powerful, for we have used it to bind the greatest power on earth—ourselves. In short, we have lost faith in ourselves, and poured it into illusions *about* ourselves. What an ironic situation! But this is a choice we made, and can change. The good news here is that we don't have to muster faith; we just need to redirect it. We don't need to change ourselves from doubting skeptics into strong believers. We are all strong believers—in something. We just need to change what that something is. Isn't that a relief?

> 6. The Holy Spirit has a use for all the means for sin by which you sought to <u>find</u> it. But as <u>He</u> uses them they lead <u>away</u> from sin, because His <u>purpose</u> lies in the <u>opposite</u> direction. He sees the <u>means</u> you use, but <u>not</u> the purpose for which you made them. He would not take them <u>from</u> you, for He sees their value as a means for what <u>He</u> wills for you. You made perception that you might choose among your brothers, and seek for sin with them. The Holy Spirit sees perception as a means to teach you that the vision of a <u>holy</u> relationship is all you *want* to see. Then will you give your faith to holiness, desiring and <u>believing</u> in it <u>because</u> of your desire.

We have spent a long time establishing and building these abilities. We painstakingly built up our faith and belief, so that we could give them to sin. We ourselves made the faculty of perception, so that we could look on sin, and so that we could choose our favorite brothers to seek sin *with*. Having built up our faith, belief, and perception, let's not set them aside as impediments to awakening. Let's use them *for* awakening. Let's allow the Holy Spirit to redirect them so that they serve the goal of holiness. This is essentially what Jesus said to Helen and Bill earlier in the Course dictation:

> You have been chosen to teach the Atonement precisely *because* you have been *extreme* examples of allegiance to your thought systems, and therefore have developed the capacity *for* allegiance. It has indeed been misplaced. Bill had become an outstanding example of allegiance to apathy, and you have become a startling example of fidelity to variability. But this *is* a form of faith, which you yourselves had grown willing to redirect. You cannot doubt the *strength* of your devotion when you consider how faithfully you observed it. It was quite evident that you had *already* developed the ability to follow a better model, if you could *accept* it. (Urtext)

> 7. Faith and belief become <u>attached</u> to vision, as all the means that once served sin are <u>redirected</u> now toward holiness. For what you think is sin

is <u>limitation,</u> and whom you try to limit to the body <u>you hate because you fear.</u> In your refusal to forgive him, you would <u>condemn</u> him to the body because the means for sin are [Ur: is] dear to you. And so the <u>body</u> has your faith and your belief. But <u>holiness</u> would set your brother free, removing hatred by removing fear, <u>not</u> as a symptom, but at its source.

8. Those who would <u>free</u> their brothers from the body can <u>have</u> no fear. They have renounced the means for sin [the body] by choosing to let all limitations be <u>removed</u>. As they desire to look upon their brothers in holiness, the power of their belief and faith sees far <u>beyond</u> the body, <u>supporting</u> vision, <u>not</u> obstructing it. But first they chose to <u>recognize</u> how much their faith had limited their understanding of the world, <u>desiring</u> to place its power elsewhere should another point of view be <u>given</u> them. The miracles that follow this decision are also born of faith. For all who choose to look <u>away</u> from sin <u>are</u> given vision, and <u>are</u> led to holiness.

What we call sin is simply the attempt to limit a brother's magnitude and worth, to cut him down to our ego's size. We are afraid of acknowledging him as a limitless spirit, and so we try to stuff him into his body. We condemn him to its tiny prison, to serve out his time there on death row. Why do we want our brothers shut up in their bodies? Because the body is the "means for sin." Its errant behavior provides daily proof that sin is the real power in the universe. That is why we have poured our faith and belief into the body—because the goal of sin dictates that we do so.

The way out of this is to first realize how much our faith in sin has limited our view of the world and everyone in it. We have stuffed everyone into little boxes. We need to be honest about this. This will spark our desire to transfer the power of our faith to something truer. And this will finally allow us to lift faith and belief from what our physical eyes show us, and place them in what vision shows us—the imageless holiness that is our brother's reality. When we do this, when we see our brothers as lights whose vast radiance extends far beyond the body, we give them miracles. We set them free. Now they have been released from seeing themselves as shut up in their body's tiny prison.

Application: Ask yourself the following questions:

Do you see that you have strong faith in the sinfulness of others and yourself?

Do you think that perhaps this faith has put everyone in a box and thus vastly limited your understanding of the world?

Given this, would you want to put your faith elsewhere, should a better point of view be given you?

Is it possible that the Holy Spirit's view of the world is a better point of view?

> 9. Those who believe in sin <u>must</u> think the Holy Spirit asks for sacrifice, for this is how they think *their* purpose is accomplished. Brother, the Holy Spirit <u>knows</u> that sacrifice brings <u>nothing</u>. He makes no bargains. And if you seek to limit Him, you will hate Him <u>because you are afraid</u>. The gift that He has given you is more than <u>anything</u> that stands this side of Heaven. The instant for its recognition is at hand. Join your awareness to what has been <u>already</u> joined [the two of you in your holy relationship]. The faith you give your brother <u>can</u> accomplish this. For He Who <u>loves</u> the world is seeing it <u>for</u> you, without one spot of sin upon it, and in the innocence that makes the sight of it as beautiful as Heaven.

We hear that the Holy Spirit is offering us the gift of vision, yet we unconsciously fill in, "Yes, but I need to make sacrifices for Him first." For we see our relationship with Him along the lines of a human bargain, in which one party sacrifices for the sake of the other, so that the other will cough up his gifts. We project our ways onto Him, but this is just our attempt to limit Him, because we actually fear Him.

Instead, we need to simply accept His gift of vision, for free. We do this by placing our faith in what that gift would show us: our brother's holiness. If we just do this one thing, He will allow us to see the world as He does, "without one spot of sin upon it, and in the innocence that makes the sight of it as beautiful as Heaven."

Application: Look around the world and imagine seeing it without one spot of sin on it. Imagine seeing it as so innocent that the sight of it is as beautiful as Heaven.

> 10. Your faith in sacrifice has given it great power in your sight; except you do not realize you <u>cannot</u> see <u>because</u> of it. For sacrifice <u>must</u> be

exacted of a body, and by another body. The mind could neither ask it nor receive it of itself [without enlisting the body]. And no more could the body. The intention is in the mind, which tries to use the body to carry out the means for sin in which the mind believes. Thus is the joining of mind and body an inescapable belief of those who value sin. And so is sacrifice invariably a means for limitation, and thus for hate.

Minds cannot really give or receive sacrifice, for sacrifice is loss, and the mind is forever whole. So, in order for the mind to engage in sacrifice, it has to use the body, which *is* able to lose in all sorts of ways. For sacrifice to work, then, the mind and body must be a single system, with each one providing its special part. Within the mindset of sacrifice, then, we see everyone as imprisoned in their bodies, and thus we see everyone as a sinner. We have so much faith in this that we don't realize that it has blinded us. We see our brother's body, but we are completely blind to who he really is.

11. Think you the Holy Spirit is concerned with this? He gives not what it is His purpose to lead you *from* [sacrifice]. You think He would deprive you [make you sacrifice] for your good. But "good" and "deprivation" are opposites, and cannot meaningfully join in any way. It is like saying that the moon and sun are one because they come with night and day, and so they must be joined. Yet sight of one is but the sign the other has disappeared from sight. Nor is it possible that what gives light be one with what depends on darkness to be seen. Neither demands the sacrifice of the other. Yet on the absence of the other does each depend.

The previous paragraph attempted to show us just how ugly the whole idea of sacrifice is. Now Jesus asks us, "Do you really think that this is how the Holy Spirit works?" You think that He wants to deprive you for your good, that He wants you to sacrifice for the sake of His greater reward. This is the traditional concept, isn't it? Yet that is like saying that He wants you to *lose* so you can *gain*, which makes Him sound very conflicted and contradictory. The truth is, He just wants you to gain. Gain is good; sacrifice is loss. Gain/good and sacrifice/loss are opposites. Saying that good *depends on* sacrifice is like saying that sight of the sun depends on sight on the moon.

12. The body was made to <u>be</u> a sacrifice to sin, and in the darkness so it still is seen. Yet in the light of vision it is looked upon quite differently. You <u>can</u> have faith in it to serve the Holy Spirit's goal, and give it power to serve as means to help the blind to see. But in their seeing they look <u>past</u> it, as do you. The faith and the belief you gave it <u>belongs</u> beyond. You gave perception and belief and faith from mind <u>to</u> body. Let them now be given <u>back</u> to what <u>produced</u> them, and can use them still to <u>save</u> itself from what it made.

By the dim light of the moon, you hazily see your body tied to a stone altar, waiting to be sacrificed to sin. But when the sun rises and you can see more clearly, the body looks very different. You see it as an instrument to serve the goal of holiness. You see it as a tool to help the blind to see. Yet once they see, they will look right past it. And you will, too. For you are in the process of withdrawing faith, belief, and perception from the body. You originally transferred them from the mind to the body. Now you are reversing that. You are putting the power back in your mind. You putting your mind in the driver's seat, where it has always been. It is what made faith, belief, and perception, and now it can use them to save itself from what it made.

IV. The Fear to Look Within
Commentary by Robert Perry

1. The Holy Spirit will <u>never</u> teach you that you are sinful. <u>Errors</u> He will correct, but this makes no one fearful. You are indeed afraid to look within and see the sin you <u>think</u> is there. This you would <u>not</u> be fearful to admit. Fear in association with sin the ego deems quite appropriate, and smiles approvingly. <u>It</u> has no fear to let you feel ashamed. It doubts not your belief and faith in sin. Its temples do not shake because of <u>this</u>. Your faith that sin is there but witnesses to your desire that it *be* there to see. This merely <u>seems</u> to be the source of fear.

Application: We may have difficulty relating to the notion that we are afraid to look within and see sin, especially to the extent that we have been influenced by contemporary spiritual attitudes of wrapping our ego in a kind of divine approval. To get in touch with this fear:

- Think about all the things you regret having done...or said... or thought.
- Think of various character traits of yours that you really wish you didn't have.
- Reflect on all the situations in which you assigned the blame to others, and consider at least some of the time you were surely denying your own responsibility.
- Reflect on all the unkind things that people have said or thought about you, and consider that their assessment of your behavior may have been more correct than you wanted to admit.

Now imagine that you could be shown the person within you from whom all these things came, that you could be shown this person unvarnished, stripped of all excuses. How would you feel about that?

Presumably, you would feel fear. In more traditional settings, this fear is looked upon as a badge of merit, a sign of true holiness. Yet the challenge of this section is to see this fear as ultimately a decoy fear, an insincere fear that serves to mask the *real* fear.

2. Remember that the ego is <u>not</u> alone. Its rule <u>is</u> tempered, and its unknown "enemy," Whom it cannot even see, it <u>fears</u>. Loudly the ego tells you <u>not</u> to look inward, for if you do your eyes will light on sin, and God will strike you blind. This you believe, and so you do <u>not</u> look. Yet this is <u>not</u> the ego's hidden fear, nor <u>yours</u> who serve it. Loudly indeed the ego claims it <u>is</u>; <u>too</u> loudly and <u>too</u> often. For underneath this constant shout and frantic proclamation, the ego is <u>not</u> certain it is so. Beneath your fear to look within because of sin is yet <u>another</u> fear, and one which makes the ego tremble.

The ego is constantly shouting, "Oh my God! I can't believe that hateful thought you just had, that callous thing you just did, that spiteful thing you just said. If I were you, I would never look within. You'll never recover from the horror of what you'll see there." In response, we think, "That voice is right. I better not look within. I better make up all kinds of stories about how I'm really the hero and everyone else is at fault. I better embrace spiritual and therapeutic concepts that tell my ego to celebrate itself." But all of this is a ruse. The ego has its own reasons for tricking you into not looking within, reasons it is not telling you.

3. What if you looked within and saw <u>no</u> sin? This "fearful" question is one the ego <u>never</u> asks. And you who ask it now <u>are</u> threatening the ego's whole defensive system too seriously for it to bother to <u>pretend</u> it is your friend. Those who have joined their brothers <u>have</u> detached themselves from their belief that their identity lies in the ego. A holy relationship is one in which you join with what <u>is</u> part of you in <u>truth</u>. And your belief in sin has been <u>already</u> shaken, nor are you now <u>entirely</u> unwilling to look within and see it <u>not</u>.

What if real self-honesty looked at the source of all our selfishness and attack, without disguise, saw its horror and said, "Huh, that's interesting. I wonder what lies past that"? What if this self-honesty then looked deeper and saw, at the center of our being, the purest holiness, as holy as God Himself? This question threatens our ego to its core, and will provoke its retaliation in some form. Yet those who have entered a holy relationship are in a new position in relation to their ego. They have a newfound openness to looking at sinlessness within, and they no longer care so much about the ego's shrill rantings.

Application: Ask yourself as sincerely and searchingly as you can, "What if the 'person' that is the source of all my selfish and unkind thoughts, deeds, and character traits is not the real me? What if it just serves to cover a me that is its opposite in every way?"

4. Your liberation still is only partial; still limited and incomplete, yet born <u>within</u> you. Not wholly mad, you <u>have</u> been willing to look on much of your insanity and <u>recognize</u> its madness. Your faith is moving inward, <u>past</u> insanity and on to reason. And what your reason tells you now the ego would not hear. The Holy Spirit's purpose was accepted by the part of your mind the ego knows not of. No more did <u>you</u>. And yet this part, with which you now identify, is <u>not</u> afraid to look upon <u>itself</u>. It knows no sin [Ur: It *knows* that it is sinless]. How, otherwise, <u>could</u> it have been willing to see the Holy Spirit's purpose as its own? 5. This part has seen your brother, and <u>recognized</u> him perfectly since time began. And it desired nothing but to <u>join</u> with him and to be free again, as once it was. It has been waiting for the birth of freedom; the <u>acceptance</u> of release to come to you. And now you recognize that it was <u>not</u> the ego that joined the Holy Spirit's purpose, and so there <u>must</u> be something else.

These paragraphs describe a part of us that seems to lie in between our true nature and our conscious mind. They describe the same part of us that was depicted in Helen's first vision leading up to the Course. Not long after she and Bill joined in a holy relationship, she experienced this inner vision:

The first of the series began with a picture of an unrecognized female figure, heavily draped and kneeling with bowed head. Thick chains were twisted around her wrists and ankles. A fire rose high above her head from a large metal brazier standing near her on a low tripod. She seemed to be some sort of priestess, and the fire appeared to be associated with an ancient religious rite. This figure came to me almost daily for several weeks, each time with a noticeable change. The chains began to drop away and she started to raise her head. At last she stood up very slowly, with only a short, unconnected length of chain still tied to her left wrist. The fire blazed with unaccustomed brightness as she rose.

I was quite unprepared for the intensity of my emotional reaction to her. When she first raised her eyes and looked at me I was terribly afraid. I was sure she would be angry and expected that her eyes would be filled with condemnation and disdain. I kept my head turned away the first few times I saw her after she stood up, but finally made up my mind to look straight at her face. When I did, I burst into tears. Her face was gentle and full of compassion, and her eyes were beyond description. The best word I could find in describing them to Bill was "innocent." She had never seen what I was afraid she would find in me. She knew nothing about me that warranted condemnation. Yet she did know many things I had never known, or at least had entirely forgotten. I loved her so much that I literally fell on my knees in front of her. Then I tried unsuccessfully to unite with her as she stood facing me, either by slipping over to her side or drawing her to mine. I noticed that she still had a few links of chain around her wrists. That, I felt, was probably the problem. (*Absence from Felicity*, pp. 97-98)

This vision of the priestess conveys the same idea that our two paragraphs are talking about. There is some part of our mind of which we have previous been unaware. It has retained its purity, but it is shackled by our identification with our ego. However, now that we have joined with our brother in the Holy Spirit's goal, its shackles are coming off. It is rising up to our conscious mind. We still fear how it sees us—what it says about who we are. But, as it turns out, it sees only *itself* in us. It sees us as perfectly innocent.

Think not that this is madness. For this your reason tells you, and it follows perfectly from what you have already learned.
6. There is no inconsistency in what the Holy Spirit teaches. This is the reasoning of the sane. You have perceived the ego's madness, and not been made afraid because you did not choose to share in it. At times it still deceives you. Yet in your saner moments, its ranting strikes no terror in your heart. For you have realized that all the gifts it would withdraw from you, in rage at your "presumptuous" wish to look within, you do not want. A few remaining trinkets still seem to shine and catch your eye. Yet you would not "sell" Heaven to have them.

These passages introduce the important topic of reason in the Course. Reason gets a bad name in many spiritual circles, but in the Course it is a key virtue. In the Course, the ego is logical, but completely *irrational*.

The Holy Spirit, on the other hand, is both logical *and* rational. The dictionary tells us that reason is "sound judgment," "good sense," "sanity," and "the power of intelligent and dispassionate thought." Does the ego have any of these things?

Jesus is clearly talking about a higher kind of reason than what we are used to. What does this reason look like? It looks like this: The Holy Spirit's purpose couldn't have been accepted by your ego, "and so there must be something else" in you besides your ego. His goal must have been accepted by another part of you, a part that *knows* its sinlessness. "How, otherwise, *could* it have been willing to see the Holy Spirit's purpose [of sinlessness] as its own?" This is the kind of reasoning Jesus wants us to engage in. Indeed, it is the kind of reasoning he has been demonstrating throughout.

> 7. And now the ego *is* afraid. Yet what it hears in terror, the <u>other</u> part hears as the sweetest music; the song it longed to hear since first the ego came into your mind. The ego's weakness is <u>its</u> <u>strength</u>. The song of freedom, which sings the praises of <u>another</u> world, brings to it hope of peace. For it <u>remembers</u> Heaven, and now it sees that Heaven <u>has</u> come to earth at last, from which the ego's rule has kept it out so long. Heaven has come because it found a home in your relationship on earth. And earth can hold no longer what has been <u>given</u> Heaven as its own.

Now that we have joined our brother, the distant strains of the forgotten song roll faintly through our mind. The ego hears these notes in terror. Yet for the other part, the holy priestess in us, this is "the song it longed to hear since first the ego came into your mind." This holy priestess has been imprisoned down here on earth for that entire time, but now it sees that Heaven has come to earth at last, "because it found a home in your relationship." Heaven has come to set its beloved priestess free.

> 8. Look gently on your brother [Ur: each other], and remember the ego's <u>weakness</u> is revealed in <u>both</u> your sight. What it would keep apart has met and joined, and looks upon the ego unafraid. Little child [Ur: children], innocent of sin, follow in gladness the way to certainty. Be not held back by fear's insane insistence that sureness lies in doubt [that you will find innocence when you look within]. This <u>has</u> no meaning. What matters it to you how loudly it is proclaimed? The senseless is not made meaningful by repetition and by clamor. The quiet way is open. Follow it happily, and question not what <u>must</u> be so.

By yourself, the ego usually gets the better of you. It sits on you like a big hairy gorilla, keeping you stuck. But when two people join, and then look on the ego from the standpoint of that joining, the perspective shifts. The huge gorilla looks instead like a tiny monkey, four inches tall. This monkey cannot stop them from doing what they want to do, and so now they are free to look within on who they are. True, the monkey shrieks continually that they better not look within. "You can be certain," it shouts, "that it's very doubtful you'll find holiness within."

That monkey is shrieking now at us. Yet just because its message is repeated over and over does not mean it's true. "The senseless is not made meaningful by repetition and by clamor." This is actually a restatement of what is known as Souder's law: "Repetition does not establish validity." The ego thinks that if it repeats something enough times, we'll believe it. But we can decide otherwise.

V. The Function of Reason
Commentary by Robert Perry

This is an important section that fully introduces what was minimally introduced in the last section: the topic of reason. All who believe that the Course is against thinking, intellect, and rationality should read this section carefully.

> 1. Perception selects, and <u>makes</u> the world you see. It literally <u>picks it out</u> as the mind directs. The laws of size and shape and brightness would hold, perhaps, if other things were equal. They are <u>not</u> equal. For what you look <u>for</u> you are far more likely to discover [Ur: *regardless* of its color, shape, or size,] than what you would prefer to <u>overlook</u>. The still, small Voice for God is <u>not</u> drowned out by all the ego's raucous screams and senseless ravings to those who <u>want</u> to hear It [Ur: to hear]. Perception is a choice and <u>not</u> a fact. But on this choice depends far more than you may realize as yet. For on the voice you choose to hear, and on the sights you choose to see, depends <u>entirely</u> your whole belief in what you <u>are</u>. Perception is a witness but to this, and never to reality. Yet it can show you the conditions in which <u>awareness</u> of reality is possible, or those where it could <u>never</u> be.

The theme of selective perception runs throughout the Course. We may think we simply observe, and perhaps pay more attention to the things that catch our eye because they are bright, shapely, or big. But that is not the case. As the image of "the messengers of perception" reminded us, perception does not observe; it *seeks*. We actively look for what we want, and we studiously avoid what we would rather overlook, even if it *is* bright, shapely, or big. As a result, we see what we want to see: our brother's sinfulness. And we hear what we want to hear: our ego's raucous shrieks. We have no idea how much hinges on this choice of what we see and hear. On this choice "depends *entirely* your whole belief in what you are." All of it is a covert operation designed to convince ourselves that we are tiny, vulnerable sinners. And it works.

> 2. Reality needs no cooperation from you to be itself. But your awareness of it <u>needs</u> your help, because it <u>is</u> your choice. Listen to

271

what the ego says, and see what it <u>directs</u> you see, and it is sure that you will see <u>yourself</u> as tiny, vulnerable and afraid. You <u>will</u> experience depression, a sense of worthlessness, and feelings of impermanence and unreality. You <u>will</u> believe that you are helpless prey to forces far beyond your own control, and far more powerful than you. And you <u>will</u> think the world you made directs your destiny. For this will be your <u>faith</u>. But never believe <u>because</u> it is your faith it makes <u>reality</u>.

Application: Think of a recent difficult interpersonal situation. Notice how readily your mind goes to what someone else did wrong. Notice how easily you listen to your ego's judgmental interpretation of what that person did. Notice how you seem to be at the mercy of the destructive power you see residing in the other person. Now realize that after seeing literally *thousands* of situations in this way, the end result is the following:

I see myself as tiny, vulnerable and afraid.
I experience depression, a sense of worthlessness, and feelings of impermanence.
I believe that I am helpless prey to forces far beyond my control, and far more powerful than I.
And I think the world I made directs my destiny.
This is where I have placed my faith.
But that does not mean that this is reality.

3. There is <u>another</u> vision and <u>another</u> Voice in Which your freedom lies, awaiting but your choice. And if you place your faith in Them, you will perceive <u>another</u> self in <u>you</u>. This other self sees miracles as natural. They are as simple and as natural to it as breathing to the body. They are the <u>obvious</u> response to calls for help, the <u>only</u> one it makes. Miracles seem unnatural to the ego because it does not understand how <u>separate</u> minds can influence each other. Nor *could* they do so. But minds cannot <u>be</u> separate. This other self is <u>perfectly</u> aware of this. And thus it recognizes that miracles do <u>not</u> affect <u>another's</u> mind, only its <u>own</u>. They always change *your* mind. There *is* no other.

All we need do is choose to place our faith in the vision of our brother's holiness and in the Voice for God, and we will be free. This vision and this Voice will witness to a whole other self in us. We will see the self discussed in yesterday's section, the self that has not lost its holiness, despite being dragged down to earth's limitations. This self sees miracles as the obvious response (we might call it the "duh response") to any supposed attack, a response as natural as breathing. This self knows that its miracles can reach directly into other minds and heal them, simply because there is no gap between minds to traverse, because there is really only one Mind.

Application: Have you had any experiences where it seemed like your mind reached directly into another mind with some kind of healing or peace? If so, realize that this other mind was not really an *other*.

4. You do not realize the whole extent to which the idea of separation has <u>interfered</u> with reason. Reason lies in the other self you have <u>cut off</u> from your awareness. And nothing you have allowed to <u>stay</u> in your awareness is <u>capable</u> of reason. How can the segment of the mind <u>devoid</u> of reason understand what reason <u>is</u>, or grasp the information it would give? All sorts of <u>questions</u> may arise in it, but if the basic question stems from <u>reason,</u> it will not ask it. Like <u>all</u> that stems from reason, the basic question is obvious, simple and remains unasked. But think not reason could not <u>answer</u> it.

We pride ourselves on our ability to reason well, yet our reasoning at its best is like the screeching of a child on a new violin, while real reason is like the playing of Itzaak Perlman. Reason is *sanity*; the words are synonyms. Even when our thinking is intellectually brilliant, it still lacks real sanity. Sanity looks clear-eyed on everything just as it is, yet our "reason" is fundamentally biased and agenda- driven. It refuses to go outside the fences erected by the ego. Indeed, it will not ask the most basic question of all: What if I looked within and saw no sin? (I think this, from T-21.IV.3:1, is the "basic question" referred to in sentence 5.)

If we were really in touch with reason, we would look upon all our viciousness, pettiness, and condemnation and say, "This definitely makes me look sinful, but what if I looked at the real core of my being and there *was* no sin there?"

5. God's plan for your salvation could not have been established <u>without</u> your will and your consent. It <u>must</u> have been accepted by the Son of God, for what God wills for him he <u>must</u> receive. For God wills not <u>apart</u> from him, nor does the Will of God wait upon time to be accomplished. Therefore, what <u>joined</u> the Will of God <u>must</u> be in you <u>now</u>, being eternal. You <u>must</u> have set aside a place in which the Holy Spirit can abide, and where He <u>is</u>. He must <u>have been</u> there since the need for Him arose, and was fulfilled in the same instant. Such would your <u>reason</u> tell you, if you listened. Yet such is clearly <u>not</u> the ego's reasoning. Your reason's alien nature to the ego [Ur: Its alien nature, *to the ego,*] is proof you will <u>not</u> find the answer there. Yet if it <u>must</u> be so, it must exist. And if it exists <u>for</u> you, and has your freedom as the purpose <u>given</u> it, you <u>must</u> be free to <u>find</u> it.

Here we see a display of real reason. Notice all the "musts" and "therefores." I will try to reconstruct the chain of reasoning presented to us here. It is a series of premises and then conclusions which logically follow from the premises. See if you can accept each premise, and then realize that once you do, you have implicitly accepted the conclusions that logically follow. Bear in mind that each new conclusion follows from both the preceding premise and the premises that went before.

Premise: God does not will apart from you, His Son. (Can you accept this?)

Conclusion: Therefore, what God wills for you, you *must* receive. (If you accept the preceding statement, you have really already accepted this.)

Premise: God willed for you a plan for your salvation. (Do you accept this?)

Conclusion: Therefore, that plan must have been received, and even *co-willed*, by you.

Premise: God's Will does not wait upon time; it is instantaneous and eternal in accomplishment. (Can you accept this?)

Conclusion: Therefore, the instant His plan was conceived, you joined with it and it was accomplished in you. (Unless you have disagreed with the above premises, you have already given your consent to this conclusion.)

Conclusion: And therefore, the place that joined with His plan is also in you now. (Try to let this in, for by accepting the preceding premises, you have already accepted this.)

Premise: The Holy Spirit has since the beginning been part of God's plan for salvation. (Do you accept this?)

Conclusion: Therefore, you must have a place in you where you received and joined with the Holy Spirit. (See how this follows from all that has gone before it.)

Conclusion: And that place must have been in you from the time the Holy Spirit was given all the way up to this present moment. (Again, try to let this in, for by accepting the preceding premises, you implicitly accepted this.)

If you accept the premises, they lead to a single logical conclusion: There is a place in you where God's plan for your salvation—for your achievement of the goal of holiness—is accomplished now and has *always* been accomplished. Can you accept this? Realize that unless you take issue with any of the above premises, you *have* accepted it. And if you have accepted it, why not accept it fully? Why not let it all the way in? If you really did that, wouldn't you feel like dancing in the streets?

Why is he working so hard to give us this conclusion—that there is a place in us where the goal of holiness has already been achieved? Maybe you've already guessed why. This is reason's answer to that basic question, "If I looked within, is it really true that I would see sin?"

> 6. God's plan is simple; <u>never</u> circular and <u>never</u> self-defeating. He has no Thoughts except the Self-<u>extending</u>, and in this <u>your</u> will [as one of His Thoughts] <u>must</u> be included. Thus, there <u>must</u> be a part of you that <u>knows</u> His Will and <u>shares</u> it. It is <u>not</u> meaningful to ask if what <u>must</u> be is so. But it <u>is</u> meaningful to ask why you are <u>unaware</u> of what is so, for this <u>must</u> have an answer if the plan of God for your salvation is complete. And it must <u>be</u> complete, because its Source knows not of incompletion.

Here we have more reasoning. God's Thoughts are always Self-extending, rather than circular and self-defeating. Your will is one of His Thoughts. Therefore, there must be a place in you—that of your true will—that is an extension of His Will, that is continuous with His Will. There is no point in asking if this is so; it *must* be so. But there is a point in asking why you are unaware of this place in you.

7. Where would the answer <u>be</u> but in the Source? And where are <u>you</u> but there, where this same answer is? Your Identity, as much a true <u>effect</u> of this same Source as is the answer, must therefore be <u>together</u> and the <u>same</u> [Together with what? The same as what?]. O yes, you know this, and more than this alone. Yet any part of knowledge threatens dissociation as much as <u>all</u> of it. And all of it will <u>come</u> with any part. Here is the part you <u>can</u> accept. What reason points to you <u>can</u> see, because the witnesses on its behalf <u>are</u> clear. Only the <u>totally</u> insane can disregard them, and you <u>have</u> gone past this.

We saw the question, "Why am I unaware of the place in me where God's plan has already been accomplished?" The answer to this question lies in God, where our real Identity is. We already know all this, and more. Yet all we need do is accept one part of what we know. As Jesus said earlier, from the ego's standpoint, a little knowledge is dangerous indeed, because with one bit of it comes *all* of it. Reason's role is to provide us with the one bit that we can accept now. Maybe what reason delivers is not knowledge per se, but it is a reflection of knowledge that opens the way to all of it.

Reason is a means that serves the Holy Spirit's purpose in its <u>own</u> right. It is not <u>reinterpreted</u> and <u>redirected</u> from the goal of sin, as are the others. For reason is <u>beyond</u> the ego's range of means.
8. Faith and perception and belief can be misplaced, and serve the great deceiver's needs as well as truth. But reason has no place at all in madness, nor can it be <u>adjusted</u> to fit its end. Faith and belief are <u>strong</u> in madness, guiding perception toward what the mind has valued. But reason enters <u>not at all</u> in this. For the perception would fall away at once, if reason were applied. There <u>is</u> no reason in insanity, for it depends <u>entirely</u> on reason's absence. The ego never uses it, because it does not realize that it <u>exists</u>. The partially insane <u>have</u> access to it, and only they have <u>need</u> of it. <u>Knowledge</u> does not depend on it, and madness keeps it <u>out</u>.

What a fascinating discussion. Imagine that someone gives you the following list:

- Faith
- Belief

- Perception
- Reason

Then you are asked these three questions:

1. Which of these are inherently of the ego, so much so that for purposes of awakening they must be set aside?
2. Which of these, though made by the ego, can (and must) be redirected by the Holy Spirit to serve His holy purpose?
3. Which of these is so inherently holy that the ego did not make it, cannot use it, and does not even realize it exists?

Ask yourself if, before reading this section, you would have answered the three questions the way Jesus does here:

1. None of them
2. Faith, belief, perception
3. Reason

The Course's reason differs from conventional reason not in being somehow anti-intellectual. It differs only in being *more* reasonable, more rational, more sane. It is still the act of carrying out sane premises in a logical way to yield sane conclusions. The only difference is that the premises are saner. What does it say about the Course that it sees reason as so holy that the ego never even touched it?

> 9. The part of mind where reason lies was dedicated, by your will in union with your Father's, to the <u>undoing</u> of insanity. Here was the Holy Spirit's purpose accepted and accomplished, both at once. Reason is <u>alien</u> to insanity, and those who use it have gained a means which cannot <u>be</u> applied to sin. Knowledge is far beyond attainment of <u>any</u> kind. But reason <u>can</u> serve to open doors you closed <u>against</u> it.

Reason lies in that other self, in that part of the mind that joined God's Will, fully accepted His plan, and allowed in the Holy Spirit. Reason is what we need now. Knowledge doesn't need it, but *we* need it to open the doors that we closed against knowledge.

10. You have come very close to this. Faith and belief have shifted, and you <u>have</u> asked the question the ego will <u>never</u> ask. Does not your reason tell you now the question <u>must</u> have come from something that you do <u>not</u> know, but must <u>belong</u> to you? Faith and belief, upheld by reason, <u>cannot</u> fail to lead to changed perception. And in <u>this</u> change is room made way for vision. Vision extends <u>beyond</u> itself, as does the purpose that it serves, and <u>all</u> the means for its accomplishment.

If you have asked the question, "What if I looked within and saw no sin?" then reason is now within your grasp to use. For that question *came* from reason. There is nowhere else it *could* have come from. This means that you are now able to use reason to guide your faith and belief, so that they can be devoted to truth, and thus produce changed perception. That changed perception will lead to vision. And vision will lead beyond itself, to that which cannot be described.

VI. Reason versus Madness
Commentary by Robert Perry

1. Reason cannot see sin but <u>can</u> see errors, and <u>leads</u> to their correction. It does not value *them*, but their <u>correction</u>. [Ur: But] Reason will also tell you that when you <u>think</u> you sin, you call for help. Yet if you will not <u>accept</u> the help you call for, you will not believe that it is yours to give. And so you <u>will</u> not give it, thus <u>maintaining</u> the belief [that it's not yours to give]. For uncorrected error of <u>any</u> kind deceives you about the power that is <u>in</u> you to <u>make</u> correction. If it [this power in you] <u>can</u> correct, and <u>you</u> allow it not to do so, you deny it to yourself <u>and to your brother</u>. And if he <u>shares</u> this same belief you <u>both</u> will think that you are damned [that you will stand forever uncorrected, unsaved]. This you <u>could</u> spare him <u>and yourself</u>. For reason would not make way for correction in you alone.

What would be the reasonable way to look on your sins? How would they look through pure, unbiased reason? They would not look like sins that call for punishment, but like errors that call for correction, that call for help.

Application: Think of one of the worst things you ever did, for which you still carry guilt, and say:

> *If I were truly reasonable, I would not see this as a sin that calls for punishment.*
> *I would see this as an error that calls for correction, a mistake that calls for help.*

If you accept that help for yourself, then you will realize that you have within you the power to give it to others. They don't think they can correct their errors. They think they are doomed to stay stuck in them. You could spare them from this. You could un-stick them. It seems like we are powerless to do this, doesn't it? But that must be because we don't accept correction for our own errors.

2. Correction cannot <u>be</u> accepted <u>or refused</u> by you without your brother. <u>Sin</u> would maintain it [Ur: you] can. Yet reason tells you that you <u>cannot</u> see your brother <u>or</u> yourself as sinful and still perceive the other innocent. Who looks upon himself as guilty and sees a sinless world? And who can see a sinful world and look upon himself <u>apart</u> from it? Sin would maintain you and your brother <u>must</u> [Ur: you *must*] be separate. But <u>reason</u> tells you that this must be <u>wrong</u>. If you and your brother are joined, how <u>could</u> it be that you have private thoughts? And how <u>could</u> thoughts that enter into what but <u>seems</u> like yours alone have no effect at all on what *is* yours [the shared mind of the Sonship]? If minds are joined, this <u>is</u> impossible.

Sin tells you that, since you and your brother are cordoned off in separate bodies, two things result. First, you can see your brother as fundamentally different from yourself. If you were truly separate, why couldn't you? Second, your thoughts don't escape your skull and affect your brother, unless they leak out in your behavior.

Reason, however, maintains that all minds are joined. Therefore, thoughts in one mind do directly affect other minds, either releasing or imprisoning them. Also, because we are all joined, how we see one of us is a decision about *all* of us. If we see a brother as sinful, we will see ourselves that way, and vice versa.

Application: Think of someone you really despise. Now say to yourself:

> *Because he is one with everyone and the same as everyone, my perception of him is a decision about everyone, including myself.*
> *Do I really want to see him the way I have?*

3. No one can think but for himself, as God thinks not without His Son. Only were both <u>in bodies</u> could this be. Nor could one mind think only for itself unless the body *were* the mind. For <u>only</u> bodies can be separate, and therefore <u>unreal</u>. The home of madness [the body] <u>cannot</u> be the home of reason [the mind]. Yet it is easy to <u>leave</u> the home of madness if you see reason. You do not leave insanity by <u>going</u> somewhere else. You leave it simply by accepting reason where madness <u>was</u>. Madness

and reason see the same things, but it is certain that they look upon them differently.

Only if we were in bodies could our thoughts not shine into the minds of others. But it's more than that. Only if our minds *were* bodies could their thoughts be private. For it is the very nature of mind to be shared and unbounded. It is the nature of body to be a separate form. All our problems stem from thinking we are inside and at one with that separate form, for it is "the home of madness." Yet we can leave it any time we want. This does not refer to suicide, nor out-of-body experiences. It doesn't refer to going anywhere else. We leave it just by seeing everything through the eyes of reason. At that point, we are no longer subject to the body. It becomes a tool we use, not a cell that holds us. Wouldn't that be freeing?

> 4. Madness is an <u>attack</u> on reason that drives it out of mind, and <u>takes its place</u>. Reason does <u>not</u> attack, but takes the place of madness quietly, <u>replacing</u> madness if it be the choice of the insane to <u>listen</u> to it. But the insane know not their will, for they <u>believe</u> they see the body, and <u>let</u> their madness tell them it is real. <u>Reason</u> would be <u>incapable</u> of this. And if you would defend the body <u>against</u> your reason, you will not understand the body <u>or</u> yourself.

We, the insane, don't really know what's in our best interests. We think that seeing a body, and listening to our madness tell us that it's all about the body, will make us happy. And when reason comes in and tells us the body is irrelevant—since it's unreal—our madness tries to drive that voice from our mind, shouting "Get out! Get out!" Too often it succeeds. However, we can choose to listen to the quiet voice of reason. And if we do, if we really listen, it will come in and take up residence. In doing so, it won't drive the madness out. It will just cause us to wake up from it, and wonder how we got stuck in such a deranged condition.

> 5. The body does <u>not</u> separate you from your brother, and if you think it does you <u>are</u> insane. But madness [insanity] has a purpose, and believes it also has the means to make its purpose real. To see the body as a barrier between what <u>reason</u> tells you <u>must</u> be joined <u>must</u> be insane. Nor <u>could</u> you see it, if you heard the voice of reason. What <u>can</u> there be that stands <u>between</u> what is continuous? And if there <u>is</u> nothing in between, how can what enters part [your mind] be kept <u>away</u> from

other parts [minds]? Reason would tell you this. But think what you must <u>recognize,</u> if it be so.

Application: Look at the nearest human body and notice how it seems to separate you from that person. If that body is scratched, that person will feel it, but you will not. Notice how that body owns things that you do not, has access to places that you do not. Notice how that body gives that person drives and needs that are separate from yours, and may even conflict with yours. Finally, notice how that body keeps its mind enclosed within a wall of privacy, almost like money in a locked vault. Unless that person tells you his or her thoughts, or physically displays them, you don't know what they are. Now say to yourself:

> *To think this body separates me from this person is insane.*
> *I only see it as having power to do so because that serves the goal*
> *   of my insanity.*
> *And that goal is sin.*
> *Let me instead listen to reason.*
> *Reason tells me that this person's mind is continuous with mine.*
> *Reason tells me that there is nothing in between us.*
> *Reason tells me that these bodies have "no power to attack the*
> *   universal Oneness of God's Son" (W-pI.137.3:5).*

6. If you choose sin <u>instead</u> of healing, you would condemn the Son of God to what can <u>never</u> be corrected. You tell him, <u>by</u> your choice, that he is damned; separate from you and from his Father forever, without a hope of safe return. You <u>teach</u> him this, and you will <u>learn</u> of him <u>exactly</u> what you taught. For you can teach him only that he <u>is</u> as you would <u>have</u> him, and what you choose [Ur: *chose*] he be is but your choice for <u>you.</u> Yet think not this is fearful. That you are <u>joined</u> to him is but a fact, <u>not</u> an interpretation. How can a fact be fearful unless it <u>disagrees</u> with what you hold more dear than truth? Reason will tell you that this fact is your <u>release.</u>

Application: Take the same person, and say the following to him or her:

VI. Reason versus Madness

By seeing you as inside your body, I see you as damned, separate
from me and from your Father, without a hope of safe return.
I condemn you to your prison, trapped in your sins forever.
And what I teach you about yourself, I teach me about myself.
Yet this final fact is a blessing, for it means that we are one.
And in that oneness lies my release.

7. Neither your brother nor yourself can be attacked alone. But neither can accept a miracle instead <u>without</u> the other being blessed by it, and <u>healed</u> of pain. Reason, like love, would <u>reassure</u> you, and seeks <u>not</u> to frighten you. The power to <u>heal</u> the Son of God is given you <u>because</u> he must be one with you. You *are* responsible for how he sees himself. And reason tells you it is <u>given</u> you to change his whole mind, which is one with <u>you,</u> in just an instant. And <u>any</u> [such] instant serves to bring <u>complete</u> correction of his errors and make him whole. The instant that you choose to let <u>yourself</u> be healed, in that same instant is his whole salvation seen as complete <u>with</u> yours. Reason is given you to <u>understand</u> that this is so. For reason, kind as is the purpose [of holiness] for which it is the means, leads steadily <u>away</u> from madness toward the goal of truth. And here you will lay down the burden of <u>denying</u> truth. *This* is the burden that is terrible, and <u>not</u> the truth.

We tend to be threatened by the idea that our thoughts directly influence 's thoughtsother people. It implies that we are at the mercy of everyone else's thoughts. Further, it feels like such a huge burden. It means we are responsible for everyone. It means we have to make sure that every thought we have is the kind that we would *want* to have go out and affect others.

But wait. Isn't this a good thing? Doesn't it mean that we have power to save others? Who of us doesn't have people in our lives that we would dearly love to help, but feel powerless to do so?

Application: Pick someone about whom you are concerned, but feel powerless to help, and say,

> *I **am** responsible for how she sees herself.*
> *And reason tells me that I can change her whole mind, which is*
> *one with me, in just an instant.*

The instant I let healing into my mind, in that same instant is her healing complete with mine.

8. That you and your brother are <u>joined</u> is your salvation; the gift of Heaven, <u>not</u> the gift of fear. Does Heaven seem to be a <u>burden</u> to you? In madness, yes. And yet what madness sees <u>must</u> be dispelled by reason. Reason assures you Heaven is what you <u>want</u>, and <u>all</u> you want. Listen to Him Who <u>speaks</u> with reason, and brings <u>your</u> reason into line with <u>His</u>. Be willing to let reason be the means by which He would direct you how to leave <u>insanity</u> behind. Hide not <u>behind</u> insanity in order to <u>escape</u> from reason. What madness would <u>conceal</u> the Holy Spirit still holds out, for everyone to look upon with gladness.

The fact that minds are joined, and influence each other constantly, is our salvation. It means that we can help each other. It means that we are free of the prison of separateness. It means that we can find Heaven again. Therefore, if we see our joined nature as a burden (as we saw in my comments on the last paragraph), it is because we see *Heaven* as a burden. And that is how Heaven looks from the standpoint of madness—no freedom, always having to be holy, everyone stuck together in one big group soup. Yet the real burden is the burden of *denying* Heaven.

We need to listen to the Holy Spirit's reason, for it would tell us the truth—that Heaven is what we want, and *all* we want. That's why they call it Heaven. I remember a Persian poem which spoke of the experience of Heaven:

> If on earth there be a Paradise of Bliss,
> It is this,
> It is this,
> It is this. (Firdausi)

9. You *are* your brother's savior. He is <u>yours</u>. Reason speaks happily indeed of this. This gracious plan was given love by Love. And what Love plans is like Itself in this: Being united, It would have you learn what <u>you</u> must be. And being <u>one</u> with It, it <u>must</u> be given you to give what <u>It</u> has given, and gives still. Spend but an instant in the glad <u>acceptance</u> of what is given you to give your brother, and learn with him what has been given <u>both</u> of you. To give is no <u>more</u> blessed than

to receive [a correction of St. Paul supposedly quoting Jesus in Acts 20:35]. But neither is it <u>less</u>.

Reason tells you that you are here to save your brother, and that this is a happy thing, not a burden. It is a plan conceived by Love. Since Love is united within Itself, it would have you learn what you are, so that you will be united within *yourself*. When this happens, you will discover that you are one with Love, and being one with Love, you must be able to give what it gives. You must be able to give salvation to your brother. And this is a inexpressibly blessed thing.

> 10. The Son of God is <u>always</u> blessed as one. And as his gratitude goes out to you who blessed him, reason will tell you that it <u>cannot</u> be you stand <u>apart</u> from blessing. The gratitude he offers you reminds you of the thanks your Father gives you for completing <u>Him</u>. And here alone does reason tell you that you can understand what you <u>must</u> be. Your Father is as close to you as is your brother. Yet what is there that <u>could</u> be nearer you than is your Self?

When we at last fulfill our function of being our brother's savior, we will learn how blessed that function is. For our brother's gratitude will go out to us and bless *us*. The blessed event we started will wrap back and envelop us. Our brother's gratitude for saving him is a distant reflection of our Father's gratitude for completing Him. Earthly gratitude may seem mundane and ordinary, but it draws our mind back toward that transcendental gratitude that is beyond what we can currently comprehend.

Application: Think of someone's gratitude to you for a gift of love that you gave. Now realize that this was a dream symbol sent to you by God to remind you of His gratitude for completing Him. See this person's gratitude as a dream symbol of your Father's eternal gratitude.

> 11. The power <u>you</u> have over the Son of God is <u>not</u> a threat to his reality. It but <u>attests</u> to it. Where <u>could</u> his freedom lie but in himself, if he be free <u>already</u>? And who could bind him but <u>himself</u>, if he <u>deny</u> his freedom? God is not mocked; no more His Son can <u>be</u> imprisoned save by his own desire. And it is <u>by</u> his own desire that he is freed.

Such is his <u>strength</u>, and <u>not</u> his weakness. He <u>is</u> at his own mercy. And where he <u>chooses</u> to be merciful, there is he free. But where he chooses to condemn instead, there is he held a prisoner, waiting in chains his pardon on <u>himself</u> to set him free.

If we can really influence others with our thoughts, if our thoughts can either hold them prisoner or free them, doesn't this mean that their reality is at the whim of outside forces? Doesn't it mean that their reality has no sure foundation, that it's just a leaf tossed in the wind? It would mean this, says Jesus, if those influencing it were really *others*. Yet in fact they are all merely parts of the *one* Son of God. Yes, there is a sense in which each part has its own faculty of choice, yet each part is also one with the whole. Indeed, each part somehow *is* the whole. And so each part's choices are choices *for* the whole, even *of* the whole. Thus, if you choose to free me, that choice, in a sense, is *our* choice. It is the choice of the one Son to free himself. Likewise, your choice to free me is really your choice to free *yourself*. In other words, whatever part of the Sonship freedom is given to, it is given to everyone. And whatever part freedom is given *by*, it is given *by* everyone. No matter what parts are involved, freedom is being given *by* the one Son *to* himself.

VII. The Last Unanswered Question
Commentary by Robert Perry

> 1. Do you not see that all your misery comes from the strange belief that you are powerless? <u>Being helpless is the cost of sin</u>. Helplessness is sin's <u>condition</u>; the <u>one</u> requirement that it demands to be believed. Only the helpless <u>could</u> believe in it. Enormity has no appeal save to the little. And only those who <u>first</u> believe that they are little could <u>see</u> attraction there. Treachery to the Son of God is the defense of those who do <u>not</u> identify with him. And you are <u>for</u> him or <u>against</u> him; either you love him or attack him, protect his unity or see him shattered and slain by your attack.

Jesus really wants you to think about that first question. So do that. *Can* you see that all your misery comes from believing you are powerless?

Then he sketches a reciprocal relationship between powerlessness and sin. First he says that powerlessness is the result of sin. Then he puts it the other way around. Only those who feel powerless, helpless, little could want the puffed up, grandiose condition that sin is all about.

Then he says that if you do not identify with the omnipotent Son of God that you are, you will inevitably be treacherous to him, betray him. That remark will become clearer as we go along.

> 2. No one believes the Son of God is powerless. And those who see themselves as helpless <u>must</u> believe that they are <u>not</u> the Son of God. What can they <u>be</u> except his enemy? And what can they do but <u>envy</u> him his power, and <u>by</u> their envy make themselves <u>afraid</u> of it? These are the dark ones, silent and afraid, alone and not communicating, fearful the power of the Son of God will strike them dead, and raising up their helplessness <u>against</u> him. They join the army of the powerless, to wage their war of vengeance, bitterness and spite on him, to make him one with <u>them</u>. Because they do not know that they *are* one with <u>him</u>, they know not <u>whom</u> they hate. They are indeed a sorry army, each one as likely to attack his brother or turn upon himself as to remember that they <u>thought</u> they had a common cause.

I've long said that this image of "the army of the powerless" is the only depiction of group behavior in the Course. I'll comment on it in full after paragraph 4.

> 3. Frantic and loud and strong the dark ones <u>seem</u> to be. Yet they know not their "enemy," <u>except they hate him</u>. In hatred they <u>have</u> come together, but have <u>not</u> joined <u>each other</u>. For had they done so hatred would be impossible. The army of the powerless <u>must</u> be disbanded in the presence of <u>strength</u>. Those who are strong are <u>never</u> treacherous, because they have no need to <u>dream</u> of power and to act out their dream. How would an army <u>act</u> in dreams? <u>Any</u> way at all. It could be seen attacking <u>anyone</u> with <u>anything</u>. Dreams have no <u>reason</u> in them. A flower turns into a poisoned spear, a child becomes a giant and a mouse roars like a lion. And <u>love is turned to hate</u> as easily. This is no army, but a madhouse. What <u>seems</u> to be a planned attack is bedlam.
> 4. The army of the powerless is weak indeed. It has no weapons and it has no enemy. Yes, it can overrun the world and *seek* an enemy. But it can never <u>find</u> what is not there. Yes, it can *dream* it found an enemy, but this will shift even as it attacks, so that it runs at once to find another, and never comes to rest in victory. And as it runs it turns against itself, thinking it caught a glimpse of the great enemy who always eludes its murderous attack by turning into something else. How treacherous does this enemy appear, who changes so it is impossible even to <u>recognize</u> him [Ur: !].

With this third paragraph on the army of the powerless, we now have Jesus' view of group behavior. What is that view? Human groups are generally collections of individuals who feel helpless, weak, and alone. They band together in mutual hatred of some vaguely defined evil power out there, whose power they both fear and envy. They hope that their superior numbers will enable them to drag this colossus down, down to their feeble condition. Yet a joining based on mutual hatred and shared weakness is not a real joining, and so this group is a fragile and delicate alliance, likely to fragment at any moment. Further, the strength they seem to gain from banding together is not real strength. Atop their core belief in weakness, they are simply *dreaming* of power. Defeating this giant enemy is just an attempt to act out their dream of power and make it real. But since this is a dream—a scenario with no reality to support it—this group behaves irrationally, like all dreams do. Each situation that seemed so sure in its meaning will mutate into another without any rhyme or reason. Therefore, underneath this army's appearance of careful planning, its actual mode is utter chaos.

Even its great enemy spontaneously mutates. For the group doesn't really know who the enemy is. He is a vague presence that is always cloaking himself in different forms. And so the group has to find him before it can fight him. First, they think they find him here, in this form, and so they run to fight him here. But then they think they spot him over there, and run there. Yet even as they run, they think they catch sight of him amidst their own ranks, and attack him there.

It seems to me that virtually every group behaves this way. Yet even if they are as confused as this sounds, the one thing that is sure is that they, the little guys, are good, while the enemy is always some looming evil out there. Also, just as the enemy is out there, the power is out there, too. Yet Jesus' portrayal turns even these universal assumptions on their head. For underneath all its disguises, the "evil" power that the little guys are battling is really the Son of God, a power that is purely loving and holy. And, even more ironic, that power is *theirs*. For they are the Son of God and have simply denied this fundamental fact.

So the next time you are part of a group, or are observing a group, as it runs to and fro, seeking the great unseen enemy, first in this form and then in that, call this image to mind. Realize that the vague, undefined enemy that is being sought within these various forms is really the Son of God, and they are trying to hunt him down because they envy and fear his power, *and* realize that his power is really their own, because they are the Son of God.

Here is an even greater challenge: Can you see your own attempts to defeat the great enemy out there in this light?

Finally, these paragraphs, with their description of the world as the battlefield of senseless, chaotic armies, have long reminded me of the closing stanza of the poem "Dover Beach" by Matthew Arnold:

> Ah, love, let us be true
> To one another! for the world, which seems
> To lie before us like a land of dreams,
> So various, so beautiful, so new,
> Hath really neither joy, nor love, nor light,
> Nor certitude, nor peace, nor help for pain;

And we are here as on a darkling plain
Swept with confused alarms of struggle and flight,
Where ignorant armies clash by night.

5. Yet hate <u>must</u> have a target. There can <u>be</u> no faith in sin without an enemy. Who that believes in sin would <u>dare</u> believe he has <u>no</u> enemy? <u>Could</u> he admit that no one <u>made</u> him powerless? Reason would surely bid him seek no longer what is <u>not there</u> to find. Yet first he must be <u>willing</u> to perceive a world where it [what is not there to find] is <u>not</u>. It is <u>not</u> necessary that he understand <u>how</u> he can see it. Nor should he try. For if he focuses on what he <u>cannot</u> understand, he will but <u>emphasize</u> his helplessness, and let sin tell him that his enemy must be <u>himself</u>. But let him only ask himself these questions, which he <u>must</u> decide, to have it done <u>for</u> him:

> *Do I <u>desire</u> a world I rule instead of one that rules me [Ur: one where I **am** ruled]?*
> *Do I <u>desire</u> a world where I am powerful instead of helpless?*
> *Do I <u>desire</u> a world in which I have <u>no</u> enemies and <u>cannot</u> sin?*
> *And do I <u>want</u> to see what [the world] I denied **because** it is the truth?*

We, the powerless, are fixated on that amorphous enemy out there. We need a target for our hate. We need someone to blame for our powerlessness. But the responsible party is nowhere to be found. Instead of tilting at the dark windmills of our own imaginings, we need to put our energy into seeing a world where there is no enemy, where no one made us powerless, and where we *aren't*.

That is the point of the four questions that Jesus lists: Are we willing to see the real world? All we need do is want to see it, and we won't have to worry about the rest. Sight of it will simply be given us.

Application: Ask yourself these four questions, slowly and consciously, and note carefully your inner response to each one.

6. You may <u>already</u> have [Ur: You have *already*] answered the first three questions, but not yet the last. For this one still seems fearful, and

unlike the others. Yet reason would assure you they are all the <u>same</u>. We said this year would emphasize the sameness of things that <u>are</u> the same. This final question, which is indeed the last you need decide, still seems to hold a threat the rest have lost for you. And this imagined difference attests to your belief that <u>truth</u> may be the enemy you yet may find. Here, then, would seem to be the last remaining hope of finding sin, and <u>not</u> accepting power.

Our reaction to the four questions was probably very much like what Jesus describes here, especially if we understand that he is referring to ruling (in the first question) and power (in the second) in a benign way, not a domineering way, which is made especially clear in the third question.

So we look at the first three questions and think, "Yeah, I like this. I don't want to live in a world where I am weak and helpless, ruled by powerful enemies that surround me." But then we get to the final question and think, "Gulp." The reason, as Jesus points out, is that in our mind truth has a lot of the characteristics of this enemy we have feared out in the world. It is big, it is authoritative, and it threatens to put us under its thumb.

> 7. Forget not that the choice of sin or truth, helplessness or power, <u>is</u> the choice of whether to attack or <u>heal</u>. For healing comes of <u>power</u>, and <u>attack</u> of helplessness. Whom you attack you *cannot* want to heal. And whom you would have healed <u>must</u> be the one you chose to be <u>protected</u> from attack. And what <u>is</u> this decision but the choice whether to see him through the body's eyes, or let him be <u>revealed</u> to you through vision? <u>How</u> this decision leads to its effects is <u>not</u> your problem. But what you <u>want</u> to see <u>must</u> be your choice. This is a course in <u>cause</u> and <u>not</u> effect.

Rather than dominating us, truth gives us power, and with that power, we heal. Sin makes us helpless, and to compensate for that, we attack. These two alternatives are mutually exclusive. We cannot want to attack and heal the same person at the same time. Another way of putting this choice is that it is really between seeing our brother through our physical eyes or seeing him through vision. Those you see with the body's eyes you inevitably want to attack, while those you see with vision you only want to heal.

As we have been told for many sections now, this choice is the only thing we need concern ourselves with. We don't need to worry about how this choice will lead to us actually *having* vision. That's the Holy Spirit's business. This is a course in cause (the choice to see our brother with vision); we should leave the effect (actually being *given* this vision) up to Him.

Note that the last line about cause and effect is not about *thinking* being cause and the *world* being effect. The cause is the *choice for vision*, while the effect is actually *seeing with vision*.

> 8. Consider carefully your answer to the last question you have left unanswered still. And let your reason tell you that it <u>must</u> be answered, and <u>is</u> answered in the other three. And then it <u>will</u> be clear to you that, as you look on the <u>effects</u> of sin in <u>any</u> form, all you need do is simply ask yourself:

> *Is this what I <u>would</u> see? Do I <u>want</u> this?*

> 9. This is your one decision; this the <u>condition</u> for what occurs [for what you end up seeing]. It <u>is</u> irrelevant to <u>how</u> it [what you end up seeing] happens, but <u>not</u> to <u>why</u> [what sets it in motion]. You *have* control of this [the choice that sets in motion what you see]. And if you <u>choose</u> to see a world <u>without</u> an enemy, in which you are <u>not</u> helpless, the <u>means</u> to see it <u>will</u> be given you.

Application: Consider carefully our hesitancy around the final question. Then let your reason tell you that you can't put off answering it forever. It must be answered. Finally, realize that by answering yes to the first three, you have implicitly answered yes to the last one (we'll see why shortly).

Now think of some frightening situation in your life, where it seems that the effects of sin are rampant, where it seems that you in your weakness face a powerful enemy (human or otherwise). Then say:

> *Is this what I want to see?*
> *Do I really **want** this?*

This is the common core of all the questions. And this is the only decision you have to make. "You *have* control of this." The rest is in the Holy Spirit's hands. Just say a truly sincere "no" to this, and He will give you the vision to see a sinless world.

> 10. Why is the final question so important? Reason will tell you why. It <u>is</u> the same as are the other three, <u>except in time</u>. The others are decisions that can be made, and then <u>un</u>made and made again. But truth is <u>constant,</u> and implies a state where vacillations are impossible. You can desire a world you rule that rules you not, and <u>change</u> your mind. You can desire to exchange your helplessness for power, and <u>lose</u> this same desire as a little glint of sin attracts you. And you can want to see a sinless world, and let an "enemy" tempt you to use the body's eyes and <u>change</u> what you desire.

The reason why the last question seems harder is that it locks you in. If you think of the world described in the first three questions as a kind of pleasant fantasy, not grounded in reality, then you always have an out. For fantasies are not binding. You make them up, and so your allegiance to them is up to you. One moment you can say, "Yeah, I'd love to see a world where sin does not exist and where nothing stands in the way of my loving power." But then you can quickly change your mind, "That dream was very nice, but right now my eyes see an enemy in front of me, and he's making me feel helpless. I better puff myself up and show him who's boss."

The plain fact is that if we see that sinless world as just a projection of our desires, then our allegiance to it will be variable, because desires change. And isn't this at least in part how we see the world that our spiritual beliefs envision? Somewhere inside, we assume that it is just an idea meant to make us feel good. Thus, if there is a time when it *doesn't* make us feel good, the winds of our allegiance blow in another direction.

> 11. In <u>content</u> all the questions <u>are</u> the same. For each one asks if you are willing to exchange the world of sin for what the Holy Spirit sees, since it <u>is</u> [Ur: For it *is*] this the world of sin denies. And therefore those who look on sin <u>are</u> seeing the <u>denial</u> of the real world. Yet the last question adds the <u>wish for constancy</u> in your desire to see the real world, so the desire becomes the <u>only</u> one you have. By answering the final question "yes," you add <u>sincerity</u> to the decisions you have

already made to all the rest. For only then have you renounced the option to change your mind again. When it is this you do not want, the rest are wholly answered.

If you say, "I want to see a sinless world" just because it makes you feel better, then when something *else* makes you feel better, that sinless world will go out the window—until you walk outside and fish it out of the bushes again. But if you say, "I want to see a sinless world because it is the truth," then you have left yourself no escape hatch. For truth *does not change*. This fact can seem like fingers tightening around your throat or like a blessing from on high. It all depends on whether you think truth is out to get you or is on your side.

The Course is leading us to the place where we realize that the truth is on our side. And the truth is that the world is sinless, and nothing stands in the way of our loving power. When we finally acknowledge this, and desire to see that true world, then we will have answered the last question. And then we will have at last "wholly answered" the first three.

> 12. Why do you think you are unsure the others have been answered? Could it be necessary they be asked so often, if they had? Until the last decision has been made, the answer is both "yes" and "no." For you have answered "yes" without perceiving that "yes" must mean "not no."

Until we have answered the final question, our answer to the first three is, "Yes, and I reserve the right to say no five minutes from now." Is that a "yes"? If someone gave you that answer in response to a marriage proposal, would you consider that a "yes"?

Application: Say to yourself, "I want to see a sinless world, where I have no enemies and nothing stands in the way of my loving power." As you say it, see which statement better reflects your attitude toward it:

> *I want this as long as it feels good to me.*

or,

> *I want this permanently and constantly because a sinless world is the truth, and only the truth makes me happy.*

No one decides <u>against</u> his happiness, but he <u>may</u> do so if he does not see he <u>does</u> it. And if he sees his happiness as ever changing, now this, now that, and now an elusive shadow attached to nothing, he <u>does</u> decide against it.

13. Elusive happiness, or happiness in changing form that shifts with time and place, is an illusion that has no meaning. Happiness <u>must</u> be constant, because it is <u>attained</u> by <u>giving up</u> the wish for the *inconstant*. Joy cannot <u>be</u> perceived <u>except</u> through constant vision. And constant vision can be given only those who <u>wish</u> for constancy. The power of the Son of God's desire remains the proof that he is wrong who sees himself as helpless. Desire what you want, and you will look on it and think it real. No thought but has the power to release or kill. And none can leave the thinker's mind, or leave him unaffected.

We like to leave our options open. We want to have freedom to suck happiness from ever-changing straws. Yet Jesus is saying that seeing happiness in this way, as an undulating, elusive shadow, is a decision to *not* be happy.

Why? Because here is how happiness comes about: We first give up our wish to leave our happiness options open, and instead wish for constancy. We wish to see a sinless world because that world is the permanent, unvarying *truth*. Out of this wish for constancy comes constant vision. We see that sinless world all the time. And out of this constant vision comes joy, which is by its very nature constant.

And that is why that last question is so crucial. It represents an unyielding commitment to constancy. And that is why we haven't answered it yet.

VIII. The Inner Shift
Commentary by Robert Perry

1. Are thoughts, then, dangerous? To bodies, <u>yes</u>! The thoughts that seem to kill are those that teach the thinker that he *can* be killed. And so he "dies" <u>because</u> of what he learned. He goes from life to death, the final proof he valued the inconstant <u>more</u> than constancy. Surely he <u>thought</u> he wanted happiness. Yet he did <u>not</u> desire it *because* it was the truth, and therefore <u>must</u> be constant.

To understand this paragraph, we almost need to start from the end. We think we want happiness, but we think it lies not in the changeless truth, but in the changing, the inconstant. This means that we value the inconstant more than the constant. Yet inconstancy is impermanency, and impermanency is death. So, within our assumption that happiness lies in the inconstant is an unseen valuing of death, a hidden request for death. And that is what we get. Our body dies as an outward statement of what we really valued.

2. The constancy of joy is a condition quite alien to your understanding. Yet if you could even imagine what it <u>must</u> be, you would <u>desire</u> it although you <u>understand</u> it not. The constancy of happiness has <u>no</u> exceptions; no change of <u>any</u> kind. It is unshakable as is the Love of God for His creation. Sure in its vision as its Creator is in what He <u>knows</u>, happiness looks on everything and <u>sees</u> it is the same. It sees <u>not</u> the ephemeral, for it <u>desires</u> everything be like itself, and <u>sees</u> it so. <u>Nothing</u> has power to confound its constancy, because its <u>own</u> desire cannot <u>be</u> shaken. It comes as surely unto those who see the final question is <u>necessary</u> to the rest, as peace <u>must</u> come to those who choose to heal and <u>not</u> to judge.

Jesus says if we could just imagine what constant joy would be like, we would want it, even though, in our current condition, we don't understand it at all. So let's try. Take a moment and imagine being joyful all the time. This joy obviously couldn't get boring, because then it wouldn't be joyful. This, then, is an ever-joyful joy. Imagine that. This joy wants to see itself wherever it looks. And since it is unchanging, it sees only the changelessly joy-inspiring in the world. Again, try to imagine that. It looks upon the truth, upon a radiance that never dims. Nothing that happens in this world can shake it, because its own desire to *be* joyful and to *see* the joyful never wavers. It automatically realizes that really wanting to see a sinless world (the first three questions from the last section) requires that you want to see that world *constantly* (the fourth question).

Can you get at least a sense for this kind of joy? Do you find that Jesus was right—that you want it?

> 3. Reason will tell you that you <u>cannot</u> ask for happiness inconstantly. For if what you desire you <u>receive</u>, and happiness <u>is</u> constant, then you need ask for it but <u>once</u> to have it <u>always</u>. And if you do <u>not</u> have it always, being what it <u>is</u>, you did <u>not</u> ask for it. For no one fails to <u>ask</u> for his desire of <u>something</u> he believes holds out some promise of the power of <u>giving</u> it. He may be wrong in <u>what</u> he asks, <u>where</u>, and <u>of</u> <u>what</u>. Yet he <u>will</u> ask because desire <u>is</u> a request, an <u>asking for</u>, and made by one whom God Himself will never fail to answer. God has <u>already</u> given all that he <u>really</u> wants. Yet what he is uncertain of [uncertain that he wants], God <u>cannot</u> give. For he does <u>not</u> desire it while he <u>remains</u> uncertain, and God's giving <u>must</u> be incomplete unless it is <u>received</u>.

There is a sure test by which you can tell if you have asked for the happiness Jesus is talking about: *if you have it.* "If you do not have it always…you did not ask for it." To really ask for it means to ask for it as a permanent, constant condition, for that is what it is.

So let's face it—none of us has asked for this happiness. But that is actually good news. If we had asked for it and still didn't have it, what would we do then? But now we have a very simple task ahead of us: to ask for/desire this constant joy. That is our only part. If we just ask for it, God will give it to us. Indeed, He already has given it to us. Yet in a sense He hasn't, for His giving is incomplete until we receive what He gave.

Application: Take a few minutes and just say over and over,

> *I want constant joy.*
> *I want to look on the constantly joyful.*

I'm not interested in the inconstant things of this world.
My desire for this joy is just as constant as this joy is.

4. You who complete God's Will and <u>are</u> His happiness, whose will is powerful as His, a power that is not <u>lost</u> in your illusions, think carefully why you have not yet decided how you would answer the final question. Your answer to the others has made it possible to help you be already partly sane [Ur: help you be but partially insane]. And yet it is the final one that <u>really</u> asks if you are willing to be <u>wholly</u> sane.

Application: Ask yourself, "Why haven't I decided how to answer the final question?" That final question, of course, was, "And do I want to see what I denied *because* it is the truth?" Other versions: Do I want to see a sinless world *because* it is the unchanging truth? Do I want to see a world without enemies, where nothing stands in the way of my loving power, *because* this world is the only truth?

You do hesitate around this question. If you didn't, you would abide in a state of profound joy that never fluctuated. So why do you hesitate? What is holding you back? You have the power to answer yes, since your will is as powerful as God's. So why don't you use that power?

5. What is the holy instant but God's appeal to you to <u>recognize</u> what He has given you? Here is the great appeal to reason; the awareness of what is <u>always</u> there to see, the happiness that <u>could</u> be <u>always</u> yours. Here is the <u>constant</u> peace [and joy] you could experience forever. Here is what denial has denied <u>revealed</u> to you. For here the final question is <u>already</u> answered, and what you <u>ask</u> for <u>given</u>. Here is the future *now*, for time is powerless <u>because</u> of your desire for what will <u>never</u> change. For you <u>have</u> asked that nothing <u>stand between</u> the holiness of your relationship and your *awareness* of its holiness.

Long before we choose the joy he is talking about, we can experience that joy in the holy instant. There, we emerge from denial and experience the joy that could always be ours. There, we are perfectly aware of the holiness of our relationship, for there we stand at the goal, at the end of the journey. There, we have finally answered that final question, and our answer is "yes."

As we exit the holy instant, we will leave that place of "yes" for our normal state of "no." But that is all right. In that instant, God had a chance to appeal to us, to make an appeal that we leave the Land of No and exchange it for the Haven of Yes, forever.

About the Circle's
TEXT READING PROGRAM

An Unforgettable Journey through the Text in One Year

The Text is the foundation of *A Course in Miracles*, yet many students find it hard going. This program is designed to guide you through the Text, paragraph by paragraph, in one year.

Each weekday, you will receive an e-mail containing that day's Text section, along with commentary on each paragraph, written by Robert Perry or Greg Mackie. The readings contain material edited out of the published Course as well as exercises for practical application. This is the material that has been presented now in book format in our series *The Illuminated Text*.

By signing up for our online program, you will also receive:

- Weekly one-hour class recordings led by Robert Perry and Greg Mackie that summarize that week's sections and answer students' questions
- An online forum for sharing with others in the program
- Related articles on key Text sections e-mailed directly to you
- Your personal web archive, with access to all your commentaries and class recordings
- An unlimited "pause feature" for pausing your program while you're away

Want to learn more? Call us today on 1-888-357-7520, or go to www.circleofa.org, the largest online resource for *A Course in Miracles*!

We hope that you will join us for this truly enlightening program!

ABOUT THE AUTHORS

 Robert Perry has been a student of *A Course in Miracles* (ACIM) since 1981. He taught at Miracle Distribution Center in California from 1986 to 1989, and in 1993 founded the Circle of Atonement in Sedona, Arizona. The Circle is an organization composed of several teachers dedicated to helping establish the Course as an authentic spiritual tradition.

One of the most respected voices on ACIM, Robert has traveled extensively, speaking throughout the U.S. and internationally. In addition to contributing scores of articles to various Course publications, he is the author or co-author of nineteen books and booklets, including the hugely popular *An Introduction to A Course in Miracles*. Robert's goal has always been to provide a complete picture of what the Course is—as a thought system and as a path meant to be lived in the world on a daily basis—and to support students in walking along that path.

Robert has recently authored his first non-ACIM book, *Signs: A New Approach to Coincidence, Synchronicity, Guidance, Life Purpose, and God's Plan*, available on Amazon sites internationally.

 Greg Mackie has been a student of *A Course in Miracles* since 1991. He has been teaching and writing for the Circle of Atonement since 1999, and has written scores of articles for A Better Way, the newsletter of the Circle of Atonement, as well as other ACIM publications. He is the author of *How Can We Forgive Murderers?* and co-taught, along with Robert Perry, the Text Reading Program and the Daily Workbook Program, which consisted of 365 recordings.

CPSIA information can be obtained at www.ICGtesting.com
Printed in the USA
BVOW07s0205111113

335968BV00002B/11/P